THE READING FOR
REAL HANDBOOK

Colin Harrison and Martin Coles provide a thorough exploration
of the 'real reading' or apprenticeship approach to beginning
reading. They bring together an emphasis on literature, meaning-
making, and enjoyment in learning to read with current thinking
and research across an important range of topics: the reading
process, the place of 'good' books in a reading programme, hearing
children read, the part parents might play, the reading–writing
connection, reading across the curriculum, supporting bilingual
readers, and providing for children who find learning to read
difficult.

The book provides an account of the current theories which
underpin reading and the teaching of reading, and also offers
guidance on how to implement those theories. Rather than simply
describing good practice, the authors offer clear pointers indicating
why the practical approaches which are offered for consideration
are theoretically sound and can be fully supported by recent
advances in theory. A series of questions is posed at the end of each
chapter, to be used as a stimulus to self-reflection and as a potential
starting point for staff discussion. An annotated booklist is also
provided which readers can use to follow up ideas contained in the
chapter.

Colin Harrison is Reader in Education at the University of
Nottingham. He is a past president of the United Kingdom
Reading Association, co-editor of the *Journal of Research in
Reading,* and a member of the national council of the National
Association for the Teaching of English. **Martin Coles** is Lecturer
in Education at the University of Nottingham. He taught for twelve
years in primary schools in England and Zambia, and was a
primary headteacher in Oxford before moving to Portsmouth
Polytechnic where he directed the Portsmouth Philosophy for
Children Project. He has published widely in the areas of young
children's language and the teaching of thinking.

THE READING FOR REAL HANDBOOK

Edited by
Colin Harrison and
Martin Coles

London and New York

First published 1992
by Routledge
11 New Fetter Lane, London EC4P 4EE

Simultaneously published in the USA and Canada
by Routledge
29 West 35th Street, New York, NY 10001

Reprinted 1993, 1995

© 1992 Colin Harrison and Martin Coles

Typeset in Baskerville by Witwell Ltd, Southport
Printed and bound in Great Britain by
Biddles Ltd, Guildford and King's Lynn

British Library Cataloguing in Publication Data
A catalogue record for this book is available from the British Library

Library of Congress Cataloguing in Publication Data
A catalogue record for this book is available from the Library of Congress

ISBN 0-415-08046-0 (hbk)   ISBN 0-415-08047-9 (pbk)

CONTENTS

CONTENTS

INTRODUCTION

Colin Harrison and Martin Coles

Current debates about the kind of texts to offer to young children learning to read are not new. In 1908 Huey said this of the prose which tended to be found in reading primers:

> No trouble has been taken to write what the child would naturally say about the subject in hand, nor indeed to say anything connectedly or continuously, as even an adult would naturally talk about the subject.
>
> (Huey, 1908)

Debate about the reading process itself and classroom methodologies that should be used to teach reading is equally longstanding. How does the reading process actually function? Should we use 'phonics' or 'look and say' approaches? Should children learning to read do so via schemes or so-called 'real books'? A book published in 1929 by a certain J. Hubert Jagger and entitled *The Sentence Method of Teaching Reading* starts with the sentence:

> The teaching of reading to little children has been a scholastic battleground for generations, a battleground that is strewn with lost causes and exploded delusions.
>
> (Jagger, 1929)

Such controversies still rage on, with teachers very often feeling themselves to be the confused and powerless civilian casualties on the periphery of this battleground.

This book attempts to inform teachers and others interested in these issues about the best in current research and practice, but it seeks to avoid taking an adversarial line in the reading debate. We hope it eschews the promotion of any single methodology. We would want to support that point of view taken by those on the Bullock Committee (DES, 1975) which was that

> the difference between good and bad reading teachers is usually not to do with their allegiance to some particular method, but to do with their relationships with children and their sensitivity in matching what they do to each individual child's learning needs. *Conclusion*

So this is not a book solely for those who are committed to a storybook approach, nor solely for those who make use of a scheme or schemes. It does, however, try to take account of the fact that we have made progress in our understanding of how children learn to read, and in doing so it attempts to bring together an emphasis on literature, meaning-making and enjoyment in learning to read, together with 'state-of-the-art' thinking and research across an important range of topics: the reading process, the place of 'good' books in a reading programme, hearing children read, the part parents might play, the reading–writing connection, reading across the curriculum, supporting bilingual readers, and providing for children who find learning to read difficult.

The book has two aims. The first is to provide, in a readable and authoritative way, an account of the current theories which underpin reading and the teaching of reading. The second is to give practical guidance on how to implement those theories. Rather than simply describing good practice, we aim to offer clear pointers indicating why the practical approaches which are offered for consideration are theoretically sound and can be fully supported by recent advances in theory. Although the book is organised in three parts with the first part putting particular emphasis on theory, each of the eleven authors draws attention to the theoretical underpinning of the practice they are advocating. It is our hope that readers will use the book to reflect on their own classroom practice in teaching reading. As an aid to this reflection there is, at the end of each chapter, a series of questions which are intended as a stimulus to self-reflection and as a potential starting point for staff discussion, as well as an annotated booklist which readers might use to follow up ideas contained in the chapter.

In the opening chapter of Part I, on theories underpinning

our overall approach to reading, Colin Harrison offers an overview of our current understanding of the reading process and learning to read. Important though they are, so-called 'psycholinguistic' theories of the reading process can no longer be accepted as fully adequate explanations, and must be integrated into a more complete description, which takes account of new research into processing of information during reading and into how children learn to read. His chapter fully endorses the need for children to have rich, early literacy experiences, but he also suggests, for example, that approaches to teaching reading which entirely ignore the need for children to develop phonemic awareness must be inadequate. The major element in these early literary experiences is the texts which children are offered. Jack Ousbey's contribution is a convincing argument that it is impossible to overestimate the importance of good literature. Children can make astonishing progress in reading when their imagination is stimulated by good books. Ousbey argues from first principles that children have a psychological need for such experiences, and that teachers should be encouraged and supported in assisting children to find them through literature. His scholarly account is informed by references to a wide range of books and authors, and some memorable quotations.

An approach which puts increased emphasis on texts chosen by the teacher needs sustaining by careful book choices, and in Part II both chapters address this issue. Gervase Phinn offers advice in the area of children's literature, not only suggesting particular books, but offering ideas about ways teachers can keep themselves informed and updated in relation to this important field. Fiction and poetry are of prime importance, but we are also gradually realising that reading for information and study skills are aspects of the reading curriculum that have been for too long ignored, especially with young children. These are aspects of reading that should certainly be given attention as soon as a child starts to become an independent reader. Such experiences are fundamental to the earliest stages of literacy, and information skills and non-literary texts are emphasised in the National Curriculum in England and Wales from Key Stage 1 through to Key Stage 4. In Alison Littlefair's chapter the ways in which non-narrative texts can be integrated into a real books approach are examined in detail and related to the important recent developments in linguistic theory.

In Part III we direct attention to the implementation of good practice in the classroom. In many classrooms the central core of the curriculum for the teaching of reading is the practice of 'hearing children read'. Martin Coles offers a principled model for classroom reading based on a matching of current theories of learning with an apprenticeship model, which is intended to broaden the reading experiences of children in classrooms. He offers a wide range of suggestions for altering the details of the teacher/child interaction in order to shift the emphasis from a 'read to me' to a 'read with me' approach, in order for the classroom to become a community of readers. A major factor in children's early literacy experiences is the social context in which learning takes place. It is now recognised that instructional practices can offer children unintentional messages about the nature of their learning. Carol Fox explores this issue in relation to reading in order that we might ask: 'Do the instructional practices in my classroom give a true picture of what literacy is, what it is for and how it works?'. Early excursions into literacy include attempts at writing as well as reading. We have only recently begun to achieve a satisfactory understanding of the nature of the relationship between early writing and early reading. Eric Ashworth puts this relationship under close scrutiny by discussing the importance of using the child's knowledge of grammar, the relationship between phonemic awareness, learning the alphabet, and early spelling, and he explains how to use current research to ensure that children's first excursions into alphabetic writing are successful.

Learning to read does not occur only at school. There is now ample evidence of the significance of parents and other caregivers in the reading development of children. Keith Topping examines evidence of the benefits to children from sympathetic parental involvement in teaching reading. He discusses the differences between parental involvement and parental partnership and outlines recommended practice in this area. Assessment is integral to the teaching process, but there is a variety of ways in which judgements can be made about children's reading, and many ways in which teachers can make use of the information gained. In her chapter, Diana Bentley discusses which methods of assessment are in keeping with our current understanding of the reading process and are, at the same time, in harmony with our understanding of both children's needs and National Curriculum requirements.

Are the approaches outlined in the preceding chapters appropriate for children with a reading delay and for those for whom English is not a mother tongue? Jean Hudson answers this question in a positive way, explaining what modified or additional strategies might be necessary in the approaches outlined in the rest of the book for use with children who have difficulty in learning to read. Guy Merchant also provides a positive answer. Learning to read and write in more than one language is a significant achievement. There are children in many parts of Great Britain from many different language backgrounds whose bilingualism means they possess a rich and varied knowledge of language. The final chapter of the book explains how teachers can support the biliteracy of these children in such a way that their confidence in reading English is not built at the expense of other languages in their repertoire.

Anyone brave (or reckless) enough to attempt to write a book on reading owes a number of debts: to the readers from whom they have learned, to the teachers from whom they have learned, and to the scholars from whom they have learned. The editors of this book wish to acknowledge the incalculable debts they owe to their children, students, friends, colleagues and mentors. They are aware that in time our understanding of the reading process will become more complete, and that with hindsight some of what is written here will seem facile, fragmentary, or plain wrong. It is their strong hope, however, that whatever changes occur in theories of the reading process and the teaching of reading teachers will never let go of their faith in the power of a book to excite children's minds, and in the value of literacy as one of the most important tools for living.

BIBLIOGRAPHY

DES (1975) *A Language for Life*. London: HMSO.
Huey, E. B. (1908) *The Psychology and Pedagogy of Reading*. New York: Macmillan.
Jagger, J. H. (1929) *The Sentence Method of Teaching Reading*. London: Grant Educational.

Part I

WHAT DOES THEORY TELL US ABOUT LEARNING TO BE A READER?

1

THE READING PROCESS AND LEARNING TO READ

What a teacher using a 'real books' approach needs to know

Colin Harrison

A CONFESSION

I've thought more about how to begin this chapter than about anything else I've written on reading over the past seventeen years. The reason is that I want to attempt to build a bridge, and I know before I start that the bridge will be a long one, and that my scaffolding and engineering skills may not be up to the task. The two islands I want to join up by this bridge do not have very good channels of communication, and those who inhabit them speak different languages.

On one island are those whose starting point in looking at the teaching of reading is a belief that learning to read is pointless unless a reader comes to value, enjoy and in some sense possess the books and stories they read. This is the island where (even if they dislike the terms) people believe in 'real books' for 'real readers'. In her book *How Texts Teach What Readers Learn,* Margaret Meek (1988) describes a project in which she and her colleagues worked with young people who had been regarded as 'unteachable', and reports: 'we gave them real books and showed them how texts teach'. Earlier in the book she lists books written by some of her favourite author–illustrators, and adds: 'Children who encounter such books learn many lessons that are hidden for ever from those who move directly from the reading scheme to the worksheet.' I share her view. I also respect the frank and professional honesty that led Liz Waterland to question her early teaching methods, which had led to her producing what she called 'a whole army of children who read well enough' but who could not remember what they had read, and gained little feeling

3

of pleasure from it. Liz Waterland's book *Read With Me* (1985) was not intended by the author to be a manual for an 'apprenticeship' approach, but it came to be regarded as one, because it answered a need, expressed with conviction and much practical good sense, for support for teachers who felt that what was crucial in their classroom were (to quote one of her chapter headings) 'Real Books for Real Readers'.

On the other island are psychologists who have studied and written about the reading process, especially the process of learning to read. Over the past ten years, I have visited this island, and have attempted to learn to speak its language, albeit imperfectly. I want to suggest that those who advocate the use of 'real books' are correct to place meaning, enjoyment and the stimulation of the imagination at the heart of reading, but that some of their accounts of how adults read, and of how children read and learn to read, have many gaps or inaccuracies, and these may seriously weaken the case for their preferred pedagogy. This is a dangerous assertion, since I am aware that to some 'real reading' advocates, accounts of the psychology of reading, particularly those from cognitive psychology, are unpalatable, both on account of their complexity and because that complexity decontextualises the reading process as it describes it. This is what makes building the bridge so difficult. But the fact remains that while I think that, for example, Denny Taylor and Dorothy Strickland's Family Storybook Reading (1986) is a wonderfully inspirational guide to leading children into literacy, I would also want to suggest that teachers of reading can support the case for such approaches much more fully than they currently do if they draw more directly upon the enormous advances in our understanding of the reading process which have been gained in cognitive psychology, especially over the past ten or fifteen years.

Among the reasons why those on the 'real reading' island feel uneasy about communicating with those on the 'cognitive psychology' island is the use made of the term 'skills' in psychology. The title alone of Usha Goswami and Peter Bryant's *Phonological Skills and Learning to Read* (1990) would be enough to convince some people that building a bridge would be an impossibility, since it is a 'skills' view of reading to which they are most opposed. Liz Waterland felt that many of her unmotivated readers were those who had been taught too many rather than too few 'skills'. Rejecting the perspectives offered in the Goswami and Bryant book

4

would, however, be very unfortunate, since I would suggest that it is one of the most important books on reading to have been published in the past ten years. What one must emphasise here is that there is a great difference between a psychologist's defining and giving close attention to one aspect of the reading process, and calling this a 'skill', and it being suggested that this 'skill' should be developed in a decontextualised way. The rationale for the present book is not to boil a 'real books' approach down to a set of 'skills' that can be taught in programmed steps; I am happy to retain the mystery and magic that are in the relationship between a child and a good book. Nevertheless, I feel that it would be immensely valuable for all teachers of reading to have a deeper insight into our current understanding of the psychology of the reading process and of how children learn to read, because this will offer a better theoretical rationale for our pedagogy, will give us a stronger defence for a 'real books' approach, and will also give us better tools for handling those cases in which children do not make a good start.

THE READING PROCESS: SMITH AND GOODMAN WERE ONLY PARTLY RIGHT

Frank Smith and Ken Goodman, by their example and by their writings, enabled many of us to become more knowledgeable about the reading process, and offered legitimacy to many of our own observations of how children read, and how they learn to read. Ken Goodman's famous dictum that reading is a 'psycho-linguistic guessing game' (Goodman, 1970) became well known and valued by teachers not simply because it seemed to ring true, but because it offered in a pithy phrase a counter-view to another description of reading that some psychologists seemed to be offering. This was the notion that reading was a letter-by-letter decoding operation, in which a person processed text in a manner similar to that in which a computer linked to a speech synthesiser 'reads' information on a disk, proceeding mechanically from letters to sounds, with meaning a low priority, something tacked on at the end of the process. This is clearly not what happens with young children. For them, meaning is paramount, and a book often seems to be not so much a text, in which every word needs to be read, as a map in which any route is permissible in the journey towards making meaning. Any account of the reading process, or of the process of learning to read, which ignores or denies this fact would be unacceptable to most of us, since it would contradict the evidence of our professional judgement.

Ken and Yetta Goodman made us aware of the importance of 'miscues' that children make while reading. They taught us how revealing a child's errors in reading can be in enabling us to see the active processes of constructing meaning which go on in the head, and they helped us find ways of monitoring and valuing such information. The Goodmans conducted many interesting studies of children's use of context in their reading strategies. They showed that some children whose word recognition was poor made highly intelligent use of context to help in the search for meaning. And this perspective gave us new respect for the reader as maker of meaning: what the reader brought to the text was just as important as what the text brought to the reader.

Equally, Frank Smith (1971, 1978) did much to make available to a wide audience the results of research into the reading process which emphasised the perspective that 'reading is only incidentally visual', though as Smith always pointed out, this interesting phrase actually came from a paper from another researcher, Paul Kohlers (1968). What Smith stressed was that in many respects the brain, with its prior knowledge of the world, of how texts are written, and of grammatical conventions, appears to contribute more information to reading than the visual symbols on the printed page. Smith argued that fluent reading is not a letter-by-letter decoding process, followed by sounding out, then word identification, culminating in comprehension. Fluent reading is too rapid for a letter-to-sound decoding process to operate all the time. Smith stressed that the fluent reader's goal is meaning. This view led him to take some rather strong positions, notably those expressed in the paper 'Twelve easy ways to make learning to read difficult' (1973), which attacked teachers who placed an overemphasis on 'phonic skills', and those who were unsympathetic towards children who attempted to guess unfamiliar words during reading. Instead, Smith advocated that we should accept that guessing and hypothesis testing were important aspects of reading. 'Learning to read is not a matter of mastering rules' wrote Smith (1975, p.184). What teachers needed to start from was the realisation that 'children learn to read by reading'.

However, while much of what Frank Smith and Ken Goodman wrote remains valid, some of what they said is now regarded by psychologists as inaccurate, and there were some crucial omissions. Where they are still thought to be right was in showing how important it is to stress meaning in reading, and that there is no point in the exercise unless it leads to meaning. Smith and Goodman are also held to be correct in stressing the intelligent use of context made by beginning readers to aid word recognition. Where they are now thought to be wrong is to do with the issue of word recognition in the reading process of fluent readers. What I shall argue is that, contrary to some of our long-held beliefs, good readers make *less* use of context for word recognition than poor readers.

The most serious omission in the writings of Smith and Goodman is in relation to the details of how children come to learn to read. Frank Smith wrote: 'children learn to read by reading'. I think that he was correct to say this, but he did not offer details of what precisely children gained from the different stages of learning to behave like a reader. On this crucial issue I shall put emphasis on some concepts which were hardly discussed in the 1970s, but which are too important for us to ignore – and these are *concepts of print, phonemic awareness,* and *analogies in reading.* Each of these topics is important enough to merit detailed treatment. Let me say at the outset, however, that nothing which follows will argue that the teaching of reading should be based on anything other than a child-centred approach, using the best books available.

THE READING PROCESS: HOW FLUENT READERS RECOGNISE WORDS

Goodman (1970) wrote that reading is 'a selective process. It involves partial use of available minimal language cues selected from perceptual input on the basis of the reader's expectations.' There are two key aspects to the reading process in this account: it is selective, and it is predictive. According to his view, the reader selects graphic cues from the text, which are held briefly in *short-term memory.* The reader then makes tentative decisions about the likely identity of the word or words read, and transfers this information to what Goodman calls *medium-term memory.* Further selective sampling of the text occurs, and the information from this is also transferred to medium-term memory. The tentative accumulated meaning is then checked for its

7

agreement with what is already held in medium-term memory. If it fits in with the prior expectations, in semantic and syntactic terms, the meaning is accepted and transferred into *long-term memory*. If, however, what is encountered next does not match the expected meaning, the reader goes back to the text and scans it again, to pick up further cues, and the cycle continues.

There are all kinds of attractions in Goodman's model. It seems to offer an explanation for the fact that often reading seems a very sloppy process. His suggestion that readers only sample the text very selectively most of the time would appear to explain why, for example, we find it extraordinarily difficult to proofread accurately, and why we not only fail to notice typographical or grammatical errors, but even unconsciously correct them. Equally, Goodman's rich descriptions of how children use context to help build meaning seem to tie in well with his notion of a reader's 'partial sampling of available minimal language cues'. No wonder, therefore, that we tend to follow Goodman in considering the ability to make intelligent use of context to be one of the marks of a fluent reader. On Goodman's view, then, a reader's sampling of the text is 'minimal'; but the reader makes maximum use of contextual information in the quest for meaning. Smith's account is very similar to this. He says, 'fluent reading does not normally require the identification of individual words' (1971, p.105), and at one point goes even further, suggesting that 'the additional stage of word identification involved in mediated comprehension is a snag, a hindrance, not a help to comprehension' (1971, p.207). For this reason, Smith and Goodman are described in the reading research literature as proponents of a 'top-down' model of the reading process. That is, their model relies heavily on information stored in memory, rather than on information derived from close attention to every word on the page.

In contrast to this view, however, the evidence currently available suggests that for fluent readers the visual processing of text is both fairly complete and very fast, and that most of the time engaging in hypothesis-testing behaviour seems to play a minimal role in the process of word recognition. This may seem surprising, but it is based on evidence collected over fifteen years, and by a number of different research groups. This is not to suggest, by the way, that reading is now thought of as a wholly 'bottom-up' process (that is, one in which reading is solely based upon a letter-by-letter analysis of the words on the page, without any input from information stored in memory). The currently accepted view of reading among psychologists is that an *inter-active* model of reading best fits the available data, with the reading process largely following a 'bottom-up' model, but with input from 'top-down' processes being used when necessary (an account of all this which is fairly technical, but worth the effort, is the extremely comprehensive book by Rayner and Pollatsek, 1989).

Evidence for the current view comes primarily from eye-movement data, much of which has become available since 1975, since which time more powerful computers, coupled with new infrared and low-powered laser technology, have permitted much more accurate recording of eye movements than had hitherto been possible (Rayner, 1983; Just and Carpenter, 1985; Rayner and Pollatsek, 1989). These new and more accurate procedures permit experimenters to know to within a single letter where a reader is fixating (fixing his or her gaze) during reading. We now know that, in normal reading, adults, far from only minimally sampling the graphic information in a text, fixate nearly all words (over 80 per cent of content words, and over 40 per cent of function words, such as *of* or *the*), and almost never skip over more than two words. Fixations on words generally last from a fifth to a quarter of a second (200–250 milliseconds), and, what is more important, it is now thought that a reader accesses the meaning of a word which is being fixated *before* moving to the next fixation. This *immediacy theory* (Just and Carpenter, 1985) is not fully accepted in every detail by all psychologists, since the theory argues that all processing, including the integration of meaning into the sentence and paragraph, is completed before the eye moves on. Nevertheless, it is broadly accepted, and this has devastating implications for the Smith and Goodman model, since it indicates that under normal conditions word recognition occurs very rapidly, generally in less than a quarter of a second, and – even more importantly – that it occurs automatically, without the reader making use of context. Indeed, just as Smith and Goodman (correctly) argued that there isn't enough time for phonemic decoding to take place in the 250 milliseconds of an average fixation, so, it is argued, there is no time for all the hypothesis generating and testing that Goodman's model implies.

The current view, therefore, is that for fluent readers in normal reading rapid, automatic, context-free word recognition is what occurs most of the time, with fixation duration largely related to the relative word frequency of different words. This model does not deny the use of context as an aid to comprehension, nor is phonemic decoding ruled out, but these are both assumed to be aids to word recognition that are often unnecessary for fluent readers. It is in this respect that reading is now regarded as an *interactive–compensatory* process.

THE 'INTERACTIVE-COMPENSATORY' MODEL OF THE READING PROCESS

In a celebrated paper, Keith Stanovich (1980) put forward the view that reading should be viewed as an 'interactive–compensatory' process. He suggested that the proportion of time given by any reader to word recognition and to comprehension was not fixed; it was variable, according to the needs of the reader. Stanovich argued that good readers recognised words rapidly because their word recognition was automatic. It was poor readers, by contrast, who needed to make the greatest use of context in order to facilitate word recognition, and they did so at the expense of needing to devote extra time to this part of the process. By 'automatic', researchers mean that the rapid word recognition of a fluent reader is not under conscious control; it therefore takes up very little processing capacity, and this is very important, since it frees up processing resources for comprehension. A fluent reader, on the interactive–compensatory model, uses very little processing capacity for word recognition, and is thus able to devote additional mental resources to interpretation. The process is compensatory in that, when necessary, readers compensate by devoting additional resources to the word recognition part of the process.

Stanovich did not, of course, say that it was *bad* to use context in order to help recognise words, only that it took up time and processing capacity. In this respect, one can see why the Smith and Goodman view was so compelling. Frank Smith (1971) made a very similar point to that of Stanovich in his account, when he talked about what he called *mediated meaning identification*, which was his term for word recognition using context or phonemic rules. He wrote:

10

Mediated word identification, then, is one way to read for meaning; it is a feasible method, but not the best. . . . I suggest that mediated word identification is used by any reader, fluent or beginner, only when he has to, and he has to when he finds the passage difficult, when immediate comprehension is not possible.

Smith, however, wrongly believed that word recognition took up too much time to be feasible in normal reading, and went instead for a model that had the reader moving directly from a light sampling of print to immediate identification of meaning. This was incorrect, but he was on the right lines to search for a model that was rapid, that did not require conscious processing for every word, and which allocated plenty of processing capacity to comprehension. The interactive–compensatory model does this, and in doing so enables us to retain the most important aspect of the Smith and Goodman view, namely that in reading the central goal should always be the quest for meaning. In their descriptions of how beginning readers or poorer readers access meaning their accounts are very close to an 'interactive–compensatory' model.

To sum up, then, where are Smith and Goodman thought to be wrong? The answer is mostly in relation to word recognition in fluent reading. Goodman is now thought to have been wrong in suggesting that in fluent reading only minimal text cues are sampled in the word recognition part of the reading process. Equally, Smith is thought to have been wrong in suggesting that word recognition is 'a hindrance' to fluent reading. What we would now say is that, in fluent reading, word recognition is automatic and rapid. When this is happening, the brain has extra processing capacity available for comprehension. When automatic word recognition is inaccurate or fails, the 'compensatory' mechanisms come into play, and the reader's behaviour approximates more closely to that described by Smith and Goodman. Smith and Goodman were correct in arguing that reading comprehension – for example, in making decisions about what type of text we are reading, or where a story is heading – is a matter of predictions and hypotheses which are modified or confirmed. But they were wrong in thinking that word recognition works in this way, except, as we have noted, when the automatic word recognition process fails.

11

What are the implications of all this? The obvious implication is that accurate, rapid word recognition is really important in fluent reading. It would, however, be unfortunate if such a realisation made some teachers discourage guessing in beginning reading, and revert to a Victorian insistence on accurate, error-free word-attack drills. This would be idiotic and counter-productive, and the reason is to do with the difference between *being* a fluent reader and *learning to become* a fluent reader. While a child is learning to read, the 'compensatory' part of the reading process is vital. When children are building up confidence, and gradually extending their sight vocabulary, they need to use all the tools available, including intelligent guesswork. Rapid word recognition is important in that it is ultimately one of the facets of good fluent reading. But it is not how we begin, nor is it a goal in its own right. The *purpose* of reading is to gain meaning, not simply to recognise words rapidly. For this reason, it seems wise to add a note on the pedagogical implications of our current view of the reading process, and this is done in the next part of this chapter.

WHY WE DO NOT NEED 10,000 FLASH-CARDS IN A BIG TIN BOX

At first sight, the realisation that one of the features that distinguishes good readers from poor readers is their ability to use automatic, context-free whole-word recognition would seem to have one inevitable implication – that we should teach children by a whole-word approach. Nothing could be further from the truth. I talked once to a large group of teachers about Stanovich's work, and after my talk, a local English Adviser came up to me and said, 'I'm sure you didn't mean this, but one of my teachers is certain that you've confirmed what she's been wanting to hear since 1960 – that look and say is back! She's ready to make hundreds of new flash-cards!'. Well, the Adviser was correct – I certainly do *not* think that look and say should be revived, and that teachers should now each have a large tin box containing 10,000 words to be used for daily whole-word recognition practice. Having a large sight vocabulary is the *result* of being a good reader, not the *cause* of being a good reader, and practising with flash-cards would not necessarily achieve anything except boredom and random guessing for many children. In the past, whole-word approaches generally stressed some useful aspects of pedagogy: they usually encouraged children to use picture and context cues, and they often put an emphasis on enjoyment. These approaches are reasonable ones to include as part of teaching reading. I cannot imagine any basis, however, on which the decontextualised study of hundreds of flash-cards could be beneficial. If anything, I would sympathise more with the use of flash-cards, on a limited basis, not to teach whole-word recognition but to teach aspects of decoding and sound–symbol correspondence, with, for example, differences between letters and letter groups in individual words being compared. For this very specific purpose, a limited amount of 'decontextualised' analysis of certain words might be defensible. It is worth adding, however, that any 'decontextualised' teaching will be pointless unless it is offered to children in a way that enables them to make connections with what they know and understand already.

HOW DO CHILDREN LEARN TO BE READERS? THE IMPORTANCE OF LEARNING TO BEHAVE LIKE A READER, AND OF ACQUIRING FOUR KINDS OF KNOWLEDGE

The most fundamental aspects of learning to read are not about skills; they are about learning to behave like a reader. Successful readers pick up books, curl up with them on easy chairs, worry or get excited about what is going to happen to the characters in a story, and later talk spontaneously about what they have been reading to their parents or their friends. As children, many of us became so keen on books that we read under the bedclothes by torchlight, risking the anger or concern of our parents and admonitions that we would ruin our sight. Why does this happen? One answer is that we must have learned that books can give some very special pleasure. Frank Whitehead (1975) argued that readers have to give more of themselves to a book they are reading than is the case if they are watching television or a film, and that this extra engagement is repaid in our becoming more absorbed, and, ultimately, in our getting closer to the characters about whom we are reading. Put a rather different way by Liz Waterland, reading is more than the sum of its parts; is like the Tardis – the time machine from the *Dr Who* television series which looked like a 'phone booth from the outside, but a spaceship from the inside. From the outside a book can look relatively innocuous, but once you get inside it, a book can be a time machine, capable of taking you anywhere, and making you a different person from the one who first entered. When Margaret Meek (1988) embarked on her project to teach 'unteachable' children to read, one of her first goals was to enable the young people to obtain some of this sense of enjoyment, of mystery, of commitment to the book they were reading, and to feel that they were doing the things that fluent readers did.

Equally, beginning readers, quite properly, want to feel that they are doing the things that children do when they are successful readers. For this to happen, however, they need to have had certain experiences, and they need to know certain things. They need to have had positive literacy experiences of the sort described in Denny Taylor's *Family Storybook Reading*. These experiences have much in common with those described by Margaret Clark in her book *Young Fluent Readers*. Taylor's book is an ethnographic account of children learning to read and write; Clark's book is written from the point of view of an educational psychologist, and the two books were written 3,000 miles apart, but many of the literacy events described in them are parallel. Taylor writes:

> For Sandy, as with the other children, reading and writing were activities to be shared. They were meaningful, concrete tasks dictated in many ways by the social setting, literate events that occurred as a part of family life, a way of building and maintaining the relational contexts of every-day life.
>
> (Taylor, 1983, p.82)

In the case of Margaret Clark's precocious readers, most had had a good deal of help with reading before the age of 4, and this had not been formal tuition; it had been embedded in the social life of the family. Clark writes: 'While half the parents felt the children were helped daily, many stressed that this help was casual rather than systematic, and that it was part of their daily life rather than something separate.'

As well as having experience of a social context in which books are valued, beginning readers need to have at least four other kinds of knowledge: knowledge of how the world works, knowledge of how language works, knowledge of how stories work, and knowledge of how books work. This is quite a tall order, but even this isn't the end of the list. If they are to learn to read without much difficulty, they need two more things, which are going to help them cope with the challenge of learning to read in English: one is not directly concerned with print, and the other has everything to do with print. The first is *phonemic awareness*; the second is an ability to learn to recognise new or unfamiliar words by generating *analogies*. Before talking about these final two aspects, let's briefly consider the four knowledge areas. A brief consideration is all that is needed in this chapter, because other chapters in this book will deal with these much more fully.

It may seem trite to mention it, but in order to understand a text, we need knowledge of the world. We are able to generate hypotheses about what's happening in a text because we know things about the world, and how things happen in it. A story which begins:

It was the day before
Frances's little sister Gloria's birthday.

(Hoban, 1968)

can only be understood if the reader or listener knows a good deal about families, and how birthdays tend to be celebrated in Western cultures. This may seem obvious, but of course children from different cultures celebrate birthdays in very different ways. So cultural knowledge and knowledge of social conventions are necessary to understand this book, and to understand the events which happen, such as writing cards and singing *Happy Birthday*, and the tug-of-war in Frances's mind between generosity and selfishness in relation to her sister's present.

The second type of knowledge needed by a reader is of how our language works. A child needs not only a vocabulary but also an understanding of how the language fits together, and a familiarity with many different syntactic structures. Russell Hoban often uses simple vocabulary to express quite complex ideas. For example:

Frances was in the broom closet, singing:
Happy Thursday to you.
Happy Thursday to you.
Happy Thursday, Dear Alice,
Happy Thursday to you.

15

'Who is Alice?' asked Mother.
'Alice is somebody that
nobody can see,'
said Frances. 'And that is why
she does not have a birthday. So I am singing
Happy Thursday to her.'

The linguistic transformations of *Happy Birthday to you* are
simple, but unusual, and the sentence *Alice is somebody that
nobody can see* is complex in structure as well as in terms of its
abstract content. The language knowledge needed here is not that
of formal linguistic description, of course; what the child needs is
a familiarity with the forms the author uses, so that it can
recognise and comprehend what is happening in the story.

Knowledge of how stories work is also very important in early
reading. Half the fun for children comes from their being able to
anticipate what might happen, and from finding that their guess
is confirmed, or, better still, finding that what follows is a
surprise, albeit an unexpected but satisfying one. This can only
happen if the author and the reader share a common 'grammar'
of story structure, in which certain events are predictable. A story
which begins:

Once upon a time there was a little girl who
didn't like going to school. She always set off
late. Then she had to hurry, but she never
hurried fast enough.

(Pearce, 1976)

is probably going to be a fairy story or a tall story, we would
guess. The little girl is doing something wrong, in always
arriving late at school, so we might guess that she is going to
have to resolve some conflict when she does arrive at school in
this story. In fact shé meets a lion, who asks her to take him to
school. Do children expect the lion to eat the little girl? No, even
very young children know that this is very unlikely, because the
girl has been introduced to us as the main character – so perhaps
it's more likely that she will do something heroic involving the
lion before the story ends, probably happily. Children's understanding of narrative structure (often very detailed as a result of
their watching television) can be very sophisticated. It certainly is
one type of knowledge which a reader needs to have, and which

16

nearly all children bring to the classroom when they start school, even if their familiarity with books is low, and upon which the teacher can draw.

The fourth type of knowledge that children need to have in order to begin to read concerns the conventions of print, and familiarity with how a book is put together. Marie Clay's *Concepts of Print* test (Clay, 1979) covers many of these conventions, running from understanding how a book is held and which way up illustrations should be, to much more complex things such as being able to point to speech marks, words, and capital letters. One important point should be made here. Knowledge of the concepts of print is quite a good correlate of early reading competence, but we should beware the causal fallacy – children who are already familiar with books do well at this test, but it would be inappropriate for a teacher to teach these concepts independently of reading good books for enjoyment. Children who have had books read to them are those who become familiar with the concepts of print. For example, a child enjoying the teacher's sharing of *Not Now, Bernard* (McKee, 1980) can readily make an informed guess as to where the word 'ROAR!' is on the page, and can begin to learn to associate speech marks with speech.

It is important for beginning readers to have these four types of knowledge, but let me emphasise once again that we should not wait for a child to acquire them before embarking upon developing that child's literacy. Children gain and develop all four types of knowledge in many social situations, from watching television to going to the shops, but teachers can also develop this knowledge systematically. A teacher who uses a book such as the wonderful *The Lighthouse Keeper's Lunch* (Armitage and Armitage, 1989) will be doing this. *The Lighthouse Keeper's Lunch*, while being a delight to read just as a story, can incidentally develop children's understanding of science, geography, and food; the book also makes fascinating use of quaint vocabulary, and has a story structure which echoes many of Aesop's fables, dealing as it does with the problem of outwitting greedy seagulls. As teachers, one of our most important goals is to help children to become skilled readers, and developing their book-related knowledge is an important part of this. However, unless we also have the goal of helping children to become enthusiastic and self-motivated readers, we may find our efforts ineffectual. Being more aware of the components of knowledge that make up reading can make us more effective teachers, so long as we are aware of the dangers of a utilitarian approach, and we work to avoid teaching the components in a fragmented and incoherent way.

THE IMPORTANCE OF PHONEMIC AWARENESS AND LEARNING BY ANALOGY IN READING – AND WHY WE DO NOT NEED DEATH BY 'PHONICS'

It is now about twenty years since I plucked up courage and asked Keith Gardner, former UK Reading Association president, what seemed at the time a very reasonable question: 'Which approach is right? "Look and say" or "phonics"?' In retrospect the question seems embarrassingly naïve. I was a seconded comprehensive schoolteacher a few weeks into work on a national reading project (I learned later that the project had been required to take on what one of the team described as 'an airy-fairy English Lit. type' – this was me). Keith Gardner smiled at me: 'Both,' he said, 'but you're asking the wrong question.' He could equally have said that the language experience approach was also 'right', developing reading through counselling was 'right', and that *Breakthrough to Literacy* was 'right', for each approach has been found to lead to children becoming successful readers, according to various researchers.

The main reason the question is so naïve, however, is because it is now generally accepted that children need to be able to use both a whole-word approach and a phonological approach in recognising words. As we have seen, they also need to be able to make use of context and all the other types of knowledge they can make available. So what's the problem? The problem is that 'phonics' and real reading have not been good bedfellows. This is because one of the prime aims of the real books movement has been to stress that reading is *not* about decoding. It is about teaching children to learn to be readers. Liz Waterland argues that conventional practice in schools concentrates on the wrong things. She refers to those who are 'obsessed with teaching decoding' (1985, p.15), and if her tone seems harsh, we should remember that she is not so much challenging the approach of other professionals as describing her own practice in earlier years.

Very few teachers would disagree with the suggestion that at some point it is valuable for beginning readers to acquire the ability to work out how to recognise words they have not met before. The issue, however, is how this ability is learned, and this leads us to a conundrum: how is it that some of the poorest readers in our schools are the ones who have had years of teaching of 'phonics'? This problem puzzled me for years, and yet the answer is simple. No child can learn what teachers call 'phonics' (a knowledge of the relationship between the letters on the page and the sounds they make) unless they have *phonemic awareness*. It is very important for us to understand that phonemic awareness is totally different from 'phonics'. Phonemes are the small units of sound which go to make up a word; phonemic awareness is the ability to hear sounds in our head and to categorise them, and is not directly about print. 'Phonics' is about the relationship between sounds and print. Phonemic awareness is what you have if you can play 'I spy'. It is what you have if you can say which of these three words (said aloud) is the odd one out because it does not rhyme: 'fish, dish, *book*'. Unless you have phonemic awareness, therefore, it is impossible to learn 'phonics'.

Many teachers who sympathise with a real books approach are uneasy about whether they should teach 'phonics' systematically. The answer is that in many respects this is the wrong question. What we need to consider is a prior question: how is it that many children come to learn to read without any instruction? What exactly have they learned, and can we help to ensure that what they have picked up without direct instruction is made available to all children? Can we provide the same types of experiences that Denny Taylor's and Margaret Clark's young fluent readers had, so that learning to read does indeed happen 'naturally', but does not happen by chance? I would suggest that we can, but that in making this happen we will be on much stronger ground if we can underpin our pedagogy by research.

We know that children who read early have had the cultural experiences described in the previous section, and that parents who read to their children pass on and develop the four types of knowledge necessary for reading. In recent years, however, we have also come to understand much more about the importance of phonemic awareness, for it is now thought that this is a vital part of the learning-to-read process. Evidence for this comes from

19

a number of sources, but the best known researchers in the field are Lynette Bradley, Usha Goswami and Peter Bryant. Since the early 1980s, these researchers have been developing three arguments through a series of projects. The first is that there is a strong correlational link between knowing nursery rhymes and acquiring phonemic awareness; the second is that there is a strong correlation between acquiring phonemic awareness and learning to read; the third is that these connections are causal ones. As we have already noted, establishing causal connections is very difficult, but Bryant and his co-workers believe that in their longitudinal studies of more than twenty schools they have established such a connection.

The good news for those who support a 'real reading' approach is that these research findings offer tremendous endorsement for the things parents and teachers already do, and indicate the importance of time spent on nursery rhymes, action rhymes and word games as crucial elements in developing literacy. The book by Goswami and Bryant (1990) referred to earlier gives a detailed account of their argument, but the position is also well summarised in a journal article. It is worth quoting from the abstract to this article, since it puts their argument in a nutshell:

> Nursery rhymes are an almost universal part of young English-speaking children's lives. We have already established that there are strong links between children's early knowledge of nursery rhymes at 3;3 and their developing phonological skills over the next year and a quarter. Since such skills are known to be related to children's success in learning to read this result suggests the hypothesis that acquaintance with nursery rhymes might also affect children's reading. We now report longitudinal data from a group of 64 children from the age of 3;4 to 6;3 which support this hypothesis. There is a strong relation between early knowledge of nursery rhymes and success in reading and spelling over the next three years even after differences in social background, I.Q. and the children's phonological skills at the start of the project are taken into account.
>
> (Bryant et al., 1989)

The causal connection is established through a somewhat complex statistical argument which is a little difficult to summarise.

It is based on a multiple regression procedure whereby the effects of a number of variables which are correlated with subsequent success in reading and spelling, such as social background, IQ and initial phonological skill, are removed, and at the final stage one is left with a relationship between the two key factors – in this case, nursery rhyme knowledge at age 3, and reading and spelling at age 6. What Bryant and his co-workers found was that children's knowledge of nursery rhymes did indeed predict success in reading and spelling two to three years later, and, more importantly, that this connection was not the result of differences in the children's intelligence or social background, or even in their initial phonological knowledge, because all these variables were controlled. What Bryant argued was that familiarity with nursery rhymes was what enabled children to become familiar with rhymes, which in turn led to their acquiring phonological awareness, which in turn helped them to succeed in reading.

The next question to consider is precisely *why* phonemic awareness is so important, and to answer it we return to one of Frank Smith's sayings, that we learn to read by reading. What exactly did Frank Smith mean? How is it that simply by reading we come to read more successfully? The answer to this question takes us to our final theoretical concept – the use of analogies in reading. What I want to suggest is that as children practise their reading not only do they develop their knowledge of the world, and widen their knowledge of language, text types, and print conventions, they also use analogies to increase gradually the store of words they can recognise easily and rapidly. This is why reading new books and rereading old favourites is so important. What are the stages in which this happens?

Initially, as most parents know, children begin by 'reading' books they know off by heart. This is indeed reading, though at an elementary level; children can match the words on the page to the words of a story they know and enjoy. A word is read as a whole, without any phonemic segmentation, and words are matched by rote association with those in the story. In the reception class, if they have not done so before, children begin to be able to read in this way. At the same time, they become more familiar with words in a wide range of contexts, as labels, on posters, on displays and in new books. The teacher reads books to and with the children, encourages the learning of letters and sounds through games, stories and poems, and begins to develop early writing activities. But at this first stage a child's reading is very context dependent. A child can read a book he or she knows, but can't recognise words from it in isolation. Equally, a child can say that a sign says 'STOP' or wrapper says 'Mars', but he or she would not recognise the word if the case of the letters was altered.

Then comes the 'click'. This second stage is in some ways the most exciting for the child, the teacher and the parents. Following models of active meaning-making which the teacher and others have provided, children begin to do three things at once: they begin to use context to make predictions about what is happening in a story, they begin to use semantic and syntactic cues to help make predictions about individual words, and they also begin to make rudimentary analogies in order to help in word recognition. This is when real reading begins, and when the encouragement of intelligent guessing is enormously helpful to the beginning reader, for there must be guessing at this stage. What will make the guessing most valuable will be feedback, discussion and encouragement. Wild guessing can lead to frustration, but if there is a supportive dialogue between the beginning reader and a fluent reader, the beginner can learn from the model of the fluent reader how meaning is built up and how guessing can best be used. The use of analogies is crude at this stage; a child may be able to guess a word using the initial letter as a clue, but little more. The analogy may be no more sophisticated than 'the word *cat* starts with a *c*, so perhaps this new word which begins with *c* is going to begin with the same sound'. Nevertheless, one can appreciate the crucial part played by phonemic awareness in making analogies even at this early stage. Children can only make this type of simple analogy if they have the ability to hear the sound of the first phoneme in a word and transfer it to another context.

The use of the term 'stages' may appear to suggest that children's reading development progresses in a fixed and regular pattern. Of course it does not. Children accelerate and regress within a stage, depending on the book they are reading and their mood. But in general this is how progression takes place, and it takes most children a year or more to move to the third stage, in which more complex analogies are made. It is in this third stage that children make tremendous progress in word recognition, using the knowledge that a word can probably be decoded by analogy with other known words. Early analogies are based on rhymes and initial letters, but later children are able to work out how to recognise a word which they have not seen before based upon other sound or spelling patterns, such as recognising *wink* from the analogous word *tank*. Equally, a word with a complex spelling pattern, such as *fight*, may be recognised by analogy with the word *light*. Over a period of perhaps two years, children use their ability to make analogies, together with other sources of information in the text, to assist in word recognition. They gradually increase the number of words they can recognise rapidly, without the need for recourse to the slower processes of using context or decoding by analogy, until they reach the final stage, which is that of the independent reader. For most children, this stage is reached between the ages of 8 and 10. The independent reader can not only analyse words into phonemes when necessary, but he or she can also use 'higher-order' rules to decode difficult words such as *cipher*, in which the *c* is soft because it precedes the letter *i*.

In order for children to become fluent readers it is not enough to be intelligent, to have supportive teaching, and to have phonological awareness. In order to become fluent readers children have to read, and they have to read widely. It is very valuable for children to reread favourite books, for enjoyment, but also because initially it is unlikely that every word will have been transferred to their rapid sight-vocabulary store. Analogies can only be made by generalising from correct, well-known and retrievable words, so rereading old favourites may have extra value in reinforcing that reservoir of words from which analogies can be made. But to become a fluent reader, a child needs to generate thousands of analogies, and clearly this cannot be done on the basis of just a few books. Here, then, is support from research for the most deeply held belief of 'real reading' teachers – that children learn to read by reading. Put the other way, you can't learn to read *without* reading; there isn't a short-cut. A child who reaches the second stage but who chooses not to read will be likely to remain at that stage, and become a poor reader, even if he or she did not start out with any reading problem.

The final point to make in this section is the importance of offering children good books which are valuable in their own right, but which also develop phonological awareness. There are dozens of such books, and in this chapter I shall mention only two, *The Cat in the Hat* and *Each Peach PearPlum*. *The Cat in the Hat* is a wonderful example of a book which teaches through fun. It is subversive, dramatic, humorous and simple to read, and children go back to it time and again, often for years, enjoying the cat's scrapes and adventures. It is easy to read because 'Dr Seuss' wrote the book in simple, uncluttered rhymes, with repetition and rhyming never obtrusively dominating the story. In a different way, *Each Peach Pear Plum* uses repetition and rhyme in a beautifully controlled manner to lead the reader on a journey in which a gallery of characters eventually meet together when Baby Bunting is returned safely home. This story is perfect in structure and wonderfully illustrated; its use of rhyme and repetition is incidental to the story, but was no accident. The story includes rhymes and themes with which many children are familiar from well before they began to learn to read, but this is why so many very young children love the book – it is precisely because of this familiarity that they can read it easily.

Many reading scheme books give special attention to offering repetition and a sequenced development of phonemes and letter clusters, in order that children are faced with a gentle slope of learning. This is entirely reasonable, but what the teacher must decide is whether the book is valuable in its own right, too. There are some delightful books in some reading schemes, and there are some awful books which are 'real books' in that they are not part of any scheme. The important point for the teacher to bear in mind is that, by one route or another, a child will need to read extensively in order to become fluent.

It should be clear now why we do not need death by 'phonics'. Instead, teachers' priorities should be first on introducing phonemic awareness, through word games, poems, 'rapping' and nursery rhymes. Second, teachers should ensure that included on their bookshelves are books which develop phonemic awareness. Third, they should ensure that children have opportunities to move through the four stages of reading described earlier in this section by developing their confidence, extending their enjoyment of books, and widening their sight vocabulary through using a wide range of reading material.

O
Reading for Real handbook

Pg 13.

Pg 25

HOW SHOULD TEACHERS SUPPORT CHILDREN IN BECOMING GOOD READERS?

Margaret Clark's young fluent readers were avid readers (1976, p.50). Their parents found it difficult to tell researchers what type of reading their child preferred because they 'devoured anything in print that was available'. These children became in many important respects independent readers before the age of 7. Every one of the children identified in Clark's study had had the good fortune to have been in the presence of 'an interested adult with time to spare to interact in a stimulating, encouraging environment'. Time is always the teacher's enemy, but allies in the form of other adults and older children can assist in offering that 'stimulating, encouraging environment'. In his book on adolescent reading, Frank Whitehead (1975) considered the factors which were associated with avid reading. He found that one factor was more important than any other – and that was the teacher. In Whitehead's study, in every case of a school in which children read many more books than the average, a teacher (and sometimes it was just one in a whole school) was identified as an important provider of encouragement, enthusiasm and resources. A teacher's enthusiasm and encouragement are the greatest gifts they can share with the children they teach, for without them any amount of resources and knowledge may be potentially barren. But knowledge and resources are important, too, and this book attempts to disseminate knowledge and identify resources.

It has been asserted by some that 'real reading' approaches are theoretically corrupt, unstructured, and dangerous. On the first point, this chapter has attempted to argue that current research and theory can firmly underpin a 'real books' approach, and in certain respects can offer a more solid, coherent and complete framework for teaching reading than would be possible for some other approaches. On the second point, I would argue that good teaching is never unstructured, and this view is shared by all the authors of the subsequent chapters, whose aim is to help provide that structure, with their own links to current theory ensuring that the foundations of the structure are firm. On the third point I plead guilty – teaching children to read certainly is dangerous, for a child who is an independent reader is a powerful person, and much more likely to have a spirit of independence as a learner. Such a reader is likely to be a challenging critic of what he or she reads, and may well learn from books that teachers and authors can be wrong. Once we teach children to read, and give them independence, we have a responsibility to help guide their reading, but we cannot teach them how to respond to what they read; we give up that right. Teachers have known for some time what always seems to come as a surprise to politicians: real education *is* dangerous.

QUESTIONS FOR PERSONAL REFLECTION OR GROUP DISCUSSION

1 Has this chapter challenged any of the views you hold? If so, which, and in what ways?
2 How does this account of the reading process tie in with your knowledge of how beginning readers read?
3 Are there any parts of this chapter with which you disagree? What sort of evidence could resolve any such disagreements?
4 What are the implications of this chapter for the teaching of reading in your classroom?
5 What is the difference between 'phonics' and 'phonemic awareness'?
6 What is the difference between teaching 'phonics' and teaching the more extensive use of analogies?
7 How is a wholehearted approach to developing reading through literature compatible with an approach which encourages the development of phonemic awareness, the use of context when necessary, and the use of analogies?

RECOMMENDED READINGS

Goodman, K. (1970) 'Reading: a psycholinguistic guessing game'. In H. Singer and R. B. Ruddell (eds) *Theoretical Models and Processes of Reading*. Newark Delaware; International Reading Association. One of the most important and influential papers on the reading process to appear in the past thirty years. Still more right than wrong.

Goswami, U. and Bryant, P. (1990) *Phonological Skills and Learning to Read*. Hove, East Sussex: Lawrence Erlbaum. Quite hard work if you're unfamiliar with the psychological literature, but it tells in detail the story of research into phonological awareness and the formation of analogies.

Rayner, K. and Pollatsek, A. (1989) *The Psychology of Reading*. Technical, authoritative and detailed. Not for the fainthearted, but one of the best in a strong field of books on the reading process. Available in paperback in an 'international student edition', which is just as well since the hardback costs over £50.

Taylor, D. and Strickland, D. (1986) *Family Storybook Reading* An American account of how to develop literacy in the home. Caring and quietly passionate about the importance of reading.

BIBLIOGRAPHY

Armitage, R. and Armitage, D. (1989) *The Lighthouse Keeper's Lunch*, Storytime Giants series. Edinburgh: Oliver & Boyd.

Bryant, P. E., Bradley, L., MacLean, M and Crossland, J. (1989) 'Nursery rhymes, phonological skills and reading'. *Journal of Child Language*, 16, 407–28.

Clark, M. M. (1976) *Young Fluent Readers*. London: Heinemann Educational.

Clay, M. M. (1979) *The Early Detection of Reading Difficulties*. Auckland, New Zealand: Heinemann Educational, for Octopus Publishing.

Goodman, K. (1970) 'Reading: a psycholinguistic guessing game'. In H. Singer and R. B. Ruddell (eds) *Theoretical Models and Processes of Reading*. Newark, DE: International Reading Association.

Goswami, U. and Bryant, P. (1990) *Phonological Skills and Learning to Read*. Hove: Lawrence Erlbaum Associates.

Hoban, R. (1968) *A Birthday for Frances*. Harmondsworth: Penguin Books.

Just, M. A. and Carpenter, P. A. (1985) *The Psychology of Reading and Language Comprehension*. Newton, MA: Allyn & Bacon.

Kohlers, P. (1968) 'Reading is only incidentally visual'. In K. S. Goodman and J. T. Fleming (eds) *Psycholinguistics and the Teaching of Reading*. Newark, DE: International Reading Association.

McKee, D. (1980) *Not Now, Bernard*. London: Andersen Press.

Meek, M. (1988) *How Texts Teach What Readers Learn*. Stroud: Thimble Press.

Pearce, P. (1976) 'Lion at school'. In D. Jackson and D. Pepper (eds) *The Yellow Storyhouse*. Oxford: Oxford University Press.

Rayner, K. (ed.) (1983) *Eye Movements in Reading: Perceptual and Language Processes*. New York: Academic Press.

Rayner, K. and Pollatsek, A. (1989) *The Psychology of Reading*. Englewood Cliffs, NJ: Prentice Hall International.

Smith, F. (1971) *Understanding Reading*. New York: Holt, Reinhart Winston.

Smith, F. (1973) *Psycholinguistics and Reading*. New York: Holt, Reinhart Winston.

Smith, F. (1978) *Reading*. Cambridge: Cambridge University Press.

Stanovich, K. (1980) 'Toward an interactive–compensatory model of individual differences in the development of reading fluency'. *Reading Research Quarterly*, 16, 32–71.

Taylor, D. and Strickland, D. (1986) *Family Storybook Reading*. Portsmouth, NH: Heinemann Educational.

Waterland, E. (1985) *Read With Me: An Apprenticeship Approach to Reading*. Stroud: Thimble Press.

Whitehead, F. (1975) *Children's Reading Interests*. London: Evans/ Methuen Educational for the Schools Council.

2

READING AND THE
IMAGINATION

Jack Ousbey

Sally Abbott is a character in John Gardner's novel, *October Light*. At one point in the book she is sitting in a room in the house reading. At first she reads without commitment, but, imperceptibly, she is drawn into the story and then:

> the real world lost weight and the print on the pages gave way to images, an alternative reality more charged than mere life, more ghostly yet nearer, suffused with a curious importance and manageability . . . . By degrees, without knowing she was doing it, she gave in to the illusion, the comforting security of her vantage point, until whenever she looked up from her page to rest her eyes, it seemed that the door, the walls, the dresser, the heavy onyx clock had no more substance than a plate-glass reflection; what was real and enduring was the adventure flickering on the wall of her brain, a phantom world filled with its own queer laws and character.

Gardner is describing here the sort of reading which occurs when the story is good enough to engage the imagination of the reader. Clearly what is happening to Sally is powerful, absorbing, influential, creative. It is the kind of reading which, once experienced, sets a standard for all other types of reading. If we want children to become lifelong readers, committed to books and aware of the satisfactions they bring, they too need to know what it is like to read in this way. And, of course, very young children (listening to a story because they are not yet independent readers) may well experience the same kind of recession as Sally Abbott, the same limber responses to the strange, new world they are encountering.

Dictionaries tell us that the word imagination comes from the Latin, *imaginare*: to form an image of; to fashion; to represent. Psychologists and philosophers appear to be both puzzled and entranced by the notion of imaginative activity, and the entries in *The Companion to the Mind* are not too helpful either. They suggest that we acquire knowledge of the external world by a kind of snapshot process which involves the production and assembly of brief images. They indicate that we achieve an orientation in space through the working of the imagination, and that we establish for ourselves sets of personal symbols by the same means. Academic research is even less rewarding. The imagination, it seems, is either amusing, quirky and unreliable, or an irritating intrusion into logical projections and carefully planned analysis. We have to turn to a poet, Ted Hughes, to get a direct and more certain view about the imagination and how it functions:

The word 'imagination' denotes not much more than the faculty of creating a picture of something in our heads and holding it there while we think about it. Since this is the basis of nearly everything we do, clearly it's very important that our imagination should be strong rather than weak. Education neglects this faculty completely. How is the imagination to be strengthened and trained? A student has imagination, we seem to suppose, much as he has a face, and nothing can be done about it. We use what we've got.

In her book, *Imagination*, Mary Warnock develops these ideas, and suggests that the images we form are also ways of thinking about the world in which we live. They take us beyond the merely sensory into 'the intellectual or thought-imbued territory of perception'. A striking example of this is found in Einstein's early investigations into relativity. His powerful, instinctive imaginings enabled him to consider what it would be like to ride a shaft of light into outer space, and led to the formulation of the famous theory. 'Imagination,' he insisted, 'is more important than knowledge.' If we also take into account a couple of other definitions – imaginative activity in its elementary form is symbolic, occurring, as it always does, inside the head; and the images prompted by our imaginings can be reactivated and reshaped – we begin to sense the importance to the learner of a vigorous, well-trained imagination.

Evidence of the influence of stories in early childhood is not easy to find. It is harder still to define the nature of the interaction when an adult reads aloud to a young child. Attempts to describe what goes on inside the child's head, for instance, have to be based on observations – the stillness, attention and responses of the listener – and to what we already know about story and imaginative activity. Consider what is happening to a small group of listeners as they encounter for the first time Antonia Barber's story, *The Mousehole Cat*, and reach the part of the tale where Old Tom, the fisherman, and his cat Mowzer put out in their small boat to face a terrible winter gale, lashed up by the Great Storm-Cat:

All day they fished in a seething sea. The waves were so high and the clouds so low that they soon lost sight of the shore.

And all the time the Great Storm-Cat played with the little boat, striking it and then loosing it, but never quite sinking it. And whenever his claws grew too sharp, Mowzer would sing to him to soften the edge of his anger.

As evening came down they hauled in the nets. Into the belly of the boat tumbled ling and launces, scad, hake and fairmaids; enough fish for a whole cauldron of morgy-broth; enough pilchards for half a hundred star-gazy pies.

'Mowzer, my handsome, we are all saved,' said old Tom, 'if we can but bring this haul home to harbour.'

But Mowzer knew that the Great Storm-Cat would strike when he saw them run for the shelter of the Mousehole.

She knew that the game serves only to sharpen the appetite for the feast to follow. It is his meal or mine, thought Mowzer, as she looked at the floundering fish in the belly of the boat. Blue, green and silver, they glistened in the greyness.

It made her mouth water to look at them.

As she thought of the morgy-broth murmuring on top of the range, the star-gazy pie growing golden in the oven, Mowzer began to purr.

And her purring rose like a hymn to home above the noise of the Great Storm-Cat's howling.

Such music had not reached the ears of the Great Storm-Cat since the dawn of Time, for when do cats purr out in the wind and the darkness?

31

Puzzled, he paused in his howling, bending his ear to catch the strange sound. It seemed to him that he had once heard such a song long before, when he was no more than a Storm-Kitten.

The Great Storm-Cat grew quiet: gone was his hunger for hunting, for making his meal of the mice-men.

Only the pleasure of the purring remained.

When we read a good story the experience is powerfully creative. The reader or listener is called on to process the text as it unfolds, not only to make sense of the chunks of language as they are read, or heard, but also to place the story, and all it consists of, on his/her personal map of experience. In the case of *The Mousehole Cat* much of what is encountered – the setting, the linguistic constructions, the literary conventions, the imagery, the vocabulary – will be new to the listener and will mean that the map has to be extended or redrawn. In a recent article Seamus Heaney spelled out his belief that:

Our capacity for imaginative sympathy and the sheer range of our linguistic receiving stations greatly exceed the given circumstances and determining logic of our social milieux

a view wholly supported by the way my young partners accommodated, without effort, Antonia Barber's marvellous account of the Cornish legend.

Insights like these, of course, fit uncomfortably into the schema of modern educational research. They cannot be replicated or validated and because they draw on the powers of the reflective spirit which first prompts question and answer, they are regarded with suspicion. Some of Michael Benton's work, for instance, carried out in the early 1980s, is based largely on the testimony of writers and readers, and uses neither research formula nor statistical device. His conclusions, nonetheless, are worth listening to. He tells us that the prime coinage of imaginative activity is mental imagery, and links this persuasively to the reading process. 'Writers and readers,' he says, 'frequently testify to the visual sense of the world they imagine. Less frequently do they refer to auditory or other images drawn from the senses.'

What are these pictures that crowd into the mind's eye, and of what use are they to us in our daily lives? Are they passive, evanescent phenomena or something much more crucial to our status as human beings? Dr David Weeks, neuropsychologist at the Royal Hospital in Edinburgh, believes that visual imagery is absolutely essential to the creative process, and that each image is capable of working on other abstract ideas to form new concepts:

> The more vivid and spontaneous the pictures in the mind's eye are, the more the person's thinking diverges from the ordinary. The capacity to see pictures of sparkling clarity is often well developed in very young children but, as we grow older, it gradually fades. Rare in adults, it appears to be lost as we acquire more abstract, verbal methods of thought.

If David Weeks is right, then what he describes is the mainspring of all human capacities - the ability to think, consider and reshape ideas; the power to build up those notions and categories we call concepts; the talent, in fact, to handle symbols.

One writer who carries readers effortlessly into the world of story is Alan Garner. His book, *The Stone Book Quartet*, has a number of marvellous set pieces, crafted, one feels, for reading aloud and sharing with children - Robert finding the mason's mark above the chapel clock; Joseph accompanying his grandfather and Damper Latham on the E flat cornet; the lovely account of the fashioning of William's new sledge; Mary climbing the spire of the village church:

> Mary hitched her frock and put the knot of the baggin cloth between her teeth and climbed the first ladder. The ladders were spiked and roped, but the beginning of the steeple was square, a straight drop, and the ladders clattered on the side. She didn't like that.
>
> 'Keep fast hold of that tea!' she heard Father call, but she didn't lift her head, and she didn't look down.
>
> Up she went. It felt worse than a rock because it was so straight and it had been made. Father had made parts of it. She knew the pattern of his combing hammer on the sandstone.
>
> Up she went.
>
> 'Watch when you change to the spire!' Father's voice sounded no nearer.
>
> At the spire, the pitch of the ladders was against the stone, and Mary had to step sideways to change. The ladders were firmer, but she began to feel a breeze. She heard an engine

get up steam on the railway. The baggin cloth kept her mouth wet, but it felt dry.

The spire narrowed. There were sides to it. She saw the shallow corners begin. Up and up. Tac, tac, tac, tac, above her head. The spire narrowed. Now she couldn't stop the blue sky from showing at the sides. Then land. Far away.

Mary felt her hands close on the rungs, and her wrists go stiff.

Tac, tac, tac, tac. She climbed to the hammer. The spire was thin. Father was not working, but giving her a rhythm. The sky was now inside the ladder. The ladder was broader than the spire.

Father's hand took the baggin cloth out of Mary's mouth, and his other hand steadied her as she came up through the platform.

The platform was made of good planks, and Father had lashed them, but it moved. Mary didn't like the gaps between. She put her arms around the spire.

'That was a bonny climb,' said Father.

'I do hope the next baby's a lad,' said Mary.

What happened to you as a reader when you went with Mary up the ladders to the platform at the top of the spire? What kind of pictures did you make inside the head? What sort of experiences, attitudes, emotions did the reading nudge into life? And where were you as you allowed the power of the tale to exercise its magic? You entered, I believe, like Sally Abbott, the phantom world of story, and what was real and believable for those few minutes was 'the adventure flickering on the wall of the brain'. Oliver Reynolds, the poet, calls it:

. . . the strangest recession:
I am there but not there.
I am reading.

My body dwindles.
Thinned by text it becomes Euclidean:
It has position but no magnitude.

An hour later, it returns;
Slowly, as if dropping by parachute.

Becoming this sort of committed reader is not just a matter of our willingness to enter this secondary world: the quality of the story on offer always affects the nature of our involvement. There is no greater barrier to entry than non-stories. Certainly the basic readers of reading schemes, with their jerky rhythms and emotionally threadbare situations, are unlikely to prove much of a draw, and, I suspect, the 'Quick Dick, Nip's been sick' style of reader is responsible for many of those children who learn to decode but have no interest in books.

A child is reading. She has tied a torch to the bed-head so that the light focuses on her book and does not disturb her younger sister, asleep in the bed next to hers. She is so absorbed in the reading she seems to have created a kind of force-field around herself, a palpable energy which holds her tightly inside the world the story-maker has created. At different times and in different ways Blake and Auden, Solzhenitsyn and Brodsky, Hughes and Heaney have reminded us that reason lives not only in facts but in possibilities. This child, not yet 7, is so open to the experiences which the secondary world of story brings she may already be changing imaginative possibility into conscious knowledge.

Good stories enable children to enter this world, and teachers who share such tales with their young children know with what ease and delight they do this. They are eager to collaborate. Unless a child is mentally impaired in a serious way, the desire to engage with imaginative literature is instinctively strong (and anyone who knows about Cushla will remember the astonishing progress, through story, of a child who was labelled mentally deficient).

What sort of stance, then, are we to take on the question of choice? When it comes to selecting stories for children, is our commitment to those books which will nourish and sustain the imagination, or are we happy to put before them the threadbare, the mediocre, the second best? It seems reasonable to suggest that this is the fundamental issue which any debate on reading must address. What kind of books? What kind of reading? What kind of readers are we promoting when we teach children to read?

That doesn't mean that reading has to be dull or limited. Michael Rosen is a brilliantly funny writer whose work rarely fails to trigger the imagination:

Quite often

35

my mum used to say to me:
'Isn't it time you had a bath?'
and I'd say:
'But I had one yesterday.'
'No you didn't,' she'd say.
'Well – the day before yesterday, then,' I'd say.
'Right,' she says – 'I'll run the water.
You be ready to get in when it's full.'

So when
the bath room was full of steam
I was ready to climb in.
One thing though –
I never get into a bath
bold and bare all over. You see,
a bath is part of the water world
and I always like to keep in touch with the dry world
till the last possible moment.
So what I do, is take off all my clothes
except my vest.

I step over and in – how's that? Owah!
as hot as feet can bear.
I kneel down
as hot as knees can bear. Oh!
Down a bit, down a bit
as hot as bottom can bear. Oooph!
Sit for one moment in the water world
with my last dry thing still on –
then, vest off, over the edge, out of sight
and I slide the rest of me into the water.

Bathtime is a marvellously comic tale, evoking that sense of childhood which all good teachers retain. It owes its success to its familiarity as well as its humour. We share the experiences with the child in the bath, having played all of those games ourselves, and we reassert our sense of what it is to be human as we encounter them again. Children need opportunities to do that – to know that they think and behave like other people; to see that their pleasures and problems are shared by the larger communities outside of home. They encounter in stories, too, experiences and attitudes which are new to them, some of which may indeed, allow them to look for better things from life than those they have met so far.

The trouble with words like 'pleasure', 'enjoyment', 'humour', 'celebration', however, is that they do not fit easily into the discourse of current educational debate. Bombarded with notions of accountability, testing, competition and quality control we resort to the publication of league tables and the frantic scramble to appear in guides to good schools. The cult of reductionism holds sway, not only in the teaching of reading but in the way schools are organised and managed. Wise teachers, like wise parents, have to redefine and defend the place of creative activities and imaginative experiences, not as options but as entitlements. A much more spacious, generous view of the developing talents of very young children is needed, as Kieran Egan, a Canadian teacher whose published work is concerned with the imagination, reminds us:

> So dealing with children's fantasies, which in turn deal with good and bad, love and hate, fear and security, and so on, we are not dealing with intellectual froth, but with the early forms and early developments of the most profound and fundamental concepts that we use to make sense of the world and of experience.
>
> Before children can walk or talk, before they can skate or ride a bicycle, they know joy and fear, love and hate, power and powerlessness, and the rhythms of expectation and satisfaction, hope and disappointment . . . . So the knowledge which comes first to people and which remains most deeply ingrained is not knowledge of 'how to do': it is of the fundamental categories upon which we learn increasingly to make sense of anything in the universe and in human experience.

Nobody can prove, or disprove, what is being said here. Good research practice wouldn't help us. We have to ask ourselves: does this make sense? Does it seem like a strong possibility even though it can't be validated? Does it sound like the true state of affairs?

One of the main differences between listening to a story being read by someone else and reading it for oneself is the flexibility which silent reading allows. We can pause whenever we feel like it, turning back the pages to check on some detail which caught our attention earlier, or we can reflect on what has happened and consider what might occur next. Sometimes these strategies are deliberate: sometimes they occur subconsciously as we move through the text. As soon as children become independent readers they operate on stories in this way, and stories, in turn, operate on them. The urge to find out what is going to happen next generates a nervy flow in the busy traffic of the imagination. We check, revise, adjust, decide, speculate as we build the story in the head, and it is imagination, then, which allows us to hold the story separate from all the other stories we know.

Ask yourself, as you read one of the best opening passages in children's literature, how the story works on you, and you on it. How do you place it in time? What experiences do you bring to the events of the tale? What is it about the language the author uses which drives the reader forward? Why are we so keen to find out what happens next?

Jackson was thin, small and ugly, and stank like a drain. He got his living by running errands, holding horses, and doing a bit of scrubbing on the side. And when he had nothing better to do he always sat on the same doorstep at the back of Paddy's Goose, which was at the worst end of the worst street in the worst part of the town. He was called Jackson, because his father might have been a sailor, Jack being a fond name for a sailor in the streets round Paddy's Goose; but nobody knew for sure. He had no mother, either, so there was none who would have missed him if he'd fallen down a hole in the road. And nobody did miss him when he vanished one day and was never seen or heard of again.

It happened when Christmas was coming on - about a week before. Dreadful weather, as hard and bitter as a quarrel. Dreadful weather, with snow flakes fighting in the wind and milk freezing in the pail.

Jackson was out in it, sitting on his doorstep with his hands cupped together just over his knees. There was a whisker of steam coming up from his mouth and another from between his hands. It wasn't his soul going up to heaven, it was a hot pie from a shop round the corner where he'd been scrubbing the kitchen since before it was light.

He couldn't make up his mind whether it was better to be warm outside or in. He couldn't make up his mind whether it would be better to keep the pie and warm his hands, or to eat it and warm his insides. So there he was, thinking hard, with his face screwed up like a piece of dirty paper, when the black dog came.

Huge: as big as a donkey, nearly, with eyes like street lamps and jaws like an oven door. Down the street it padded, with a glare to the right and a glare to the left, and a savage twitch of its great black nose. Somebody opened a window and threw a bucket of dirty water down; and the black dog snarled with rage. Up it came to the doorstep where Jackson sat and steamed. It glared and growled while the snow flakes fried on its nose.

'Shove off!' wails Jackson, hiding his pie and shaking in his shoes – or, rather, in his feet as he had no shoes worth mentioning. 'I got no food and I'm only skin and bone myself so I'll taste as sour as leaves!'

'Liar!' says the dog; not in words but with its terrible eyes and rattling teeth.

'I'm froze and hungry!' wails Jackson, wishing he'd eaten the pie.

'And I'm froze and hungry!' says the dog; not in words but with its lean sides and smoking breath.

'All right,' says Jackson, seeing there's no help for it. 'Fair's fair. Half for you and half for me.' And he breaks the pie and the dog swallows down half with a fearful guzzle and growl. 'Fair's fair,' says Jackson; and eats what's left. 'Now shove off!'

But the black dog just stands, and bangs at the falling snow with its tail. Then, big as the night, with its street-lamp eyes, it comes straight at Jackson; and licks his face. Not because it loves him, but because Jackson smells as much of pie as he does of drains.

'You're spifflicating me!' howls Jackson, and tries to push the monster off. He gets his hands round its tree of a neck and then cries out: 'Hullo! You got a collar on! You must belong to somebody. Hullo again! You got something under your collar. What you got? What you got? Stone the crows! You got a key!'

By inclination I am a list-maker. I am not sure how useful summaries are to anyone other than the maker, but a review of the key features of reading and the imagination seems to me to be worth stating:

- imaginative activity involves holding and inspecting pictures inside the head;
- this is the basis of nearly everything we do;
- the images we shape can be recalled and reorganised;
- the activity is symbolic and thought-imbued;
- visual images are much more important than other forms;
- good stories create pictures on which the imagination can operate;
- children are better at 'picturing' than adults;
- all children have the ability to receive and process stories;
- conceptual learning arises when images, and the ideas they sponsor, work on each other;
- skilful story-makers create secondary worlds;
- children enter these worlds easily and naturally;
- inside this world we encounter familiar and new experiences;
- as we read we check, reflect, picture, compare, consider, confirm, speculate, anticipate, question and decide;
- children need to encounter stories which extend, challenge, puzzle and engage their attention;
- good stories deal with the fundamental categories of human experience.

It is a sad reflection on our society that the small number of schools which recognise the qualities and truths that real stories provide are branded woolly theorists and their approach regarded as damaging imposture. Those influential and strident people who tell us that structure and schemes, and well-tried, traditional methods will soon sort things out, would do well to consider whether or not a lack of reflectiveness is an even greater illiteracy than being unable to read well. Maybe they should confront their own comprehensive ignorance first, by reflecting on the words of Bruno Bettelheim:

> The time is long-gone when learning to read was directly related to learning about the supernatural and magic, about the dangers of sin and the hope of salvation. That is why many children, although they have the requisite intelligence for learning to read, fail to do so. Even if they do learn, reading remains emotionally empty and unappealing

to them. For them reading is not supported by its power to stimulate and satisfy their imagination, in respect to what, to them, are pressing and urgent issues; nor has it created a strong appeal through its magical meaning. If it has not become attractive during the child's formative years, it may never seem attractive, even when its practical value is recognised.

I suspect that we would all agree on which are the formative years in a child's development - those years before, and immediately on, entry to school. If the child is fortunate he/she will have parents who know about stories and their importance, and will then go to a school where reading appeals through its magical meaning: if not, if the parents don't bother with stories, and the school puts its efforts into those anaemic formulations which masquerade as stories, society will continue to deplore the decline in standards. More importantly, the failure to link reading and the imagination will be ours.

QUESTIONS FOR PERSONAL REFLECTION OR GROUP DISCUSSION

1 Do you share the writer's views about the centrality and importance of good stories in the teaching of reading?
2 Should schools which are involved in early reading work have an agreed, articulated policy for book selection?
3 What kind of criteria would form the basis for such a selection?
4 Is it important for every teacher of young children to be enthusiastic and knowledgeable about children's literature?
5 Is it possible to list ways in which teachers can develop their understanding of children's literature?
6 What specific activities and initiatives would help to bring children and books together before statutory schooling begins?
7 What steps can a school take to create an attractive, positive reading environment?
8 What can be done in the classroom to help children know about books and authors?
9 How well do the claims publishers make, for the stories in their reading schemes, match up to your criteria? And to the list made by the writer at the end of this chapter?

10 Compare half a dozen books from a reading scheme with a similar number of top-quality stories provided by your Education Library Service, considering not only the quality of each story, but also the layout, illustrations and attractiveness of the books.

11 Working in small groups, present readings of children's stories to each other, accompanied by assessment, commentary and evaluation.

RECOMMENDED READINGS

Butler, D. (1979) *Cushla and Her Books*. London: Hodder & Stoughton. An astonishing, inspirational account of the power of story to sustain and nourish a severely handicapped baby.

Fox, G. *et al.* (1976) *Writers, Critics and Children*. London: Heinemann. This excellent collection of views and insights into children's literature includes the seminal essay by Ted Hughes, 'Myth and education'.

Gregory, R. (ed.) (1987) *The Companion to the Mind*. Oxford: Oxford University Press. A dictionary which details recent investigations into the psychological and philosophical operations of the mind, including sections on imagery and the imagination.

Heaney, S. (1980) *Preoccupations*. London: Faber & Faber; (1989) *The Government of the Tongue*. London: Faber & Faber. Heaney writes with great perception and style, about influences, the writer's voice, other poets, childhood, and the way language operates; though not explicitly about teaching or reading these essays inform and illuminate the territory.

Inglis, F. (1981) *The Promise of Happiness*. Cambridge: Cambridge University Press. This book was written to answer the question: which books should children read? Inglis is forthright, uncompromising, clear sighted and unswerving in his commitment to good books.

Iser, W. (1974) *The Implied Reader*. London: Johns Hopkins University Press. The final chapter, 'The reading process', offers a clear and comprehensive picture of what happens when a reader makes contact with a good story.

BIBLIOGRAPHY

Benton, M. (1983) 'Secondary worlds', *Journal of Research and Development in Education*, vol. 16, no. 3.

Bettelheim, B. (1987) *A Good Enough Parent*. London: Thames & Hudson.

Egan, K. (1988) *Primary Understanding*. London: Routledge.

Gardner, J. (1977) *October Light*. London: Cape.

Heaney, S. (1990) 'Poetry review', *Sunday Times*, December 1990.

Hughes, T. (1976) 'Myth and education'. In G. Fox *et al. Writers, Critics and Children.* New York and London: Agathon and Heinemann.
Reynolds, O. (1985) *Skevington's Daughter.* London: Faber.
Warnock, M. (1976) *Imagination.* London: Faber.
Weeks, D. (1989) 'Brainplan', *The Observer,* 1989.

Quotes from children's stories

The Mousehole Cat, Antonia Barber, ill. Nicola Bayley, Walker Books, London, 1990.
The Stone Book Quartet, Alan Garner, reissued by Collins, London, April 1992.
Quick, Let's Get Out of Here, Michael Rosen, ill. Quentin Blake, Deutsch, London, 1983 and Puffin, Harmondsworth, 1985.
Fair's Fair, Leon Garfield, ill. Brian Hoskin, Simon & Schuster, Hemel Hempstead, 1990.

Part II

WHICH BOOKS SHOULD WE USE?

3

CHOOSING BOOKS FOR YOUNG READERS
Habituated to the Vast
Gervase Phinn

I read every book that came my way without distinction – and my father was very fond of me, and used to take me on his knee, and hold long conversations with me. I remember, that at eight years old I walked with him one winter evening from a farmer's house, a mile from Ottery – and he told me the names of the stars – and how Jupiter was a thousand times larger than our world and that the other twinkling stars were Suns that had worlds rolling round them – and when I came home, he shewed me how they rolled round. I heard him with a profound delight and admiration; but without the least mixture of wonder or incredulity. For from my early reading of Faery Tales, and Genii etc. etc. – my mind had been habituated to the Vast.

(From *Letters 1, 1780*, and quoted in *Coleridge: Early Visions* by Richard Holmes, 1990, p.18)

A favourite with young children is the wonderfully warm and sympathetic story of *The Great Sharp Scissors* by Philippa Pearce. It contains all the qualities of this fine writer's other books: big open characters, a fast-moving plot, spareness in the prose and sharp, clear dialogue. The twelve-page story is full of wit, wisdom and suspense. It begins:

Once there was a boy called Tim who was often naughty. Then his mother used to say 'Tim!' and his father shouted 'TIM!' But his granny said, 'Tim's a good boy really'.

The reader's interest is immediately aroused. Tim resents being left alone while his mother visits his sick granny.

He scowled and stamped his foot. He was very angry.

His mother warns him not to let anyone into the house but when a strange man calls and offers to sell him a most remarkable pair of great sharp scissors which will cut anything, Tim cannot resist:

'I'll have them,' said Tim.

With the great sharp scissors in his hand he now has the opportunity to give vent to his feelings. He *snip snaps* the buttons off his father's coat, he cuts the carpet into hundreds of little pieces, he chops the legs off tables and chairs, and the clashing blades slice through the clock on the mantelpiece.

> By now Tim knew that the great sharp scissors would cut anything. They would cut through all the wooden doors and floors. They would cut through all the bricks of all the walls, until nothing was left. Nothing. Tim went and sat on the bottom step of the stairs and cried.

Fortunately his second visitor, a strange woman who smiles kindly at him, exchanges the scissors for some special glue. When Tim's mother arrives back from granny's, Tim has repaired everything and the house is back to normal. The story ends on an ironic but immensely warm and reassuring note which is never missed by the little listeners.

> 'Granny's much better, and sends her love. I see you've been a good boy, Tim. Everything neat and tidy. . . . ' She made a pot of tea, and she and Tim had tea and bread and butter and raspberry jam. In the middle of it, Tim's father came home, and he had some of the raspberry jam too.

The Great Sharp Scissors has all the qualities which are important when thinking about the books to present to children. This powerful and carefully crafted story has an immediate appeal. Children enjoy hearing about someone very much like themselves. They love tales about boys and girls like Tim who have moods and get angry as they do, who are sometimes naughty and get into trouble but who, in the end, receive the reassurance of being loved and wanted. They enjoy sharing the experiences and emotions which a well-written story triggers and willingly project into it their own feelings of fear, insecurity, anger, joy and relief.

One of Philippa Pearce's greatest qualities as a writer for children is that she never patronises her young readers. She knows well that children are curious, eager and sharply observant and that they love stories that absorb their attention and which make demands upon them. Such stories are important in developing children's language but are more important in their emotional development.

Stories like *The Great Sharp Scissors* that explore ideas of right and wrong, where good finally triumphs over bad and which feature kind and understanding parents, are the type of texts the beginning reader needs and ones which will be remembered.

> I knew nothing of myself till I was five or six. I do not know how I learnt to read. I only remember my first books and their effects upon me; it is from my earliest reading that I date the unbroken consciousness of my own existence.
>
> (From *The Confessions* by Jean-Jacques Rousseau, 1781)

A reading of *The Great Sharp Scissors* will often prompt the kind of response from young children shown in Figure 3.1.

This is quite simply what those of us in education should be about: exposing children from the earliest age to books which arouse their interest in, and develop a love of, reading; to present them with a rich variety of stories and poems to make them laugh, sometimes sad and scared and which will encourage them to ask for more. Bruno Bettelheim, the renowned child psychologist, argued that from the very start books should have a real literary quality with the power to engage the child's active interest:

> What are needed are beginning texts that fascinate children and convince them that reading both is delightful and helps one to gain a better understanding of oneself and others – in short, of the world we live in and of how to live in it. To achieve this, primary texts should stimulate and enrich the child's imagination, as fairy tales do, and should develop the child's literary sensitivities, as good poems are apt to do. The texts should also present the child with literary images

ROTHERHAM METROPOLITAN BOROUGH COUNCIL
EDUCATION DEPARTMENT

Aston Hall J. & I. School,
Church Lane,
Aston,
Sheffield S31 0AX

HEAD TEACHER: Mrs. B. Gibson
Telephone Sheffield 879811

Dear Mr Phinn

Thank you for reading us a
story. We liked it when Tim cut his
dads buttons off and then he cut the
carpet and then he cut the TV set
up. If I did that I would get done by
my mum. Then a man knocked on the
door and he give Tim some glue to
mend the things that he broke. I wish
I had some glue like that. I liked the
voices that you made. It made me and
Helen laugh. Sometimes it made me and
Jane sad and scared. Our mummies
laughed. Mrs Lumb laughed until tears
fell down her face
Please will you come and tell us a
story again soon.

With love from all our class in Aston
Hall School.

Figure 3.1

of the world, of nature and of man, as these have been created
by great writers.

(From *On Learning to Read: A Child's Fascination with
Meaning* by Bruno Bettelheim and Karen Zelan, 1982, p. 263)

There cannot be a teacher in the country who would not
subscribe to this view or who would dispute the recommendations contained in the National Curriculum which endorse it:

Teaching should cover a range of rich and stimulating texts and should ensure that pupils regularly hear stories, told or read aloud, and hear and share poetry read by the teacher and each other . . . . Reading should include picture books, nursery rhymes, poems, folk tales, myths, legends and other literature. . . . Both boys and girls should experience a wide range of children's literature.

(From *English in the National Curriculum, Programme of Study for Reading, Key Stage 1, Paras 6 and 7,* Department of Education and Science, 1989)

But where does the teacher start? What books in particular should be presented to children? Which material is appropriate? What are the qualities of 'a good book'?

Before selecting books for the young reader there are a number of questions one should ask:

1 Is the book appealing and eye catching? Picture books with bright, colourful and beautifully illustrated covers – such as those listed below – demand to be picked up, opened and read:

Little Beaver and the Echo by Amy MacDonald, with illustrations by Sarah Fox-Davies (London: Walker Books, 1990)
Dinosaurs, Dinosaurs by Byron Barton (Hemel Hempstead: Simon & Schuster, 1990)
Ellie's Doorstep written and illustrated by Alison Catley (London: Beaver Books, 1990)
The Chocolate Wedding written and illustrated by Posy Simmonds (London: Jonathan Cape, 1990)

2 Is the story worth telling? Does it read well aloud and bear a rereading? Is it entertaining and challenging? Does it contain some excitement and suspense? C. S. Lewis argued vehemently that:

No book is really worth reading at the age of ten which is not equally worth reading at the age of fifty – except of course information books. The only imaginative works we ought to grow out of are those which it would have been better not to have read at all.

(From an essay in *The Cool Web* by C. S. Lewis)

Picture books like the following will enthral the young reader:

Aunt Nina's Visit by Franz Brandenberg (London: Bodley Head, 1986). A captivating and amusing account about not wanting to go to bed.

The Tunnel by Anthony Browne (London: Julia MacRae, 1989). Tense, thoroughly engrossing and ultimately reassuring and happy, this tale tells of a shy little girl who goes in search of her brother lost in the dark, mysterious tunnel.

Cupid by Babette Cole (London: Hamish Hamilton, 1989). An extremely funny account centring on the antics of the mischievous little archer.

3 Is the language appropriate, natural and meaningful? Does it encourage children to predict what will happen, to anticipate and become involved in the narrative? Is there a richness in the expression and an imaginative use of words? Does the writer make some demands on his or her readers in terms of language? Good books expose the child to language in its most complex and varied form, presenting the thoughts, emotions and experiences of others in a vivid and dramatic way.

> Aesthetic properties of language are to be found more than anywhere in literature. Literature is nothing if not language formed in highly deliberated ways. From the earliest pre-school stages of development, children are interested in forms of language. . . . Wide reading, and as great an experience as possible of the best imaginative literature, are essential to the full development of an ear for language.
> (From *The Report of the Committee of Inquiry into the Teaching of English Language: The Kingman Report*, Department of Education and Science, 1988, Chapter 2, Para 21)

Such is the range of good quality material now available that there is no need for children to put up with anything less than the best. Children are entitled to books by such authors as: Janet and Allan Ahlberg, Quentin Blake, John Burningham, Eric Carle, Eric Hill, Shirley Hughes, Pat Hutchins, Ezra Jack Keats, Hugh Lewin, Arnold Lobel, David McKee, Graham Oakley, Helen Oxenbury, Rodney Peppe, Jan Pienkowski, Tony Ross, Maurice Sendak, Brian Wildsmith and many, many more fine writers.

4 Is the dialogue appropriate to the characters? Is it clear and

understandable? Does it capture the rhythms of real speech? Does it reflect the speech patterns of those for whom it is intended?

'I can't,' said Nanna.
'You will,' said her mother. 'Sleep well, Nanna.'
'Can't,' repeated Nanna.
'Cuckoo!' sang the bright-eye in the dusty clock.
'Whoomph!' barged the wind.
'Pitterpitterpitter,' pattered the attic mice . . . .
(From *Sleeping Nanna* by Kevin Crossley-Holland, 1989)

5 Do the illustrations enhance the story, adding meaning to the words rather than detracting from them? Do the pictures link closely to the text? A recommendation contained in the Bullock Report is:

that all early reading material should be attractive not only in presentation but in content. The words and pictures should complement each other in such a way that the child needs to examine both with equal care.
(From *A Language for Life: The Bullock Report*, Department of Education and Science, 1975)

The most accomplished and original illustrators include: Paul Adshead, Reg Cartwright, Philippe Dupasquier, Susan Hellard, Sonia Holleyman, Charles Keeping, Colin McNaughton, Peter Melnyczuuk, Kathryn Meyrick, Jennifer Northway, Teresa O'Brien, John Steptoe and Beatriz Vidal.

6 Is the subject appropriate to the children in terms of age and maturity? Does it avoid being moralistic, overly sentimental and patronising?

In *Why Do You Love Me?* by Martin Baynton (1990), a little boy is taken out for a walk with his father. The simple straightforward text is richly evocative:

Do you love me?
Yes, I love you very much.
Why do you?
Oh, lots of reasons.
Do you love me because I'm strong?
Mmmm, perhaps.

7 Are the characters rounded and convincing? Do they live and

breathe on the page, develop and grow in the reader's mind? Can children readily identify with the characters and enter into their lives?

> When they brought my baby brother home, everyone fussed over him.
> It wasn't fair.
> 'What about me?'
> 'You're a big girl now,' my mother said.
> I'm not THAT big.
> People are always doing things for him.
> I have to do things for myself.
> It's not fair!
>
> (From *It's Not Fair!* by Anita Harper
> with illustrations by Sue Hellard, 1988)

8 Is the print clear, well spaced and of an appropriate size?
9 Is the story the work of a real writer, not merely a book especially written to teach children to read?

> Authors who genuinely want to write for children do not count the words in a sentence. They know instinctively where phrases start and stop because they shape narratives and incidents.
>
> (From *Learning to Read* by Margaret Meek, 1982)

10 Is the story of real interest to the teacher? Does he or she enjoy reading and rereading it, presenting it to and discussing it with his or her children?

> There was once a man who wanted to live for ever. His name was Bodkin, and his home was a small village which lay beside the river in a sheltered valley surrounded by green and gentle hills.
> One day he went to see . . .
>
> (From *The Man Who Wanted to Live For Ever* retold by
> Selina Hastings and illustrated by Reg Cartwright, 1988)

Asking such questions about *The Great Sharp Scissors* and then the old-style reading scheme books will show a stark contrast. The latter would sound ludicrous read aloud. The plots were arid, the language stilted and unnatural and the characters wooden. There existed little if any connection between one sentence and another, no narrative style, no humour and sadness, suspense or excitement. The Bullock Report contained the following sharp observation:

> The authors of the older reading schemes sacrificed important considerations in restricting the vocabulary and repeating words frequently. They produced prose so unrealistic that it cannot be regarded as an effective basis for reading instruction.
>
> (From *A Language for Life: The Bullock Report,* Department of Education and Science, 1975)

In their day these schemes served a purpose – after all, many of us learned to read using them. But children are entitled to much better, more interesting and demanding material. They deserve, as Brough Girling so passionately argued at The Twelfth Woodfield Lecture:

> Books that are so good that they have to fight for existence and success on retail bookshelves: books with super covers, good stories, with plots that make you want to turn the page over.
>
> (From *The Woodfield Lecture XII,* 1989)

Before recommending such books I need to restate the obvious: teachers must be *reading* teachers if they hope to promote the reading of the children they teach. Research has revealed again and again that teacher influence on children's book choices and on their language development is considerable. The two most important factors in fostering children's reading are teacher influence and the provision of a wide range of material. So teachers must be readers themselves. There is no short-cut, no easy answer, no definitive booklist. Teachers need to have read the books they present to children, they need to select them with care and knowledge and be skilled in judging when and how to use them. Keeping up with the plethora of material available is time consuming and demanding but it is also highly enjoyable and rewarding.

Teachers might keep up with their reading in a number of ways:

1 By having close and regular contact with the Schools Library Service. The librarians advise on and recommend titles, organise courses, workshops and book reviewing groups, and

produce fiction and poetry lists. Teachers might try to visit the Schools Library Service HQ on a regular basis and depart with a small collection for reading: a couple of picture books, a poetry collection, a short story anthology, some recently published non-fiction texts, perhaps a controversial children's story about which the librarian wants an opinion, and one or two books that the librarian feels might be of interest.

2 By keeping in close and regular contact with a good bookshop. Suppliers who specialise in children's literature like Sonia Benster of the Children's Bookshop in Lindley, near Huddersfield, and Madeleine Lindley of the Acorn Centre in Oldham are widely read and select books with knowledge and care. They will send material, recommend titles, tell their customers what new publications have come on the market and which are the most popular with children, and attend teachers' in-service courses and parents' evenings to mount displays and sell books.

3 By reading the reviews. Over the school holidays teachers might catch up on the new publications reviewed in such journals and booklets as those produced by the Thimble Press and the School Library Association. Two essential guides are: *Children's Books of the Year*, published by Andersen Press, London, and The Children's Book Foundation; and *The Good Book Guide to Children's Books* published by Penguin Books, Harmondsworth, and Braithwaite & Taylor Ltd.

4 By listening to the children and finding out what they enjoy reading. Some writers like Roald Dahl have a universal appeal, others are an acquired taste and some they learn to like given time. The stories children enjoy reading depend on a number of factors: age and maturity, ability, environment, experience and interests, even the mood they are in at a particular time. Like adults children have preferences and a story which one child will read avidly will have little impact on another.

Now to some recommendations. This list is very selective and contains only a small number of the 60,000 or so children's books in print. Last year alone over 5,000 new titles were published. The books listed are those that many children have read and enjoyed, which fulfil the criteria outlined earlier in this chapter, and in some measure represent the great variety of reading material now available. The selection is not necessarily the best and I guess that some readers will feel many well-tried favourites and much-loved books have been omitted.

PICTURE BOOKS

The greatest teachers of reading and writing in Britain today are David McKee, Shirley Hughes, Anthony Browne, Graham Oakley, John Burningham, the Ahlbergs, Jan Pienkowski, and a host of others like them. Their intensive courses are very modestly priced and come 'packaged' at two or three pounds a time in the form of wonderful picture books.

(Jeff Hynds, quoted by Liz Waterland, 1988)

Fortunately there is now a vast range of picture books, varied in design, story and illustration. Good picture books, like the ones described below, foster the skills of reading, stimulating and supporting the early reader as he or she struggles to decode the print.

Fred by Posy Simmonds (London: Jonathan Cape, 1987). This warm, funny story with beautifully vivid illustrations is an effective blend of comic strip and picture book. When Sophie and Bick's cat dies they discover that the sly creature has been leading an outrageous double life as a rock star. *Lulu and the Flying Babies* and *The Chocolate Wedding*, also by Posy Simmonds, are as richly illustrated and equally memorable.

Six Dinner Sid by Inga Moore (Hemel Hempstead: Simon & Schuster, 1990). Sid has six owners, lives in six houses and eats six dinners a day. Life is wonderful for the clever cat until he is found out. This is an affectionate and witty tale with wonderfully rich and humorous illustrations.

Monsters by Russell Hoban (London: Gollancz, 1989). Monsters! Monsters! Monsters! John just cannot stop drawing them. His obsession leads to strange and disturbing events! *Bread and Jam for Frances,* by the same author, with pencil drawings by Lilian Hoban, is another captivating and sympathetic story, this time about a little badger who will only eat bread and jam.

Each Peach Pear Plum by Janet and Allan Ahlberg (Harmondsworth: Picture Puffin, 1989). A delightfully simple and fascinating collection of rhyming couplets featuring familiar nursery rhyme characters like Cinderella, Baby Bunting, the Three Bears and Mother Hubbard who are all hiding craftily in the pictures.

Willy the Wimp by Anthony Browne (London: Julia MacRae, 1984). Poor, lonely Willy is frightened of everybody. When the suburban gorilla gang pick on him and call him Willy the Wimp he decides that action is called for. Exercise, special diet, aerobics, boxing and body-building transform Willy into a force to be reckoned with. Written by a favourite children's author, this is a delightfully sharp, sophisticated and amusing story.

Ten Little Swimming Crabs by Beverley Randell with illustrations by John Canty (Walton-on-Thames: Nelson, 1984):

> Ten little swimming crabs,
> Found a fishing line.
> One caught it with its claw . . .
> And then there were nine.

A joining-in book with a simple catchy rhythm and fresh lively illustrations. Also in this series, first published in Australia in 1984, are *Ten Small Koalas, Did You Ever, A Day at the Beach* and *Down by the Water-hole*.

Just a Minute by Anita Harper with illustrations by Susan Hellard (Harmondsworth: Puffin, 1989). Illustrated with witty panache, this is a cleverly written and good-natured tale about the little kangaroo whose parents respond to his excited questions and comments with, 'Just a minute . . . .' Children love to join in and delight in the humour.

Just Awful by Alma Whitney with illustrations by Lilian Hoban (London: Collins, 1976). When little James cuts his finger his teacher sends him to the school nurse. His heart sinks when he hears he has to receive the 'three-part-treatment'. A warm and appealing story with lively, colourful and humorously detailed drawings.

Half a World Away by Arlette Lavie (Swindon: Child's Play, 1988). The children force their elders to take action when a strange purple cloud covers a far-off land. A poignant allegory beautifully illustrated by the author.

Which Shoes to Choose by Bronwyn Elsmore and illustrated by Tracey Clark (Walton-on-Thames: Nelson, 1989). The clown just cannot decide which pair of shoes to choose and the elephant is not much help. A brisk and appealing story written in verse, with clear, bold print and big bright illustrations.

Dr Xargle's Book of Earth Hounds by Jeanne Willis and illustrated by Tony Ross (London: Andersen Press, 1989). Dr Xargle sent his class of aliens to study 'earth babies' (in *Dr Xargle's Book of Earthlets*). Now his extraterrestial pupils revisit Earth to look at 'earth hounds', those lively little creatures who are called man's best friends. Offbeat, amusing and original, this story is enhanced superbly by the quirky and endearing illustrations.

More suggestions for beginning readers:

Hi Cat by Ezra Jack Keats (Harmondsworth: Picture Puffin, 1973)
Look at the Little Ones by Mary Cockett (Knight Books)
The Princess and the Dragon by Audrey Wood (Swindon: Child's Play, 1982)
The Chicken that Could Swim by Paul Adshead (Swindon: Child's Play, 1988)
On My Way to School by Celia Berridge (London: Andrew Deutsch, 1976)
New Clothes for Alex by Mary Dickenson (London: Hippo, 1986)
All in One Piece by Jill Murphy (London: Walker Books, 1989)
The Sad Story of Veronica Who Played the Violin by David McKee (London: Beaver Books, 1988)
I Want an Ice Cream by June Melser and Joy Cowley (Walton-on-Thames: Nelson Story Chest, 1981)
The Baked Bean Queen by Rose Impey and Sue Porter (Harmondsworth: Puffin, 1988)
Tyrone the Horrible by Hans Wilhelm (Hippo, 1989)
Peabody by Rosemary Wells (London: Picturmac, 1987)
The Thorn Witch by E. J. Taylor (London: Walker Books, 1989)
In the Night Kitchen by Maurice Sendak (London: Picture Lions, 1971)

NOVELTY AND POP-UP BOOKS

Pop-up books have never been more popular but they're often frowned upon, and with reason, by reading experts. Unless carefully chosen, they offer a play experience, rather than a reading one.

(From *The World of Children's Books: a Guide to Choosing the Best* by Michele Landsberg, 1988, p.36)

Despite the frowning experts, children are delighted and fascinated by many pop-up books; they love the cleverness and originality and enjoy the element of surprise. The worst kind of pop-up books are mass produced and fall apart after just a few readings. The prose is mechanical and the illustrations garish. The very best pop-up books are sturdy with well-written texts. They are designed to stimulate and support the beginning reader through lively narrative, lyrical repetition of language, verbal jokes, bright original illustrations and paper engineering.

The most comprehensive and original selection of pop-up and die-cut reading books is produced by Child's Play International, Swindon. The range includes:

Beware of the Pog by Kees Moerbeek (1988). A menagerie of crazy creatures jump from the pages. Children are encouraged to mix and match the tops and bottoms and create their own animals. There are happy, gentle, greedy, bad-tempered and many more strange creatures which will chase you, like you, lick your face and sit on your lap.

The Fox in the Farmyard by Keith Moseley and illustrated by Ann Wilson (1986). By pulling the tabs the rowdy chorus of farm animals comes to life every time the sly fox appears.

If Pigs Could Fly by Peter Seymour with illustrations, design and paper engineering by David A. Carter (1988):

> If pigs could fly and Frogs liked pie
> and there were Unicorns,
> If Worms could leap and Sheep could creep,
> and Bulls could wiggle horns . . .

The lively rhythms continue through the sturdy book enhanced by dancing ducks, snoring butterflies and great golden fish that wink from the page.

Ruth's Loose Tooth by Nicholas A. Kerna with illustrations by John Wallner (1987). Ruth is a great brown cow with an old wiggly tooth. Everyone tries to help her to pull it out. The mouse and the goat, the fish and the crow and a variety of other helpful animals and birds tug and toil through the text, each of them heaving on a long piece of string which stretches from page to page. This delightfully clever little book is part of the *Child's Play Action Books Series*. Others include *Curious Kittens*, *The Peek-o-Boo Riddle Book* and *Hide and Seek*.

Patrick and the Puppy by Peter Seymour and designed by Keith Moseley and illustrated by Carol Wynne (1985). A delightful little finger-puppet book. The reader has to help Patrick find the puppy something good to eat. The little finger-puppet wags, nods and shakes his head through the text.

Missing Dad by Carla Dijs (1990). 'Help I am lost. I want my dad!' cries the tiger cub raising a sad little head. He asks the great lumbering polar bear, the ostrich that lifts an enormous neck, the crocodile which snaps long green jaws and rattles a set of sharp teeth, until at last he finds his dad. 'Dad am I glad to see you?' he squeals in delight. 'There is no one like you in the whole world.' A deceptively simple and appealing story guaranteed to bring a lump to the throat. *Missing Mum* is in the same series.

There Were Ten in Bed (1980). When the little one says: 'Roll over!' the children tumble out of bed. The big bold illustrations by Pamela Adams cover the brightly coloured pages.

Zebra Talk by Vanessa Vargo (1990). Can the zebra survive? The question is posed through simple, powerful prose and stark black and white illustrations. Children will 'read the signs' and 'get the message' in this clever and compelling book.

Little Red Riding Hood, illustrated by Kees Moerbeek (1988). Open the book and close it slowly and the characters talk. The wolf opens wide his great toothy jaws and emerges from the page with quite frightening realism.

What's in the Cave by Peter Seymour and illustrated by David A. Carter (1985). A delightfully original and witty pop-up book where children are encouraged to find out what is lurking in the cave by lifting a series of flaps. There is a lazy lizard, a fat bat, a sneaky snake, a friendly frog, a sly spider, a broody bird, a busy beetle and finally a multi-coloured monster which always makes the little ones gasp.

More suggestions for pop-up books:

Surprise by Ron and Atie van der Meer (London: Hamish Hamilton, 1987) and in the same series *Things That Work* and *Playthings*

Dinner Time by Jan Pienkowski (London: Orchard Books, 1989) and also *Little Monsters* and *Small Talk* in the same series

Dinosaurs by Dot and Sy Barlowe (London: Collins, 1988)

The Gingerbread Man retold and illustrated by Irana Shepherd (London: Collins, 1977)

See You Later Alligator by Tony Bradman and Colin Hawkins (London: Methuen, 1986)

Are You my Mother? by P. D. Eastman (London: Collins, 1982)

The Most Amazing Hide-and-Seek Alphabet Book by Robert Crowther (Harmondsworth: Viking Kestrel, 1977)

Is Anyone Home? by Ron Maris (London: Julia McRae, 1985)

Peepo by Janet and Allan Ahlberg (Harmondsworth: Puffin, 1983)

Who Eats the Bone? Who Lives Here? by Ron and Atie van der Meer (London: Methuen, 19??)

POETRY BOOKS

There is no doubt that the combination of rhythm, rhyme and striking illustration brings the reader the closest to a successful and satisfying reading that he or she has ever known. The lines unfold effortlessly once the text has been heard once or twice and the new reader experiences a flow and fluency that may hitherto have been elusive. Then the reader is liberated to enjoy poetry's particular way of saying things.

(From *Developing Readers* by Judith Graham and Elizabeth Plackett, 1987)

Poetry according to Coleridge is 'the best words in the best order' and to Kenneth Koch poetry 'makes children feel happy, capable and creative'. Young readers are quick to appreciate the importance of order and they come to love the rhymes and rhythms of the nursery rhymes read and recited by parents and teachers. There is an enormous range of rich, colourful and appropriate poetry collections available. The following small selection includes poems that are witty, sad, moving, magical, saucy, arresting, contemplative, clever and provocative, written and edited by some of the finest and most popular poets:

Rabbiting On by Kit Wright (London: Fontana Lions, 1978)

Unspun Socks by Spike Milligan (Harmondsworth: Puffin, 1982)

Smile Please by Tony Bradman (Harmondsworth: Puffin, 1989)

That'd Be Telling by Michael Rosen and Joan Griffith (Cambridge: Cambridge University Press, 1988)

The Mighty Slide by Allan Ahlberg (Harmondsworth: Puffin, 1989)

Seen Grandma Lately? by Roy Fuller (London: Andre Deutsch, 1979)

An Imaginary Menagerie by Roger McGough (Harmondsworth: Viking Kestrel, 1990)

A Footprint on the Air by Naomi Lewis (Knight Books, 1985)

The Clever Potato by Vernon Scannell (London: Hutchinson, 1988)

Moon Whales by Ted Hughes (London: Faber & Faber, 1988)

Ask a Silly Question by Irene Rawnsley (London: Methuen, 1988)

A Very First Poetry Book by John Foster (Oxford: Oxford University Press, 1985)

Figgie Hobbin by Charles Causley (Harmondsworth: Puffin, 1979)

Is a Caterpillar Ticklish? by Adrian Rumble (London: Robert Royce, 1986)

Boo to a Goose by John Mole (Calstock: Peterloo Poets, 1987)

Over the Moon by Shirley Hughes (London: Faber & Faber)

Lizard Over Ice ed. Gervase Phinn (Walton-on-Thames: Nelson, 1990)

There's a Poet Behind You by Morag Styles (London: A. & C. Black, 1988)

All Together Now by Tony Bradman (Harmondsworth: Viking Kestrel, 1989)

All the Small Poems by Valerie Worth (New York: Farrar, Straus & Giroux, 1989)

All the Day Through by Wes Magee (London: Evans Brothers, 1982)

Inkslinger by Morag Styles and Helen Cook (London: A. & C. Black, 1990)

Madwhale Midiwhale by Wes Magee (Harmondsworth: Viking Kestrel, 19)

The Jungle Sale by June Crebbin (Harmondsworth: Viking Kestrel 19)

FOLK AND FAIRY TALES

There are some stories that no child should miss: fairy tales, legends and myths. Fairy stories are genuine children's literature, and we know that there are deep and abiding links

63

between the childhood of mankind as preserved in these stories and the early life of each of us.

(From *Learning to Read* by Margaret Meek, 1982)

The familiarity of the fairy tale, the magic and fantasy, the wild, wonderful and exaggerated characters, the fast action and the terrible events, the constant repetitions and finally the happy ending, all combine to create a powerful and fascinating story which captures the child's imagination and remains with him or her long after it has been heard and read.

There are many wonderful and beautifully illustrated tales, traditional and modern, in single editions and in collections, which offer insights into other cultures and into other times:

Fairy Tale Treasury by Raymond Briggs (Harmondsworth: Puffin, 1987)

The Faber Book of Nursery Verse by Barbara Ireson (London: Faber & Faber, 1983)

The Woman in the Moon by James Riordan (London: Hutchinson, 1989)

The Miracle Child by Elizabeth Laird *et al.* (Glasgow: Collins, 1985)

Fairy Tales by Terry Jones illustrated by Michael Foreman (Harmondsworth: Puffin, 1983)

Gods, Men and Monsters of the Greek Myths retold by Michael Gibson (Wallingford: Peter Lowe, 1977)

The Fairy Tales of Oscar Wilde illustrated by Harold Jones (London: Gollancz, 1987)

The Brothers Grimm Popular Folk Tales illustrated by Michael Foreman (1987)

Tales from Grimm retold by Ulla Dolt and Geoffrey Summerfield (London: Ward Lock)

Hans Andersen: His Classic Fairy Tales translated by Erik Haugaars and illustrated by Michael Foreman (1987)

English Fairy Tales by Joseph Jacobs illustrated by Margery Gill (London: Andre Deutsch, 1987)

The Lost Merbaby and the Wishing Nut Tree by Margaret and Mary Baker (Harmondsworth: Puffin)

The Elephant Headed God and Other Hindu Tales by Debjani Chatterjee, illustrated by Margaret Jones (Littleworth, 1989)

The Kingdom Under the Sea and other stories by Joan Aiken,

illustrated by Jan Pienkowski (Harmondsworth: Puffin, 1973)
Fairy Tales of Urekean by W. B. Yeats selected by Neil Philip
Sir Gawain and the Loathly Lady retold by Selina Hastings and
illustrated by Juan Wijngaard (London: Walker Books, 1987)
Mouth Open, Story Jump Out by Grace Hallworth, illustrated
by Art Derry (London: Methuen, 1987)
Ears and Tails and Common Sense Stories from the Caribbean by
Philip M. Sherlock and Hilary Sherlock (London: Macmillan,
1983)

The traditional tales in *The Story Chest Series* (published by
Thomas Nelson, Walton-on-Thames) come from many countries
and different sources. Gambia, Egypt, Brazil, Japan, Vietnam,
China and India are only a few of the countries represented. As a
collection it provides a splendidly rich resource for reading aloud
and for classroom work. Children are encouraged to listen, watch
and join in with the natural lively language of the stories. They
have been carefully selected and underpinned by a clear philosophy:

> Traditional tales are not without problems. Male and
> female roles are often more robustly and separately defined
> than is accepable today, and issues of race may be presented
> in a challenging way. The attitudes and ideas expressed
> in many of the stories are thought-provoking even for
> adults.
>
> The stories provide an ideal opportunity for discussion
> and for exploration of the underlying theme of the text; it
> may be goodness, honesty, truth or the victory of the weak
> over the strong.
> (From *The Story Chest Teacher's File* by Pam Hutchinson
> *et al.*, 1991, p. 203)

STORY BOOKS

Books that celebrate the range of life's possibilities, books
that acknowledge and delight in the variety of human
experience, books that by their virtuosity of language make
the reader share in that curiosity and excitement – these are
the books that enhance children's lives, that give them food
for thought, pique their imaginations and sensibilities and

arouse their sense of wonder.

(From *The World of Children's Books: A Guide to Choosing the Best* by Michele Landsberg, 1988, p. 222)

The range of story books is vast: fantasy, ghosts, science fiction and animal stories; adventure, mystery, family and schools stories; cartoons, nature, evolution, hobbies, sport, history – the list is endless. As teachers it is our responsibility to bring children and books together and give them a range worth their time and attention.

The following small selection might form the core of a classroom library for early readers:

A Bear Called Paddington by Michael Bond (London: Fontana Lions, 1988)

The BFG by Roald Dahl and illustrated by Quentin Blake (Harmondsworth: Puffin, 1984)

The Magic Finger by Roald Dahl (Harmondsworth: Puffin, 1989)

Danny, the Champion of the World by Roald Dahl (Harmondsworth: Puffin, 1984)

The Shrinking of Treehorn by Florence Parry Heide (Harmondsworth: Puffin, 1975)

Dinner at Alberta's by Russell Hoban (Harmondsworth: Puffin, 1987)

Stanley Bagshaw and the Short Sighted Football Trainer by Bob Wilson (Harmondsworth: Puffin, 1987)

Father Christmas by Raymond Briggs (Harmondsworth: Puffin, 1975)

Flat Stanley by Jeff Brown (London: Methuen, 1974)

My Dog Sunday by Leila Berg (Harmondsworth: Puffin, 1979)

Brother Dusty Feet by Rosemary Sutcliff, illustrated by C. Walter Hodges (Oxford: Oxford University Press)

Chips and Jessie by Shirley Hughes (London: Fontana Lions, 1987)

Grump and the Hairy Mammoth by Derek Sampson (London: Methuen, 1971)

The Little Prince by Antoine de Saint-Exupery (London: Piccolo, 1982)

Five Children's Stories by E. Nesbit (Harmondsworth: Puffin, 1984)

The Princess and the Goblin by George Macdonald (Harmondsworth: Puffin, 1984)

Finn Family Moomintroll by Tove Jansson (Oxford: Windrush, 1989)

The Phantom Fisherboy by Ruth Ainsworth (London: Andre Deutsch)

Worst Witch Books by Jill Murphy (Harmondsworth: Puffin)

The Ramona Books by Beverley Cleary (Harmondsworth: Puffin)

Ursula Bear by Sheila Lavelle (London: Hamish Hamilton, 1977)

Tales of Oliver Pig by Jean Van Leeuwen and illustrated by Arnold Lobel (London: Fontana)

Meg and Mog Books by Helen Nicoll and Jan Pienkowski (Harmondsworth: Puffin)

The *Banana Books* (published by Heinemann, Oxford) offer a wide range of early reading material: stories about animals, school, science fiction and ghosts. They have bright, attractive, hard covers and include stories by Kevin Crossley-Holland, Dick King-Smith, Sheila Lavelle, Anne Fine, Marjorie Darke, Rose Impey, and Floella Benjamin.

Toppers (published by Malin/Deutsch, London) are a collection of lively, clever, enchanting, witty, moving and endearing stories which provide lots of reading fun for early readers.

The Story Chest Selection (published by Thomas Nelson, Walton-on-Thames) is a comprehensive primary reading programme which offers a rich variety, breadth, depth and genuine engagement. The stories are infinitely varied in subjects, ideas and situations. There are sad, strange, humorous, tender, touching, exciting, warm, vivid stories from different cultures, in varying styles, of contrasting moods. At the end of most of the stories is a picture of the author with interesting biographical details.

The following texts are for the teacher's bookshelf and contain stories ideal for reading aloud and sharing with others:

Lion at School and other stories by Philippa Pearce (Harmondsworth: Puffin). A collection of nine fresh, funny and lively stories which contains *The Great Sharp Scissors*.

It Shouldn't Happen to a Frog and other stories by Catherine Storr (London: Piccolo). These warm-hearted and satisfying stories are about Lisa – a modern girl caught up in the traditional fairy tales of the Frog Prince, the Three Bears, Bluebeard and Cinderella. They give a modern twist to the favourite children's tales and are lively, inventive and great fun to read aloud.

More Stories from Listen With Mother (London: Sparrow Books/BBC). A treasure house of early children's literature full of sparkling language, lively dialogue, shrewd insight, excitement and humour. Authors represented include Eugenie Summerfield, Jean McKenzie, Ann Das, Gordon Snell and Elizabeth Robinson.

Stories from Around the World from the Federation of Children's Book Groups (London: Hodder & Stoughton). Over 21,000 children from all over the world took part in the testing of these short stories. The aim of this collection is 'for families and teachers to share these stories with children in the hope that it will bring our love of storytelling to others'. The fifteen stories range from the affectionate and humorous to the sad and touching and they are written by some of the finest writers: Anita Desai, Grace Hallworth, Edna O'Brien, Alf Proysen, Joan Aiken, and Virginia Hamilton.

Stories for Christmas by Alison Uttley (London: Faber). Twelve splendid magical stories which capture the atmosphere of the season. Written with great emotional honesty and warmth by a fine storyteller.

Scottish Highland Tales selected by Ian Crighton Smith (London: Ward Lock). Tall tales about the great mountains and desolate lochs drawn from traditional and original sources to stimulate children's imagination and encourage lively discussion. They are magical, dreamy and mysterious and include eerie tales about giants, birds transformed into men, seals changed into women, the brown bear of the green glen and the serpent's stone. Enhanced with delightfully robust line drawings by a variety of illustrators.

A Necklace of Raindrops and other stories by Joan Aiken (Harmondsworth: Puffin). Eight enthralling, ingenious and magical stories all told with economy and poetic intensity by a masterful storyteller.

Tilly Mint Tales by Berlie Doherty (London: Fontana). An absolutely sure-fire, read-aloud collection of short stories. Amusing, good hearted and gripping, wildly funny and verbally inventive.

The Magic Doll and other stories by Naomi Lewis (London: Methuen). Poignant, sensitive, endearing stories from an author who has a fine understanding of children's feelings and concerns.

INFORMATION BOOKS

Non-fiction texts should include those closely related to the world of the child and extend to those which enable children to deepen an understanding of the world in which they live. (From *English in the National Curriculum, Programmes of Study, Key Stage 1, Para 7*, Department of Education and Science, 1989)

Publishers which offer a comprehensive list of clear, well-written and attractively illustrated, non-fiction material for the early reader include the following:

Wayland (Hove)

A series of interesting topics are explored in a clear and imaginative way. The language is simple and readable, the print, illustrations and diagrams bright and generous. There are *Starting Science* books about animals, floating and sinking, food, sound, music, waste and weather, *Wayland Topics* about great disasters, maps, money and peoples of the world, and individual titles on a range of subjects. Recently published texts include:

Wood by Graham Carrick (1989). The different kinds of wood and woodworking tools are described clearly and simply along with some imaginative projects for children to undertake.
Leather Shoes by Wayne Jackman (1990). Why do we wear shoes? How are they made? All is explained in this clear, factual text which is brightly illustrated with colour photographs.
Design by Catherine McDermott (1989). Within the forty-eight pages the writer manages to cover many aspects of design from Victorian times up to the present day. The style is clear and very readable and enhanced by bright illustrations and photographs.
Let's Look at Books. Rhona Nottridge, the editor of this series, writes in a simple, clear and lively style which will appeal to the young. There are twelve books in the series covering many of the topics teachers of young children deal with: bikes, castles, colours, farming, sunshine and transport. Brightly coloured illustrations, line drawings and clear diagrams illustrate the texts and there are useful contents, glossary, and 'books to read' sections in each.
Topics by David Lambert. For the slightly older child who can

cope with a more complex language, these books are ideal. Sixteen topics are considered in some detail and depth. Bright illustrations, colour photographs and clear sharp maps, diagrams and charts enhance a well-written text printed in clear bold type.

Great Lives. A wide collection of famous people from Shakespeare to Elvis Presley, Magellan to Mother Teresa, is considered in this series. The biographies are sharply observant and fascinating and contain a wealth of interesting information. The format of each book is clear with useful pages devoted to contents, dates and events, glossary, books to read and index.

Franklin Watts (London)

Clear, well-explained texts offer a wealth of information on the principles of how things work as well as practical advice for children for developing their own ideas.

Typical of the texts in this excellent series is *Muscles and Machines* by Neil Ardley. Children will be fascinated by this clever and very readable book which explores how things move. We learn about gravity, friction and energy in a language which is carefully and simply used. Bright, clear and appropriate diagrams and photographs help to clarify the more difficult concepts.

Nelson (Walton-on-Thames)

The *Stepping Stones Series* adds a non-fiction strand to the *Story Chest Reading Resource* and offers a range of information book features. The poet Wes Magee takes a fascinating look at 'collections' – everything from the contents of a matchbox to a children's library. Dr Barrie Wade, the author and educationist, describes children's lives in a series of photographic biographies and Andrea Bradshaw, an experienced infant teacher and writer, considers kites, bells, the countryside, machines and the solar system. Each text has been carefully vetted by a subject expert (Patrick Moore in the case of *The Solar System*) and a linguist who has a special expertise in the language of information books for young children. The subject matter in these bright, readable and fascinating little books supports the National Curriculum Key Stage 1 Science, Geography and History, as well as English.

Other useful and well-written non-fiction selections are the *First Sight Books* (London: A. & C. Black), the *Longman First Look at ...* books and the bold, colourful and very popular texts published by Usborne (London).

A READING ENTITLEMENT

The National Curriculum stresses the importance of providing a range of rich and stimulating texts, both fiction and non-fiction. All pupils are entitled to hear and read for themselves picture books, nursery rhymes, poems, folk-tales, myths, legends and other literature.

Children should

> encounter an environment in which they are surrounded by books and other reading material presented in an attractive and inviting way.

Activities should

> ensure that pupils hear books, stories and poems read aloud ... as well as rhymes, poems, songs, and familiar stories (including traditional stories from a variety of cultures).
> (From *English in the National Curriculum, Programmes of Study, Key Stage 1, Paras 7 & 10*, Department of Education and Science, 1989)

If we provide children with this variety of stimulating texts, with stories and poems that fascinate, excite, intrigue and amuse, that give them new insights, that open their minds and imaginations and that introduce them to the wonderful richness and range of language, then we offer the very best models for their own writing. It is axiomatic but worth stating: all great writers are or were great readers. The poems and stories which follow were written by children who are avid, eager readers, who work in rich reading environments, helped, encouraged and supported by sensitive and skilful teachers.

Debbie is 6 and in her lively description of the clever tortoise (Figure 3.2) we see how her writing has been influenced by the amusing and sophisticated stories she has heard. Debbie's teacher makes the sharing of stories a pleasurable experience building on the oral language and knowledge her children bring from home.

The aims stated in the school's 'Language Development Policy' include:

- to enable children to become confident, independent and fluent readers;
- to develop children's skills in reading competence by exposing them to a wide range of appropriate texts;
- to acknowledge and value pre-reading skills, including 'pretend' reading;
- to give children the opportunity to read for pleasure and information;
- to give children the opportunity to share their reading with others;
- to encourage children to use a variety of reading strategies to decode text including contextual, visual, letter/sound features of words and phonic cues;
- to ensure that the reading material presented takes account of continuity and progression;
- to monitor and assess the children's reading.

Elizabeth is nearly 6 and has been in her infant school for less than a year. Much of her writing demonstrates an unusual zest, freshness and originality (Figure 3.3). Her self-esteem as a reader and a writer is high and she speaks with confidence about her work: 'I'm very good at stories,' she said. When asked why she was such a good writer she replied that her mummy wrote poems, her daddy read stories to her and her grannie often told her stories. She receives books as presents at Christmas and on her birthday and visits the local library regularly.

In Elizabeth's school there is a clear, whole-school approach to reading. A useful policy document includes the following objectives:

Early readers should:

- read an increasingly wide variety of books, including poetry and non-fiction;
- be actively encouraged to become more independent in their reading;
- recognise letter/sound correspondence – the phonic alphabet;
- understand how and why punctuation is used;

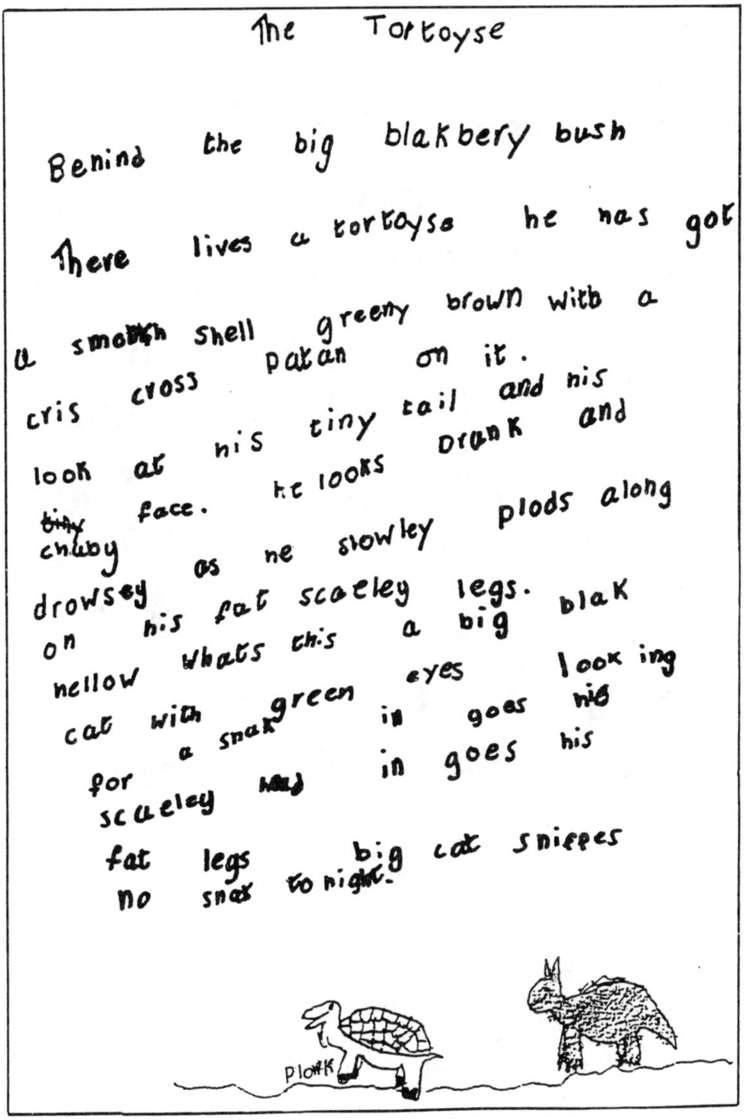

The Tortoyse

Benind the big blakbery bush

There lives a tortoyse he has got

a smolish shell greeny brown with a cris cross patan on it. look at his tiny tail and his tiny face. he looks Drunk and chuby drowsey as he slowley plods along on his fat scaeley legs. blak hellow whats this a big cat with a snak green eyes looking for a snak in goes his scaeley head in goes his fat legs big cat snieees no snak tonight.

plonk

Figure 3.2

73

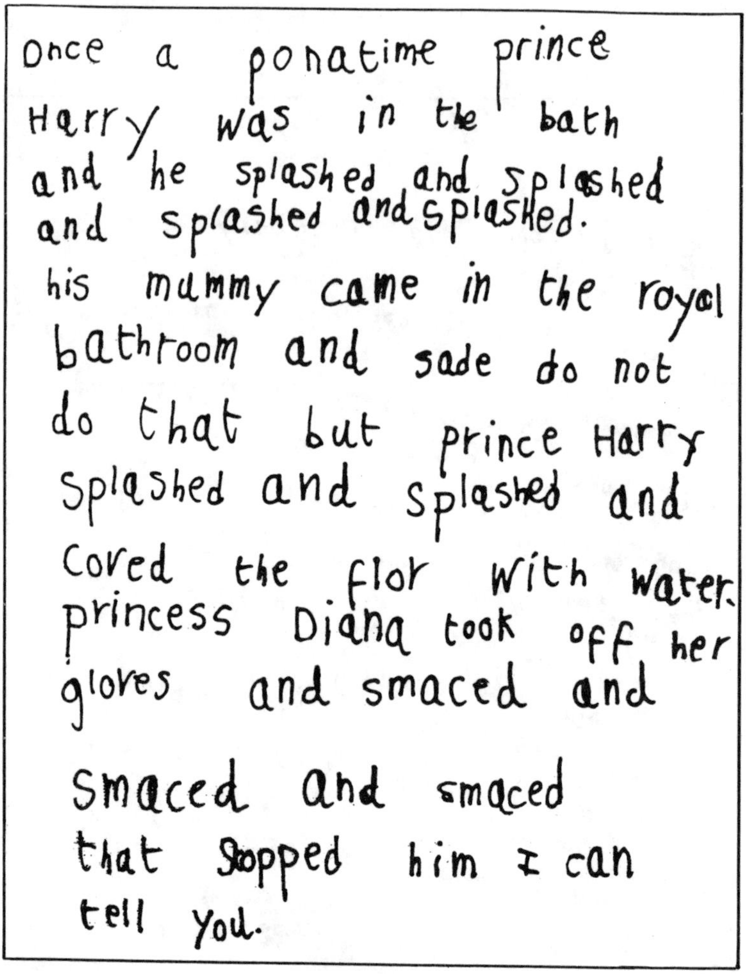

Once a ponatime prince
Harry was in the bath
and he splashed and splashed
and splashed and splashed.
his mummy came in the royal
bathroom and sade do not
do that but prince Harry
splashed and splashed and
Cored the flor with water.
princess Diana took off her
gloves and smaced and

smaced and smaced
that stopped him I can
tell you.

Figure 3.3

- develop the habit of reading quietly;
- be heard to read by the teacher on a regular basis;
- be encouraged in their reading to use pause and expression;
- listen and respond to a variety of stories and poems read aloud by the teacher;
- become more reflective and critical about what they have read.

Mark is 9 and an articulate (Figure 3.4), lively and interesting

My Nan.

I like my Nan.
She's raund and rinkly and powdery
And smells of flowers and soap.
She's as comfy as a coshen to sit on.
When my Mom shouts at me
I go to my Nan.
She cuduls me and says
Never mind love
Your Mum was like that
When she was a littel girl
A real grumpybum.

Mark

Figure 3.4

boy. His teacher actively encourages all the pupils in her class to read, building on the children's success so that they clearly see themselves as young readers who turn naturally to books for pleasure and for information. Mark's teacher ensures that:

- the children are surrounded by bright, glossy backed and appealing books and encouraged to read for meaning;

- the children hear stories and poems read regularly and are encouraged to discuss them and read them for themselves;
- the children receive reassurance, respect and sensitive help;
- reading experiences are carefully structured, purposeful and enjoyable;
- the children discuss and evaluate the organisation, form and style of what they read and relate this to their own writing;
- good literature is presented to the children through the teacher, visiting writers and librarians, cassette tapes, radio and television broadcasts;
- a range of simple and appropriate dictionaries and non-fiction books is available;
- a practical and cumulative system of assessment is used.

Dominic is 11 and excited about moving to the comprehensive school next term. His nose is never out of a book and he has a growing collection of novels, stories and poetry anthologies in his bedroom at home. Most of the books he buys from the school bookshop. All through his primary school career Dominic has found the work he has undertaken challenging and interesting and he has been fortunate to have been taught by sensitive, sympathetic and enthusiastic teachers with wide reading interests – helping, stimulating, discussing, challenging, reading and recommending. His poems (Figures 3.5 and 3.6) are full of the surprises and sly humour of Michael Rosen's verse and his stories are as boisterous, sharply observed and inventive as those written by Philippa Pearce.

If as teachers we endeavour to encourage children to turn to books as sources of great pleasure, we must ensure that it is matched by our own professional commitment. We must know the range of books available, what kind of poems and stories interest individual pupils, and be in a strong position to advise and help in the choice of reading material. Just as non-reading children are made by non-reading parents so the problem is compounded by non-reading teachers. Unless our pupils see us enjoying reading and hear us talk with knowledge and enthusiasm about books it is hardly likely that we will 'habituate them to the Vast'.

We read books to find out who we are. What other people, real or imaginary, do and think and feel . . . is an essential

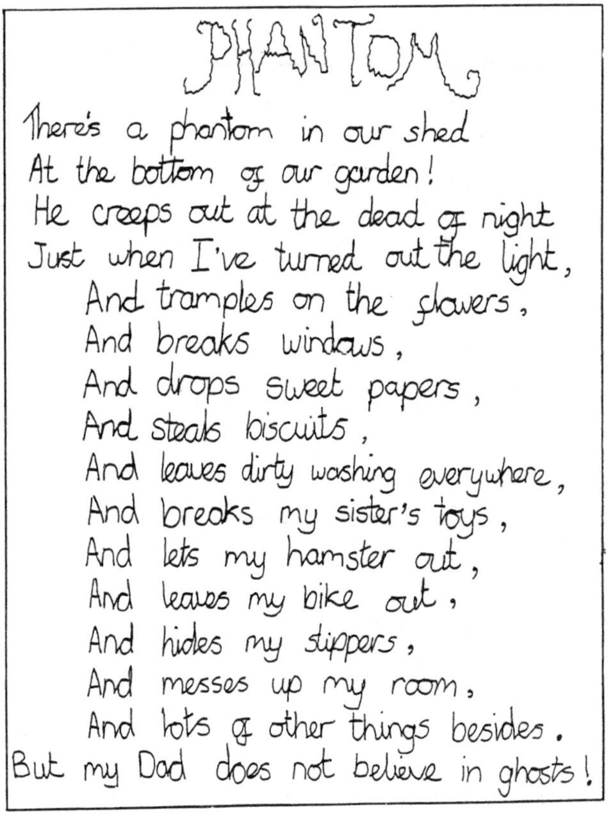

> # PHANTOM
>
> There's a phantom in our shed
> At the bottom of our garden!
> He creeps out at the dead of night
> Just when I've turned out the light,
>   And tramples on the flowers,
>   And breaks windows,
>   And drops sweet papers,
>   And steals biscuits,
>   And leaves dirty washing everywhere,
>   And breaks my sister's toys,
>   And lets my hamster out,
>   And leaves my bike out,
>   And hides my slippers,
>   And messes up my room,
>   And lots of other things besides.
> But my Dad does not believe in ghosts!

Figure 3.5

guide to our understanding of what we ourselves are and
may become.

(From *The Language of the Night*
by Ursula K. Le Guin, 1989)

QUESTIONS FOR PERSONAL REFLECTION OR GROUP DISCUSSION

1   In more schools, heads need to develop clear, well-
formulated policies which are subscribed to by the whole
staff and which form the basis of a planned programme of
reading.

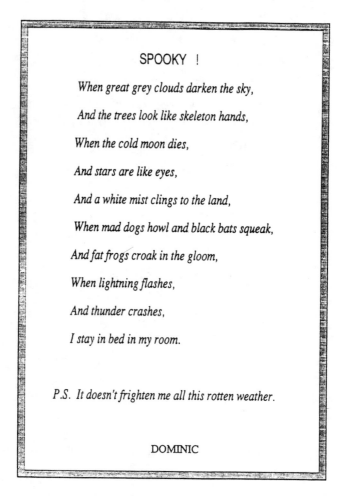

Figure 3.6

(From *The Teaching and Learning of Reading in Primary Schools: A Report by HMI, Para 80*, Department of Education and Science, 1990)
Few schools have consistent policies which ensure that children receive a suitably broad and balanced experience of good literature, including poetry, from year to year.
(From *Aspects of Primary Education: The Teaching and*

Learning of Language and Literacy, an Inspectorate Review by HMI, Para 21, Department of Education and Science, 1990)

As a staff, examine your school's English Policy Document. Does it include an agreed plan for reading development? Are there clear and well-understood aims and a description of the methods for achieving them? Is there a book selection policy? Are there procedures for assessing and recording progress?

2 In the HMI report, *The Teaching and Learning of Reading in Primary Schools,* certain characteristics were listed of those schools which achieved high standards of reading. One characteristic was that the schools *had a wide variety of appropriate books and other materials, effectively organised and matched to individual needs* (Para 6, xii). The report concluded that: *Good standards of reading cannot be achieved without adequate and suitable resources* (Para 86).

How do you as a staff decide what is adequate and suitable for the pupils in your school? How do you keep up to date with children's literature? For example, does each member of staff review books and report back to colleagues? Discuss and write down the ways in which you could keep yourselves better informed about children's literature.

3 Look at the book corner in your classroom. Is it attractive and inviting? What are the weaknesses in the stock of books? Does it contain a full range of reading material including:

- books without words
- big books
- poetry
- non-fiction and reference material
- books suitable for the struggling reader
- books suitable for the gifted reader?

4 Devise an annotated booklist for parents which includes advice on the selection of books.

5 Devise a set of guidelines for children about the selection of suitable books.

6 Conduct a small-scale survey of the children in your class to discover what they read and the factors which influence their choice of books. You might consider such areas as:

- book jacket

- subject matter
- illustrations
- familiarity with author
- print layout
- paperbacks v. hardbacks
- teacher influence
- parental influence
- influence of television (adaptations etc.)

RECOMMENDED READINGS

Bennett, Jill (1975) *Learning To Read with Picture Books.* Stroud: Thimble Press. This short book has become a standard source of ideas about and inspiration for changes in the way young children are helped to become readers. It focuses on books themselves supplying a comprehensive annotated selection of real books for beginning readers which is updated as new editions are printed.

There are a number of useful journals which will help you to increase your knowledge of children's books and keep you in touch with the world of children's books:

Books for Keeps, six times a year. Feature articles and short reviews.
Books for Your Children, three times a year. A lively journal aimed at parents.
Dragon's Teeth, four times a year. The anti-racist children's book magazine with features and reviews, mainly on multicultural books.
Language and Learning, three times a year. Contains articles from teachers on the work in the classroom they are doing in the field of language.
Language Matters, three times a year. Contains articles on language and literacy teaching in school.
Signal, three times a year. Reflective articles on various aspects of children's literature.

Also: Book Trust Touring Exhibitions provide a focus of interest, offering children and parents the opportunity to look at, handle and read carefully selected children's books, e.g. *Children's Books of the Year* - an annual exhibition of over 300 titles for children of all ages (Book Trust, Book House, 45 East Hill, London SW18 2QZ).

BIBLIOGRAPHY

Baynton, Martin (1990) *Why Do You Love Me?* London: Walker Books.
Bennett, Jill (1982) *A Choice of Stories.* School Library Association.
Bettelheim, Bruno and Zelan, Karen (1982) *On Learning to Read: The Child's Fascination with Meaning.* London: Thames & Hudson.
Bradman, Tony (1986) *Will You Read Me a Story? The Parent's Guide to*

Children's Books. Wellingborough: Thorson's Publishing Group.

Butler, Dorothy (1986) *Five to Eight*. London: Bodley Head.

Cass, Joan E. (1984) *Literature and the Young Child*. Harlow: Longman.

Chambers, Aidan (1985) *Booktalk: Occasional Writing on Literature and Children*. London: Bodley Head.

Children's Book Foundation (1990) *Children's Books of the Year*, selected by Julia Eccleshare. London: Andersen Press.

Colwell, Eileen (1991) *Story Telling*. Stroud: Thimble Press.

Crossley-Holland, Kevin (1989) *Sleeping Nanna*. London: Orchard Books.

DES (1975) *A Language for Life: The Bullock Report*. London: HMSO.

DES (1988) *Report of the Committee of Inquiry into the Teaching of English Language: The Kingman Report*. London: HMSO.

DES (1989) *English in the National Curriculum*. London: HMSO.

DES (1990) *Aspects of Primary Education: The Teaching and Learning of Language and Literacy, an Inspection Review by H.M.I.* London: HMSO.

DES (1990) *The Teaching and Learning of Reading in Primary Schools: A Report by H.M.I.* London: HMSO.

Girling, Brough. (1989) *The Woodfield Lecture*, given at the University of Loughborough, under the sponsorship of Woodfield and Stanley Ltd, Huddersfield.

Graham, Judith and Plackett, Elizabeth (1987) *Developing Readers*. School Library Association.

Harper, Anita (1988) *It's Not Fair*. Harmondsworth: Picture Puffin.

Hastings, Selina (1988) *The Man Who Wanted to Live For Ever*. London: Walker Books.

Holmes, Richard (1990) *Coleridge: Early Visions*. London: Hodder & Stoughton.

Hutchinson, Pamela, *et al.* (1991) *The Story Chest Teacher's File*. Walton-on-Thames: Thomas Nelson.

Koch, Kenneth *Wishes and Dreams*.

Landsberg, Michele (1988) *The World of Children's Books: a Guide to Choosing the Best*. Hemel Hempstead: Simon & Schuster.

Leeson, Robert (1985) *Reading and Writing: the Past, Present and Future of Fiction for the Young*. London: Collins.

Le Guin, Ursula (1989) *The Language of the Night*. London: Women's Press.

Lewis, C. S. (1977) in Meek M., Warlow A., and Barton G. (eds) *The Cool Web: The Pattern of Children's Reading*. London: Bodley Head.

Meek, Margaret (1970) *How Texts Teach What Readers Learn*. Stroud: Thimble Press.

Meek, Margaret (1982) *Learning to Read*. London: Bodley Head.

O'Connor, Maureen (1990) *How to Help Your Child Through School*. London: Harrap.

Phinn, Gervase (1986) 'Fiction in the classroom'. In Roy Blatchford (ed.) *The English Teacher's Handbook*. London: Hutchinson.

Phinn, Gervase (1987) 'No language to speak of: Children talking and writing'. In Tony Booth, Patricia Potts and Will Swann (eds) *Preventing Difficulties in Learning*. Oxford: Basil Blackwell/Open University.

Raban, Bridie and Moon, Cliff (1978) *Books and Learning to Read*. School Library Association.

Rosen, Betty (1988) *And None of it Was Nonsense: The Power of Storytelling in School*. London: Mary Glasgow.

Rousseau, Jean-Jacques (1781) *The Confessions*.

Waterland, Liz (1988) *Read With Me: an Apprenticeship Approach to Reading*. Stroud: Thimble Press.

4

READING AND WRITING ACROSS THE CURRICULUM

Alison Littlefair

LEARNING TO READ AND READING TO LEARN

In all the argument about how reading should be taught little is said about how far learning to read is related to reading to learn. It has often been assumed that once children can read narrative adequately they can transfer that skill and read information with equal competence. Yet this confidence is not necessarily shared by teachers of older children. Research some years ago by Lunzer and Gardner (1979) suggested that secondary school teachers had such little faith in the reading ability of their pupils that they consistently avoided giving their pupils reading tasks. Indeed, the average 'burst of reading' undertaken by first-year secondary school pupils was given as under 15 seconds. We do not have up-to-date research to compare with this data but we are aware that many teachers have thought it prudent to simplify more difficult subject texts by producing worksheets. This solution may have eased problems for our pupils but the result has been that we have not grappled with the task of teaching children to read a range of texts.

We know that story is a very powerful influence on children's development both as readers and writers. We also know that most children will require equal competency in both reading and writing non-narrative texts if they are to manage the demands of later education and indeed of adult life.

Much of the discussion and concern about teaching reading centres on how children achieve initial competency which is usually taken to mean the ability to read stories. Of course this is of prime importance, but the discussion rarely continues to consider how we help readers to develop that ability so that they can read a variety of texts with understanding. If we are to extend our children's reading we require a comprehensive reading curriculum which takes into account both narrative and non-narrative texts.

We all know of children who are fascinated by information books. Non-narrative books are commonly displayed in classrooms for children to 'dip into' or use with more purpose because they relate to a specific topic. Many children, however, will not progress beyond glancing at the illustrations in these books. Our task is to guide all young readers so that they become familiar with the way non-narrative texts are written.

DIFFERENT TEXT PATTERNS

Non-narrative texts are not organised in the same way as narrative. Katherine Perera (1984) contrasts the unfamiliarity of non-narrative with the fact that stories are part of our oral culture. Children are able to predict what will happen in a story because they know the kind of arrangement of ideas and language used by story writers, but we do not recognise non-narrative texts in the same way, which means that 'children cannot bring to them the structural predictions that they are able to bring to their reading of stories' (Perera, 1984, p.325).

Both psychologists and linguists have discussed how the pattern within texts or discourses is created. The overall structures of texts are sometimes seen as 'macro-structures' (van Dijk, 1977) which are dictated by the type of text which is involved. But we cannot imagine that there are different texts for every kind of content that is written about. The organisation of texts must be related to the sort of thinking which is involved. So the organisation of a story is different from that of an explanation because the writer's thinking is different. Needless to say writers use language as they organise their text and express their meaning.

LINGUISTIC INSIGHTS

If we have some linguistic understanding of how writers choose language for their varying purposes we have valuable insights which can greatly inform our teaching of both reading and writing across the curriculum. It is not sufficient simply to expose all children to a wide range of texts. We have to help young readers not only to read the content of the text but also to become aware how that content is organised. In other words our concern is to teach children how language varies as we read and write for different purposes.

Fortunately we now have the benefit of considerable research into ways in which we use language in a range of situations. Most of this research has followed the thinking of M.A.K. Halliday. Even more fortunate is the fact that many of these linguists are studying the relevance of this work for teaching and learning language within schools.

Writers' purposes and the genres of texts

A group of Halliday's colleagues have quite specifically studied the various ways in which we communicate in both spoken and written language (Martin et al., 1987). They suggest that we do not organise spoken and written texts in an *ad hoc* manner but rather we choose a form of genre of language which we have learned within our culture.

We know a great deal implicitly about language for we are experienced language users. As soon as we wish to read or write we choose a form or genre of writing which we think is appropriate. This is the overall organisation or form of our text. For example, we will probably not write a letter to the tax inspector in the same form as we would write a recipe for a favourite dish. Our purpose for writing would be quite different. So there is a connection between our purpose for writing and speaking and the form of the text we choose.

Let us relate this linguistic thinking to kinds of text organisation which we find in non-narrative books. The author who plans an explanatory book will probably organise information into some kind of logical structure; the author who plans to write instructions for an activity will probably organise the information into some kind of list. Competent readers recognise these two kinds of text structures and predict the kind of meanings which are involved. It is reasonable to suggest that we explain to young readers the implication of different text forms when it is appropriate. In other words, we can point out that the purpose of a sequential form of text we find in a story is not the same as that of a non-sequential text form we may find in an information book.

CHRONOLOGICAL AND NON-CHRONOLOGICAL LANGUAGE

Our understanding of the complexity within texts is perhaps made clearer by Katherine Perera's reference (1984) to chronological and non-chronological writing. Chronological writing refers to a sequential organisation of text. When we read narrative we are carried along by some kind of chronological sequence of events, by the actions of the characters. Stories grip our interest. We follow the events in the same way as we watch events unfold on the television whether on the news or in the action of a play. Indeed, our everyday conversations very often relate events.

But we must be careful not to equate chronological writing only with narrative. Non-narrative texts can themselves have a chronological pattern as in some book reviews or in a description of an activity. There is a distinct sequence of events in this extract from a non-narrative book:

> *Studying cells* You can see the cells of an onion quite easily with a microscope.
> Cut a slice of the onion, carefully peel off a tiny piece of the thin skin. Lay this skin on a microscope slide. Place a drop of water on the centre of the skin. Gently put a coverslip over it. What does the onion skin look like under the microscope? Can you see the tiny boxlike cells?
>
> (Jennings, 1986, p.13)

Many non-narrative texts follow a 'non-chronological' pattern. If we look at the following extract we can see that there is a general statement about the topic which is followed by more detailed description. So we can alert pupils to recognise something of the way in which the meaning is organised.

> *Air and the Human Body*
> Humans must breath air to live. It is essential for our survival that our bodies receive the oxygen that is contained in the air. We obtain this oxygen through a process called *respiration*.
>
> In this process we breathe in, or inhale, air through our noses or our mouths. The air goes down a tube called a *windpipe* to our *lungs*, two large spongy bags in our chests.

Our lungs take oxygen from the air and mix it with our blood. The oxygen is then transported to all parts of the body in the blood-stream. The body uses up the oxygen and produces a waste gas called carbon dioxide. This gas is passed out of the body, or exhaled, when we breathe out. There is extra moisture as well as the extra carbon dioxide in the air we breathe out.

(Carter *et al.*, 1990, p.8)

Registers of language

But it is not only the form of these kinds of text which may be unfamiliar; it is also the language which the author uses within the text. When we write or speak we choose vocabulary and grammar which we think is appropriate for our purpose and our situation. But how do we choose that variety or 'register' of language?

Certainly our choice of language is not entirely free. Halliday (1989) suggests that we are constrained by three factors: what we wish to write about (the field), how we want to use language (the mode) and by our audience (the tenor). It is these interactive factors which result in a register of language. Of course we can defy the norms of appropriateness in any way we like but we would have a purpose for doing that!

Children learn at quite an early age that we speak differently in different situations for they hear differences all around them – at home, in school, on the television. They soon come to know that the language of the playground is not necessarily the language of the classroom. Yet we cannot rely on the same awareness of the meaning of written registers of language. Research (Chapman, 1987; Littlefair, 1991) suggests that the majority of children do not spontaneously develop an implicit awareness and under-standing of different varieties or registers of written language.

The impersonal registers in many non-narrative texts

At first pupils read the language of simple storybooks, which is reasonably close to the language of speech. As they read more complex storybooks they meet language which is increasingly removed from their everyday spoken language.

We have already seen that when we speak we respond to our situation and to the interaction of our listener(s). Writing, however, is not such a spontaneous activity. Even if we write about personal experiences we write in retrospect for the experience is past and so we recollect and reflect. The language we use is, therefore, far more deliberate than spoken language. The differences between spoken and written language increase in formality as we read and write for information. Language refers less and less to the immediate environment. It becomes 'decontextualised' (Donaldson, 1978) and even abstract. As children begin to read more advanced explanations and descriptions they meet increasingly decontextualised language.

Almost twenty years ago, Halliday (1975) noted that many children meet a new function of language when they enter school, that of representing ideas and opinions. In the same year the Bullock Report (DES, 1975, p.31) urged greater intervention by teachers in children's language development:

> This involves creating situations in which, to satisfy his own purpose, a child encounters the need to use more elaborate forms and is thus motivated to extend the complexity of language available to him.

Reading and writing across the curriculum provide us with this kind of learning and teaching situation.

PREPARING FOR READING ACROSS THE CURRICULUM

Listening to non-chronological language

The National Curriculum for Reading (DES, 1989) is somewhat vague in its reference to non-narrative texts. Nevertheless, the importance of reading for information is stressed and there is emphasis on teaching reading skills such as skimming and scanning, and the awareness of lists of contents, indexes and glossaries. These competencies are important, but facts are 'embedded' in texts and it is the texts themselves which are unfamiliar. If we are to help young readers to extend their competence in reading narrative to competence in reading non-chronological texts then we must begin early in the primary school to familiarise children with the rhythm of these genres of writing, for it is very different. As Margaret Meek (1988, p.21) says:

The most important single lesson that children learn from texts is the nature and variety of written discourse, the different ways that language lets a writer tell, and the many and different ways a reader reads.

Our first strategy then is to read non-narrative to young children and to discuss new knowledge with them. This is perhaps not so straightforward as it seems. Later in their school life children will read and write more formal information texts and will be expected to contribute to discussion about ideas and concepts. In order to prepare children for these complex tasks we might begin to discuss with them matters outside their personal experience. In this way the direction of our teaching moves away from the world of imagination and personal involvement and enters the world of facts and ideas. We can help to introduce a model of the language of explanation or description if we ourselves gradually introduce more factual description into our discussions about science or other areas of knowledge with our children.

Early reading of non-chronological texts

We may well have problems when we come to select non-chronological books to read to young children. Many authors are reluctant to write non-chronological language, and without doubt it is a difficult task to simplify explanations and descriptions. In addition, some authors hold the view that information should be presented to children in the form of a story. We then find that such writers produce chronological text which is not helpful. Not only is this text a limiting model for children's own writing, it may also create difficulties for readers who search the text for information. So we must be careful that our selection of non-narrative books includes not only the kind of subject matter we require but also the linguistic expression which is suitable for our purpose.

The same problem arises when we select information books for young children to read themselves. If we have some linguistic knowledge we can choose simplified information books which will provide a realistic introduction for young readers to the language of explanation and description. We also have to be aware of whether authors write about their subject so that readers are informed as well as entertained. Reading across the curriculum involves learning about matters which are increasingly outside children's own common sense or general knowledge. We know that learning should be within a meaningful context, but sometimes writers are so concerned to relate scientific knowledge to everyday knowledge that they may actually sacrifice real information. Unsworth (1990) indicates to us that a scientific understanding of the world may not be the same as a common-sense understanding. If authors try to relate one with the other too closely they may present scientific knowledge inadequately.

Reading across the curriculum

As children read non-narrative they are introduced to various subjects across the curriculum. In the primary school we find many history books which are written as narrative:

> It was the spring of AD 101. The Roman frontier along the Danube was in ferment. The hastily repaired roads were crowded with troops moving into the area. Barges were being towed up the Danube, full of supplies from the Black Sea for the massive army that was assembling. Auxillary troops kept a constant vigil from the many newly-built watch-towers and forts that lined the southern bank of the great river Danube, in case the Dacian tribes on the opposite bank launched a surprise attack. The name of Trajan was on every tongue, for news had arrived that the emperor was on his way north.
>
> (Connolly, 1988, p.4)

Of course, many children's interest will be captured by this kind of writing but we have also to remember that each subject area has its own individual way of expression or 'discourse'. We must therefore introduce children to the language of history, of geography, and of science.

Linguists have looked closely at the characteristic features of different subject discourses which children will meet in more advanced texts. We can only really help children to read effectively across the curriculum if we know what kind of texts they will eventually have to cope with. While we cannot plunge most readers immediately into these kinds of expression we should be careful that we do in fact gradually introduce them to these kinds of formats.

For example, Eggins *et al.* (1987) have described features of history books. Writers about history select facts which they interpret and from which they make generalisations. These meanings are expressed in non-chronological language which becomes increasingly complex not only because of technical vocabulary but also because of grammatical intricacy. Here is an example:

> The historical period begins with the unification of the whole of Egypt into a single political unit under the control of one king. The king was Narmer, the date about 3100 BC. It is at this time that Egyptian writing, hieroglyphic, first appears, as well as the first monumental architecture. Egyptian rulers are divided into dynasties though these were not used by the Egyptians themselves and were coined by a later historian called Manetho, a native Egyptian writing in Greek.
>
> (Watson, 1987, p.5)

It is clearly valuable to introduce less experienced readers gradually to more impersonal language:

> The first railway in London was the London and Greenwich, opened in 1834, but the horse and the ship were still the main means of transport. Some 1,500 stage coaches a day left London, and the rich had their own post-chaises and carriages. By 1897 London contained several major London termini and an underground railway, and the first petrol-driven cars were being used.
>
> (Rawcliffe, 1985, p.3)

Wignell *et al.* (1987) describe writers of geography books as grouping, classifying, analysing and explaining geographical facts. These texts probably include many technical terms and definitions which means the reader has to comprehend quite a lot of information which is condensed into a relatively small space. The organisation of this complexity is helped by clear use of headings:

> *Industry – Exports and Imports*
> Australia is one of the world's leading industrialised nations. Its manufacturing industry developed after 1945 and now employs about one-quarter of the country's work-

91

ing people. As in other industrial countries, service indus-
tries have also grown to become the largest employer. Two-
thirds of the working population of Australia have jobs in
offices, shops, banks, schools, universities and government
departments. Fewer than one in 10 works in agriculture.
Food processing is the biggest manufacturing industry, in
terms of both value and employment. This is followed by
machinery, cars, aircraft and shipbuilding. In the past 10
years the production of steel, aluminium, refined copper,
lead, zinc and tin has expanded rapidly and now accounts
for one-quarter of all Australia's exports.

(Crashaw, 1988)

Of course, not all writers of non-narrative texts write explanation
or description. As we have noted many non-narrative books
contain the chronological language of instructions or of lists of
facts. We cannot take for granted that all readers will follow this
kind of arrangement. We may have to point out the seemingly
obvious sequencing which in many cases will be signalled by
technical signs. Christie and Rothery (1990) suggest that aspects
of science textbooks need discussion – tables of contents, indexes,
chapter headings, subheadings and points at which information
is summarised.

Many non-narrative books contain some explanation as well as
lists of facts or instructions and we should highlight the different
purposes of the author. Examples from books about science
earlier in this chapter illustrate that subject texts may contain
both chronological and non-chronological writing. In addition,
within these genres come diagrams, maps, illustrations, photographs, graphs – all of which should act as links within the text
and help to make it coherent.

When children select a reference book such as an encyclopaedia
or a dictionary they meet a list of items but also sometimes
complex explanations or definitions of each item. We must judge
the demands of these kinds of reference books which we may all
too easily just hand out to children with the expectation that they
will understand this particular genre of writing.

So we have responsibility to prepare children for the reading
demands of different subject discourses and for the range of
chronological and non-chronological writing within non-
narrative books. If children are to have adequate introduction to

92

non-chronological texts we have to select books which introduce these forms of text to 'apprentice' readers. Our purpose is to place children in a position to distance themselves from texts across the curriculum so that they can reconstruct them for their own purpose. In this way we are not simply helping children to comprehend a text but to relate that text to their own learning.

WRITING NON-NARRATIVE ACROSS THE CURRICULUM

We have already seen that children need to listen to the rhythms of non-chronological language and experiment in using those rhythms as they discuss information with their peers and teachers. They also need to write about information, for children gain insight into how texts are constructed when they come to write similar texts themselves. Kress (1986, p.111) has made this important point:

> Readers, in other words, need as much training as do writers. Some of the best training is, of course, to make all readers into fully competent and fully aware writers.

Children's ability to write personally and to write stories may not be reflected in their ability to write about information. Early writing usually reflects children's own experience but the purpose of writing about information becomes one of describing and explaining.

We can give young children opportunities to begin to write appropriately about information from an early age. If children are always left to write about information in their own way, the majority are not likely to write in ways which will aid their own understanding. Indeed, once children have gathered facts they are often uncertain as to how to relate the facts on paper. The fact that attractive drawings or other illustrations accompany the writing does not always mean that children have learned very much about how to write effectively in a non-narrative form. It is a good idea to keep a check on the kind of writing done by individual children in topic work. It is all too easy for children to restrict themselves to one kind of expression within a busy topic-based lesson.

In order to avoid limiting learning and to familiarise children with more formal language it seems reasonable to intervene and teach forms of expression. Rothery (1984) suggests that children can be effectively introduced to specific genres of writing. Such a proposal is not purely formulaic. Rather it is a teaching strategy which enables children to extend their awareness of writing strategies. In other words children should be aware of their options and be able to discuss forms of writing which are appropriate for their purposes. In addition, discussion of how we write within different genres can complement children's own reading of a range of genres.

O'Connell (1989, pp.53–6) has described teaching the writing of reports to a mixed ability group of Year 4 Australian children. Here the term 'report' indicates description or explanation of topics of interest. She encouraged children to discuss the ways in which reports they read had been written and to say how they differed from a story form. She reports some of the children's responses:

> They're true.
> It's usually about one thing only. It's like facts.
> It tells you the most important facts. It gives you information.
> You pick out the most interesting things so people will want to read it.
> It goes from most important to least important.

Group writing work followed as the children brainstormed ideas about bicycles, put together the ideas and then drafted paragraphs. After that O'Connell and her pupils together organised the paragraphs into a logical sequence and then wrote an introduction and conclusion. Together they produced the following:

Bikes

A bicycle is a two-wheeled machine that is pedal-operated. A bicycle has two wheels with spokes and rubber tyres. It also has a solid chrome frame, with a seat on the top for the rider and a chain which helps the pedal move the wheels. Handlebars help you steer. A chain which is on a frame is powered by the pedals. When the pedals are turned by our feet, they move the chain which causes the wheels to turn. To keep your bike clean, oil the chain, ride it regularly and get your parents to check the brakes.

There are many types of bikes. Some examples are: B.M.X., children's racing bikes, racer bikes for adults, fold-up bikes, ladies' bikes and trainer bikes which have two extra wheels. Some types of B.M.X. are: Diamond Back, Red Line and Crusader.

To keep your bike safe, you must check it regularly. Some safety precautions are: not riding on the footpath, wearing a safety helmet, don't wear thongs, always watch carefully where you're going and don't double.

Doubtless further collaboration would have improved the composition of this report, but individual work followed as children wrote their reports about their individual interests. This extract was written by a child of average ability:

Piano

A piano is a musicle insterment.

The sound is made by strings inside the piano. So when you hit the key a wooden hammer joined to the key hits the string and the strings vibrat to make a sound . . .

There are all sorts of music you can play on a piano. Sometimes you may hoin a band and make music. If you begin piano you start with eezy. You must practice 6 days a week and realy try hard. So practice makes perfect.

It is quite common for children to try to write in a procedural form as they put together a list of instructions. Again we can model this form of writing, discuss with children whether they have written instructions which could be followed and how far this form of writing differs from explanations or descriptions. Derewianka (1990, pp.32-3) illustrates how difficult it can be for children to write in this genre. Here is the first attempt of a group of children to write instructions to make a pulley for a message:

Instructions to Make a Pulley

Things you need

2 points
string
box
2 operators

Method

Wind the string around the points.
Attach the box.

Pull the string.

Another group of children decided that they could not really follow these instructions and after further conferencing both groups of children finally wrote:

<u>Instructions for Making a Message Pulley</u>
Purpose: to send messages to a friend in the classroom
<u>Materials</u>
at least 2 points around which to loop the string e.g. sticks (approx. 2 cm wide and 30 cm long), table legs or chair legs strong non-twisting string, twice the length of the distance to be covered
at least 1 carrier of a suitable size to carry messages e.g. small light box
masking tape
at least 2 operators
<u>Method</u>
1 Measure the distance between the two points.
2 Cut the string to twice this distance.
3 Loop the string around the points.
4 Tie the ends of the string in a knot so that the string is stretched firmly between the points.
5 Attach the box/boxes to the string with masking tape.
6 Test the pulley out by the operator pulling one side of the string.

Of course we are concerned that children should be able to relate new knowledge to their existing understanding. Their writing, however, is restricted if we always try to achieve this purpose by suggesting children translate knowledge into personal experience. For example, when we ask children to write a diary as though they were a Roman soldier on Hadrian's Wall we are not giving them experience of writing non-chronological text. We are converting knowledge into narrative. There may be good reason to organise children's writing in this way but we must also make sure that those children have equal experience of writing *about* the Roman soldiers on Hadrian's Wall. The same observation can be made of a task which asks children to write about a scientific experiment in the form of a newspaper report.

Christie and Rothery (1990, p.90) warn of the dangerous myth that 'children write scientific information in the form of stories or other "imaginative" or "self-expressive" genres' on the grounds that they enable pupils to use their own language in writing science, presumably graduating – at some never clearly specified point in the future – to writing the harder genres of science. Learning to write in the imaginative or expressive genres is essential and natural, but in itself it may not be enough. A child who can also read and write passages in more formal genres has access to more information and a wider range of audiences. Learning to handle these genres is too important to be left to chance – the teacher should ensure that he or she provides opportunities to deal with these harder genres, and scaffolding for the student who is approaching them.

READING FOR INFORMATION: ENCOURAGING CHILDREN TO FORMULATE THEIR OWN QUESTIONS

Children most commonly read and write for information when they are engaged in topic work. Topic work usually involves finding out information from books or other material and recording this information in a variety of ways. Here is an opportunity for dynamic interaction of reading and writing if this work is carefully planned. Sometimes, however, young readers have vague ideas about what it is they want to find out. This point is noted in the Programmes of Study for Reading in the National Curriculum (DES, 1989, pp.16,23): 'Pupils should be encouraged to formulate first the questions they need to answer.' We can encourage an approach which requires children to write down the questions they have in mind so that they answer those questions directly.

Directed reading activities

Florence Davies (1986) described the work of the Schools Council Reading for Learning Project which produced 'Directed Activities Related to Text (DARTS)'. These activities direct children to look at text in order to categorise, evaluate or summarise the text so that they can more easily access the information required. In this work the teacher sets purposes and a framework of activity, and collaborates with children. So instead of looking for specific words and sentences children's attention is drawn to chunks of information. They look at the way in which different points are linked in a text. This analytical work can lead to group discussion about the information they find and how they might continue their research. The information is sometimes recorded in tables and diagrams, which enables more efficient writing or reconstructing of facts. In other words, here is a method which is far more realistic and meaningful than asking children simply to rewrite that information in their own words.

'Write in your own words'

When we instruct children to write in their own words we are really asking them to bridge the gap between written language which is close to their spoken language and the formality of the language of many information books. Yet, as we have seen, the language of non-narrative books may be far removed from some children's experience of language.

For many years we have frowned upon copying from an information book but the ease with which we say, 'Write it in your own words' suggests this is a simple task. We are really asking children to undertake a complex linguistic task: that they read more formal text, extract information from various sources, reorganise that information and rewrite it in a way we think is appropriate.

We should be aware of various problems. The children will almost certainly use books which will contain different registers. The language of the books may be quite complex and even quite abstract. If the language is that of a specific subject area it may be too unfamiliar and difficult to express 'in your own words'. So the child has two problems, one of rewriting part of the text and one of fulfilling the aims of the teacher. Some children quite reasonably invent their own strategies because the task is so complex. Children have told me that they write in their words by 'mixing it around a bit' or by 'chopping it about'. These children are coping with the task by looking at single sentences rather than at longer texts. We will do well to remember that when we ourselves study we often get round such difficulties by quoting. Why should we not teach children how to quote from books properly and encourage them to do this occasionally?

Wignell (Eggins *et al.*, 1987, p.16) describes asking children to write in their own words as 'one of the ironies of education'. So our common instruction 'in your own words' means to change formal writing into your own kind of words. Surely it is possible that children understand what they are reading although they might not be able to rephrase it. We are asking children to translate possible abstraction and other linguistic complexities into a register which is more familiar to them. We might consider the importance of a stage intervening in this process by asking children to discuss information they have found out so that their thoughts are clarified and developed.

IMPORTANCE OF READING AND WRITING ACROSS THE CURRICULUM

Reading and writing across the curriculum involve sharing common literacy concerns. Writing is not just a means of recording but of learning how to write in different forms and understanding what kinds of meaning those forms represent. Reading is not just a means of comprehension but of becoming aware of how writers express meaning and becoming able to reconstruct those meanings for our own understanding.

We need the broad canvas of work across the curriculum if we are to develop reading and writing competencies in ways which reflect a real understanding of effective use of language within a range of contexts. In fact we have little time to lose. As Margaret Donaldson (1989, p.29) warns:

Primary teachers have a crucial role to play in ensuring that the bases of this kind of competence with the written word are well established when a child crosses the secondary school threshold for the first time. If it is not done by then, it will very likely be too late.

QUESTIONS FOR PERSONAL REFLECTION OR GROUP DISCUSSION

1 Take a look at some examples of information books in your school. What can you say about the way they are written? You may wish to consider some of the following: vocabulary, prose, organisation, illustrations.
2 Do the books you have examined make demands on the reader which are different from those of stories? If so, how do they

differ? Can children cope with them? What evidence do you have for this?

3 Do you have a reading curriculum in your school? If so, what is the place of non-fiction within it? How does this relate to the National Curriculum?

4 Do you teach children to handle non-fiction texts? If so, how? If not, how might you do this?

5 What types of writing do children undertake in your school? Collect examples, and categorise them in relation to the type of writing. Some possible text types are: story, list, description, process, instructions. Do you teach and encourage children to attempt different types of writing? If not, how might this be done?

6 What are DARTS? How might these be used to develop children's comprehension?

7 Under what circumstances is it reasonable or useful to ask children to express the information from a book 'in their own words'?

RECOMMENDED READINGS

Carter, R. (ed.) (1990) *Knowledge about Language*. London: Hodder & Stoughton. The book is a tangible result of the LINC Project. Some chapters will prove helpful in extending a general awareness of language in use.

Christie, F. (ed.) (1990) *Literacy For A Changing World*. Australia Council for Educational Research, Windsor: National Foundation for Educational Research. Frances Christie is a key writer and thinker about genre ideas. In this book she draws on recent linguistic research in Australia. Here are accounts of the kind of understandings about language which these linguists believe we must have if we are to prepare children adequately for the demands of a rapidly changing world.

Donaldson, M. (1989) 'Sense and Sensibility', Occasional Paper No. 3, Reading and Language Centre, University of Reading School of Education. Perhaps one of the most significant papers to emerge from the reading debate. Margaret Donaldson succinctly argues that children must be introduced to impersonal ways of thinking and expressing themselves.

Gilham, B. (ed.) (1986) *The Language of School Subjects*. London: Heinemann Educational. A pre-National Curriculum book which looks at language across the curriculum in a practical way and, in particular, at the language of different subjects. Here also is a broader approach to reading for information than simply encouraging study skills.

Halliday, M.A.K. and Hasan, R. (1989) *Language, context, and text: aspects of language in a social-semiotic perspective.* Oxford: Oxford University Press. A very important theoretical description of how we use language in different social contexts. Teachers who do not have specialist linguistic knowledge need not be daunted by this book.

Littlefair, A.B. (1991) *Reading All Types of Writing.* Milton Keynes: Open University Press. I hesitate to recommend my own book but, as far as I know, it is the only one published in this country which looks at the educational implications of looking at register and genre as separate linguistic concepts.

BIBLIOGRAPHY

Chapman, L.J. (1987) *Reading: from 5 to 11 years.* Milton Keynes: Open University Press.

Christie, F. and Rothery, J. (1990) 'Literacy in the curriculum'. In F. Christie (ed.) *Literacy For A Changing World.* Australia Council for Educational Research, Windsor: National Foundation for Educational Research.

Davies, F. (1986) 'The function of the textbook in sciences and the humanities'. In B. Gilham (ed.) *The Language of School Subjects.* London: Heinemann Educational.

Department of Education and Science (1975) *A Language for Life.* A Report of the Committee of Inquiry Appointed by the Secretary of State for Education and Science under the Chairmanship of Sir Allan Bullock FBA. London: HMSO.

Department of Education and Science (1989) *The National Curriculum for English.* London: HMSO.

Derewienka, B. (1990) *Exploring how Texts Work.* Primary English Teaching Association: Sydney.

Donaldson, M. (1976) *Children's Minds.* Glasgow: Collins.

Donaldson, M. (1989) 'Sense and sensibility', Occasional Paper No. 3, Reading and Language Centre, University of Reading School of Education.

Eggins, S., Wignell, P. and Martin, J.R. (1987) 'The discourse of history: distancing the recoverable past'. In *Working Papers in Linguistics,* Writing Project Report No. 5, Linguistics Department, Sydney University.

Halliday, M.A.K. (1975) *Learning How To Mean.* London: Arnold.

Halliday, M.A.K. (1989) 'Context of situation'. In M.A.K. Halliday and R. Hasan (eds) *Language, context, and text: aspects of language in a social-semiotic perspective.* Oxford: Oxford University Press.

Kress, G.R. (1986) 'Reading, writing and power'. In C. Painter and J.R. Martin (eds) *Writing to Mean: Teaching Genres Across the Curriculum.* Papers from the 'Writing to Mean' Conference held at the University of Sydney, May 1985.

Littlefair, A.B. (1991) *Reading All Types of Writing.* Milton Keynes: Open University Press.

Lunzer, E. and Gardner, K. (1979) *The Effective Use of Reading*. London: Heinemann Educational.

Martin, J.R., Christie, F. and Rothery, J. (1987) 'Social processes in education: A reply to Sawyer and Watson (and others)'. In *The Place of Genre in Learning: Current Debates*. Victoria: Deakin University.

Meek, M. (1988) *How Texts Teach What Readers Learn*. Stroud: Thimble Press.

O'Connell, E. (1989) 'Writing reports in Year 4'. In J. Collerson (ed.) *Writing for Life*. Primary English Teaching Association, Sydney, Australia.

Perera, K. (1984) *Analysing Classroom Language*. Oxford: Blackwell.

Rothery, J. (1984) 'Teaching writing in the primary school: A genre based approach to the development of writing abilities'. In *Working Papers in Linguistics*, Writing Project No. 4, Linguistics Department, University of Sydney.

Unsworth, L. (1990) 'Learning the culture through literacy development: information books for beginning readers'. Paper presented to The Thirteenth World Congress of the International Reading Association, Stockholm, July 3-6, 1990.

van Dijk, T.A. (1977) *Text and Context: Explorations in the Semantics and Pragmatics of Discourse*. London: Longman.

Wignell, P. (1987) 'In your own words'. In *Working Papers in Linguistics*, Writing Project Report No. 5, Linguistics Department, University of Sydney.

Wignell, P., Martin, J.R. and Eggins, S. (1987) 'The discourse of geography: ordering and explaining the experiential world'. In *Working Papers in Linguistics*, Writing Project Report No. 5, Linguistics Department, Sydney University.

Non-narrative books mentioned

Carter, C., Nitert, R. and Ritchie, I. (1990) *Air*. Australia: Macmillan.

Connolly, P. (1988) *Tiberius Claudius Maximus The Cavalryman*. Oxford: Oxford University Press.

Crashaw, P. (1988) *People and Places. Australia*. London: Macmillan.

Jennings, T. (1986) *The Young Scientist Investigates The Human Body*. Oxford: Oxford University Press.

Rawcliffe, M. (1985) *Finding Out About Victorian London*. London: Batsford Academic and Educational.

Watson, P.J. (1987) *Costume of Ancient Egypt*. London: Batsford.

Part III

HOW SHOULD WE ENCOURAGE CHILDREN TO BE READERS?

5

DEVELOPING AND EXTENDING THE CONCEPT OF APPRENTICESHIP

Sharing reading in the classroom

Martin Coles

I intend in this chapter to consider just one aspect of the review a school might undertake of the methods it uses for developing children's reading – the organisation and practice of reading in the classroom.

One of the recurring themes of this book is to do with an understanding that those schools which decide to move away from reading via publishers' schemes cannot simply change the texts they offer children. Principled planning for such a change demands that schools review not only the approach they take to the whole of the reading curriculum, not simply the texts used, but also the reading instruction offered by the teacher, the classroom organisation of reading, methods of assessment and record keeping, and the involvement of parents. Such a review is a necessary part of any move towards a 'reading for real' approach. I want to look at the notion of the beginning reader as an apprentice sharing reading in the classroom with the teacher. What does it imply for classroom practice, and in particular what does it imply in relation to the practice of 'hearing children read'?

Waterland (1985) explains her understanding of the concept of apprenticeship as it relates to beginning readers thus:

> I came to adopt instead, a view of the learner not as passive and dependent like a cuckoo chick but rather as an active and already partly competent sharer in the task of learning to read. Here the model is apprenticeship to a craftsman. Consider the way apprenticeship works; the learner first undertakes the simplest parts of the job, then gradually the more complex ones, increasing the share he can cope with

and all the time working alongside, under the control of, and with the help of, the craftsman. The apprentice does not sit passively with his mouth open; he works actively with the tools of trade in his hand.

On the face of it this last sentence indicates a weakness in the analogy. Traditional apprenticeship occurs in the field of manual tasks. Reading on the other hand is a mainly cognitive activity. Even recognising the place of cognitive plans in motor skills and the necessity for a certain level of hand–eye co-ordination in reading, drawing parallels between tasks which are different in so many respects might well lead to inappropriate descriptions of beginning reading. There are other problems too with Waterland's brief analysis. She asks us to consider the way apprenticeship works: 'the learner first undertakes the simplest parts of the job then gradually the more complex ones'. Now this is certainly how some classrooms work. Tasks and problems can be chosen to suit the stage of learning that the child is at. Teachers can, for instance, slowly increase the complexity of reading tasks and materials provided for children. But traditional apprenticeship is set in the workplace and the problems and tasks that are given to learners arise from the demands of the work-place. Tasks are therefore clearly and obviously purposeful; but letting the job demands select the tasks for students to practise is still one of the great inefficiencies of traditional apprenticeship.

So in traditional apprenticeship the tasks are selected either by job demands, or by the 'master', who takes the job demands into account. Yet many advocates of 'real reading' suggest allowing the child, not the teachers, to specify the task in reading apprenticeship. Children choose their own books. In this way at least, the child is in charge and controls the actions of the adult, a reversal of the traditional master–apprentice relationship.

Furthermore, apprenticeship often works on the basis of building subskills to the point where they can be integrated in the efficient performance of the target task. But, as Colin Harrison explains in Chapter 1, reading is not a series of discrete skills; it is not a simple process whereby an individual takes a situation detail by detail and meticulously builds up a whole. For instance, in order to fulfil the basic goal of creating the meaning of a text, interpretations must be made that go well beyond the text itself, however simple the text. Nevertheless, the ability to do this cannot be separated from the ability to recognise the individual words within the text.

Criticisms of this kind imply that apprenticeship cannot be used as an exact model for teaching and learning reading. Perhaps it is more sensible to consider apprenticeship as a suggestive rather than an exact analogy. If we look at apprenticeship in this way, as suggestive, what are the structural features of traditional apprenticeship and what lessons might it have for teaching and learning reading in the classroom? There are I think some essential features of traditional apprenticeship which can be usefully applied to learning to read and which carry implications for classroom practice. Those features are to do first with observation, coaching and practice, and second with social context. These features point up ways of sharing reading in the classroom. They are both ways of seeing teaching and learning reading in the classroom as assisted performance.

Apprenticeship highlights methods for carrying out a task. Apprentices learn their methods through observation, coaching and practice. The apprentice repeatedly observes the master carrying out a task, modelling the process. An apprentice then attempts to execute the same process with help and guidance from the master, i.e. coaching. A key aspect of this coaching is aid in the form of reminders and other help that the apprentice needs to complete the task. Once the apprentice has a grasp of the skill, the master reduces participation, providing only limited hints and feedback to the learner who continues to practise until the skill approximates to that of the master.

If we follow this model it becomes obvious that an apprenticeship approach is not a matter of *laissez-faire*. It is not simply a matter of 'catching' reading as if cognitive skills could be caught in the same way as one catches a cold. An apprenticeship approach following this paradigm does not mean just providing children with good books and assuming that it is enough simply to apprentice children to the authors and illustrators, important as good books are. Rather it is a case of being apprenticed to a teacher, of sharing reading. The pattern is one where, broadly, the child moves from listening to the adult read (observation), through reading with the adult (coaching), to reading independently (practice).

This is the path through what Vygotsky called the zone of proximal development which is the distance between the actual developmental level as determined by individual problem solving and the level of potential development as determined through problem solving under adult guidance or in collaboration with more capable peers

(Vygotsky, 1978, p.86)

i.e. it is the gap between a child's ability working on his or her own and that ability working with assistance.

In the zone of proximal development assistance is provided by the teacher, the adult, the expert, the more capable peer whatever the activity and through this assistance learning awakens a variety of internal developmental processes that are able to operate only when the child is interacting with people in his environment and in cooperation with his peers. Once these processes are internalized, they become part of the child's independent developmental achievement.

(Vygotsky, 1978, p.90)

OBSERVATION

Good reading teaching must be to do with assisting performance along a pathway through the zone of proximal development. The pathway starts at the point of observation where the child has a very limited understanding of the concept of reading, the reading task, or the goal to be achieved; at this level the teacher offers a model and the child's response is acquiescent observation. Only gradually does a child come to an understanding of what it might mean to read. The child gains some conception of the overall performance through listening, through conversation about a book, through questions and feedback. In this way the teacher is providing what the psychologists would call cognitive structuring in order to encourage the learner's belief that he or she can turn print into sense. So the child's notions of what it is to read and what it is to be a reader are both in the zone of proximal development. Knowing what reading is all about is the most crucial first lesson of all.

Several points are worth emphasising here. Traditional apprenticeship works in domains where the skills are usually external and readily available in both learner and teacher for observation. Applying apprenticeship methods to largely cognitive skills requires an externalisation of processes which are usually carried out internally in order that the learner can observe the expert strategies that the teacher is using. Of course, at the stage of observation, this means reading aloud, but also implies incidental conversation about the text and a commentary on the reading aloud in any one-to-one situation. So, for instance, teachers might mention their change of voice as the speech marks provide a signal; they might at a certain point ask for a summary of the passage since summarising forms the basis for comprehension monitoring; they might ask questions of the text which require the reader to predict in order to encourage an overall reading strategy of hypothesis formulation and testing. Teachers might sometimes model these activities for the learner by summarising themselves or, in a conversational way, making a prediction about the way the story is going in an attempt to reflect the fact that skilled reading involves developing expectations and evaluating them as evidence accumulates from the text. They might too offer some interpretative comments on the text as a demonstration that meaning is not somehow all in the text, to be extracted entirely through decoding, but relies to some extent on the reader's response.

Of course all this has to be done with some sensitivity remembering that the eventual goal is for the teacher to fade from the scene, though when and whether this happens will depend entirely on the text and context. The zone is always with us! There is an important sense in which even undergraduates studying English are being taught, or are learning to read. The teacher becomes less obtrusive but certainly has not disappeared. Nevertheless the learner must be helped to move from observation, through coaching to practice, and overwhelming interruption from the text itself is unlikely to help motivate a reader or allow pleasure to be gained from the book. Judging the what, when, and how of intervention, and matching this to the learner's experience calls for sensitive, informed judgement. In practice a sensible compromise has to be reached between the need for commentary on the reading process and the need to provide a pleasurable and coherent reading experience. Still, it is the case that there is a need to sensitise learners to the details of expert performance which can be done by highlighting with skilful verbal description.

What else might be said about the observation stage? Well most obvious is the need for interesting materials that make sense to the learner. This point has been discussed at some length in Chapter 3. It is sufficient here to remind ourselves that if the texts used are interesting and meaningful to the child then they will not only offer motivation but also teach about 'the nature and variety of written discourse' (Meek, 1982). Bamberger (1976) talks about the chief task of the teacher being to 'lure' children into reading. Teachers of the youngest children begin this luring process by storytelling and reading aloud so that children know the delights to be obtained from books.

> A book, a person, a shared enjoyment: these are the conditions of success.
>
> (Meek, 1988, p.9)

Reading to children should not be confined to fiction. Interesting material is available in a variety of forms. To become attuned to this variety of genre children must have early experience of texts other than simple narrative. Even young children might listen to newspaper accounts of current events. Comics, with their direct relationship of story to visual display through captions, stimulate a lively interest in most children. Children's own interests and hobbies might be a starting point for gathering other material.

Above all, though, children benefit from hearing the shape and form of written language which good stories, read well, offer. Reading aloud is a skill which all teachers ought to develop continuously. There may well be a place for story reading which is carried out by a classroom assistant or other adult in the school, but story reading is a skilled job which ought not to be delegated lightly. Good reading will supply intonation and emphases which offer a message of meaningful reading. It is also important that children observe in the teacher an adequate image of a literate adult. Children who observe their teacher genuinely enjoying the stories he or she is reading will begin to see reading as something personal, not something which is carried out simply for the sake of instruction. It is important that young children do not see reading as a performance simply for the teacher's sake, irrelevant and purposeless outside the classroom. In this respect the teacher's role and attitude are crucial. Skilled readers show apprentices what it is like to be a reader, show them what kinds of choices are made about reading, demonstrate the whole task complete.

Sometimes this reading aloud might be from an enlarged text, preferably in book form though sometimes perhaps enlarged by using overhead projector transparencies of books children can read for themselves, or even hurriedly produced text on large sheets or flipcharts with felt-tips. Making large text this way does have the benefit of allowing the teacher to tailor the text to the particular needs of the group, perhaps underlining certain phrases, or highlighting particular words or letters in different colours. In this way the book becomes an enjoyable shared experience which easily allows discussion about the way language is written down, about the elements of language which children recognise or about what is happening in the information text or story that is being read. Holdaway (1979), noticing the difficulty of matching the ideal of individualised teaching with the reality of large class sizes, points out that corporate learning (for instance, in initiation ceremonies, playground games and church services) has always been a powerful mode. The examples he offers have in common a lack of competitiveness; rather 'they are entered into to be *like* other people . . . if we can achieve this corporate spirit, there is no reason why a large class cannot learn together'. The group reading experience then has the advantages of a co-operative social occasion in which participants share mutual enjoyment of the reading. This practice is an obvious way to connect story-time, the teacher reading, the enjoyment of narrative, the excitement of shared experience, with the child's 'learning-to-read' process. It should avoid the misunderstanding evident in this story told by Helen Arnold (1982, p.14):

> A child who was able to read, with natural intonation, at a normal rate, many books at home, took a copy of the reading scheme home to his mother and chanted it out word by word to her. When asked why he was reading it out in such a 'funny' way, he replied that that was how you were supposed to read your book at school. 'Everybody does it like that.'

It is worth saying again that this kind of reading does not have to be confined to fiction. The sharing of songs and rhymes ought to be a fundamental part of any early reading curriculum. The benefits of early familiarity with rhyme have been dramatically demonstrated by the work of Bryant and Bradley (1985). Familiar stories and rhymes from the whole range of cultures represented in the classroom can be shared orally and then in written form, perhaps as large 'home-made' books.

Sometimes the teacher will select books to share which have no words, so that children will 'read' the story through the illustrations. Sometimes he or she will share the children's own writing in books which have been placed in the book corner collection of books. Sometimes the teacher will read from the collection of books that children are able to read independently. Doing this will familiarise children with the form and language of the story and make independent reading easier.

It is important here to point out that the sequence of observation, coaching and practice is descriptive of a sequence of learning phases, but these phases are not simply linear in terms of time and it should not be assumed therefore that they offer a simple guide to a sequence of teaching activities. So, for instance, reading aloud to a class should not be confined to young children and certainly should not stop when children can read independently. In any apprenticeship learning there is always movement back and forth between the stages of observation, coaching and performance. Perhaps Bruner's (1966) notion of the spiral curriculum, in which children continually return to the same piece of learning but at a more sophisticated level, is a useful one to keep in mind here.

COACHING

We have so far considered the stage of observation, but of course listening and watching are not enough to turn an apprentice into a skilled craftsman. It is crucial that running alongside classroom practices which offer opportunities for observation are chances to practise with coaching. Learners must try out the skilled activity for themselves. So what defines this stage of coaching?

Here we need to return to the Vygotskyian theory of teaching as assisted performance and remind ourselves of the main tenets of the theory. Assisted performance defines what a child can do with help, with the support of the learning environment, with others and of the self. The contrast between assisted performance

112

and unassisted performance identifies the most important space between development and learning, which is the zone of proximal development. For Vygotsky assistance should be offered in those interactional contexts which are most likely to generate joint performance. During the earliest periods in the zone of proximal development the child may have only a limited understanding of the task or goal to be achieved. The teacher offers a model and the child responds by observing and imitating. Gradually the child comes to understand the point and purpose of the activity and the way different parts of the activity relate to one another.

In terms of reading this happens through all those activities outlined above. Then when some conception of the overall performance has been acquired the child can be assisted by other means, by joint performance, feedback, questions and further cognitive structuring. For instance, even before interacting with a child a teacher assists by age-grading materials. The selection of appropriate texts for an apprentice reader is one of the most important features of assisting performance.

During the coaching stage there should be a steady decrease in the teacher's responsibility for the task performance and a steady increase in the learner's proportion of responsibility. This is Bruner's 'handover principle' – the child who was once an observer, now becomes a participant (Bruner, 1983, p.60). Children gradually take over the structuring of the task themselves, for instance by asking questions of the adult – 'what does that say?' – rather than only responding to adult questions, or by making choices about their own reading materials. The adult's task is to tailor assistance accurately to the child by being responsive to their current effort and understanding. The child's questions – 'what does this mean?' – assist the adult to assist.

Attempts by skilled assisting adults to assess a child's readiness for greater responsibility are most often subtle rather than explicit, more usefully embedded in the ongoing interaction than separated out as assessment activities. Careful reflective listening and attention will allow appropriate coaching 'input'. This is the most essential skill in being a good teacher of reading.

In a good master–apprentice relationship the teacher graduates the coaching in response to the child's performance: the more the apprentice can do, the less the master does so that the coaching task is accomplished when responsibility for tailoring assistance and performing the task itself has been effectively handed over to the learner.

All this is theory. What does it mean for classroom practice? Essentially it means that at the stage of coaching the teacher will read *with* the child, sharing and helping and enjoying the book.

> The adult's job is to read with him what both can enjoy, to let him see how the story goes, to help him observe what there is to be read and to tell him what he needs to know when he finds it difficult.
>
> (Meek, 1982)

Reading with a child then is not at all the same as 'hearing a child read'. It is not just a regular check on quantity read, nor just a way of making individual contact with a child. It is not an activity in which a teacher listens to a child perform, but rather a joint performance, a collaborative activity. It occurs as part of the longer but less frequent pupil–teacher conference advocated by the Schools Council Report (Southgate *et al.*, 1981). Helen Arnold (1982) describes this activity, in what she calls a 'shared reading interview' as 'a relaxed and enthusiastic dialogue between teacher and pupil'. She offers (1982, p.82) a particular recipe for the activity, made up of the following ingredients:

> Teacher reads some of the text.
> Child reads some of the text.
> Teacher sets a purpose at beginning of interview to encourage skimming and scanning to find certain elements in text.
> Teacher asks child to read a paragraph silently first and then to read it aloud.
> Teacher asks child to read a paragraph silently and then questions them on it.
> Teacher encourages a child to ask questions about a text that has just been read.
> Teacher discusses decoding problems with child.
> Teacher and child discuss contents of text in terms of appreciative/emotional response.
> Teacher discusses child's difficulties in reading in general, attitudes, likes, dislikes, and so on.

Arnold does point out that these ingredients would vary from reading to reading, and would very much depend on the text that had been chosen.

A particular element which Arnold omits from her recipe is that in which the child and teacher read together quite literally. The child reading with the teacher gradually gains confidence and begins to take over more of the reading. The child's contribution is supported by teacher guidance of the sort contained in the list above so that the child becomes more autonomous. In this way children achieve an understanding of the interaction of print and text, start to build a sight vocabulary, and learn to make informed guesses based on semantic, syntactic, graphophonemic, and bibliographic information, bringing to the activity all they know and can do in order to make the text meaningful.

It is this kind of interaction which occurs in the best parent/child story-reading times. Minns (1990) demonstrates that in the best domestic situations the parent approaches the activity

> with warmth, confidence and intelligence. Most notably perhaps they make no outward distinction between reading and learning to read, and thus put no pressure on the child to become word-perfect . . . . Their aim, whether stated explicitly or not, is to involve the child as much as possible in understanding the author's words. They recognise that the child needs to talk about the story and give them time to do this. So the words of the story become intertwined with conversational talk; there are regular pauses to laugh at the funny bits, to enjoy repetitions aloud and to talk about things the story reminds them of.

There are of course difficulties with shared reading of this kind. It would be foolish to pretend that the sustained one-to-one contact of shared reading is easy to achieve in the classroom. However, many teachers do organise their classrooms for such interactions to occur, mainly by creating a classroom ethos of self-reliance, so reducing the constant call on the teacher's attention. It is perhaps a question of priorities in terms of classroom organisation.

In shared reading the essential role of the teacher is to be an opportunist, a guide rather than an instructor, just as the master craftsman is a guide who provides feedback to the apprentice who is practising. Southgate (1972) suggests how this relationship between the master reader and the reading apprentice should work in these terms:

Likewise, teachers need to acquire an extensive knowledge of what requires to be learned if the skills of literacy are to be effectively mastered. Their expertise could be considered as a store of background knowledge from which they could draw at appropriate moments, rather than as an elaborately detailed curriculum of which every item has to be earnestly taught. The teacher would thus be in a strong position when the moment for a small amount of direct teaching arises to help the child to take the next minute step forward and so channel learning towards the ultimate goal of efficient reading.

What specific advice might be offered in regard to this kind of coaching and guidance? The following list is offered on the assumption that teachers will have taken on board the important point made by Southgate above, i.e. the list must be part of a store of background knowledge to be drawn upon at appropriate moments. It must be remembered too that the major objective in any reading session is to retain interest in and enjoyment of the text and so teaching must be sensitive to the danger of destroying the essential element of attending to and appreciating the reading experience. This does not have to be an alternative to an emphasis on cognitive learning. Showing children what the reading process is and how to use the cueing systems available to them does not destroy reading enjoyment. Indeed it should positively influence motivation towards the task as the apprentice readers observe their own improvement and increasing success. So what follows are five pieces of practical advice about shared reading coaching:

1 In any master–apprentice relationship the master's job is eventually to make himself redundant as a teacher. Likewise, in reading coaching the eventual goal should be nil intervention (although it is worth repeating what was said before that when this might happen will depend very much on text and context). Do not always interrupt the reader to correct errors. To do this is to risk offering the child a message that reading is to do with pronouncing rather than comprehending. Rather, take note that some 'errors' or 'miscues' are productive of comprehension while others are a hindrance. Some miscues, as for instance in 'the child went back to his home' for 'the

116

child went back to his house', provide evidence that the child is on the right track in the search for meaning.

2 Offer children a range of strategies which they might use to work out the meaning of unknown words. Sometimes this might be by 'cloze' technique, encouraging children to make intelligent guesses from the rest of the sentence using both syntactic and semantic clues. Sometimes it might be by pointing out the initial sound of the unknown word, or some other letter/sound association. Sometimes it might be by demonstrating how long words can be broken into constituent syllables, as in cat-a-ma-ran. Sometimes a scrutiny of an illustration may provide a clue. Sometimes comparison with a more familiar word may present a clue, for example, 'starts like', 'ends like' or just 'like'. Very often it will be appropriate simply to offer the word to the child in order to maintain fluency and motivation. Reliance by the teacher on a single strategy will encourage a similar narrow attack on the part of the child. In particular the earlier a word appears in the sentence, or the greater its isolation from a familiar grammatical context, the more necessary will be alternative cues.

3 Stop occasionally in the reading and ask questions about the text as part of the reading conversation, in order to cause the reader to interact with key ideas and information. An example question might be 'What do you think will happen next?'. Sometimes it is a good idea to offer questions prior to the reading in order to direct attention to the text rather than asking the reader to use memory after the reading has finished. So, for instance, 'As we read together I want you to listen very hard for the parts of the story that tell us . . .'. Sometimes it might be appropriate to follow simple cohesive chains to trace the events of a story, perhaps playing 'detective', following clues to answer questions such as 'How do we know that the author means this or that person?'.

4 Reading support with new texts is offered if some preparation takes place before the reading begins. A context for the story, or information passage, can be provided by talking about the setting and characters in the story, or discussing the background to some new information, building up the general meaning of the text. Sometimes at the end of the session the child might be asked to investigate specific problems to do with the text as part of private reading; perhaps to answer

questions which would encourage scanning rather than word-by-word reading; perhaps to answer questions which would allow a start to be made in appreciating the different levels of interpretation which can operate in fully understanding a text.

5 The way a learner approaches a task is crucially important. In reading the way the text is approached will influence an understanding of what is read. In forming their strategies for reading children may have ideas about what they should do, but actually do something completely different. So in any shared reading act the teacher ought to take note of the child's overall attitudes and styles of learning in order to tailor the coaching more appropriately to individual needs. Arnold (1982) gives some examples:

> For instance a child who initially lacked confidence in word-attack skills may have found the teacher ready to prompt quickly on each hesitation. He may have become over-dependent, unwilling to hypothesise, waiting for help. Other children may appear anxious not to appear as poor readers, and will anxiously hazard guesses, usually employing only the first phoneme of a word as a cue. Concentration – or the lack of it – is again easily observable.

PRACTICE

We need once again now to return to our apprenticeship model of observation, coaching, practice. The move from coaching to practice comes once the task has been internalised, when assistance from adults or more capable peers is no longer needed. Indeed 'assistance' now might be disruptive since once this stage is reached instructions can be irritating and counter-productive. At this point self-consciousness, attempting an awareness of strategies being used, is detrimental to the smooth integration of all elements of the task. Of course, dependent on the context and material, a child may be at more than one stage at a time as I have pointed out earlier. The child who can read certain stories independently might still be in the zone of proximal development when it comes to understanding exactly how to extract information from a non-fiction text. Reading is a highly complex skill. It must be regarded as a continuously developing skill and thus the apprenticeship is a long one that continues through all levels of schooling and sometimes beyond.

Thus once children have mastered particular reading skills they should not have to rely solely on 'internal mediation'. They should be encouraged to ask for help when stuck. Any good reading classroom must allow for situations where, when children are having difficulty, they may seek out more competent others.

So, the more competent children become, the closer they move to the stage of independent practice, the more the coaching must become responsive, contingent and patient; the more the child can do, the less the adult should do. 'Assistance' offered at too high a level is not effective teaching. Constant and careful assessment of where the child is in reading ability relative to the zone of proximal development is required. But at the 'internalised' stage practice should be the chief ingredient. One study (Bamberger, 1976) reveals the paradox that many teachers intuitively understand: that 'many children do not read books because they cannot read well enough. They cannot read well enough because they do not read books'. There needs to be a balance between the three elements of apprenticeship. Concentration on coaching is important, but equally, if not more important, is to develop children's reading through the development of a reading habit where pupils read regularly their own stories and favourite books. There certainly needs to be an understanding in the class that silent, individual or group reading activities are central to the learning-to-read process, not merely supplementary to reading aloud to the teacher. Whether a child is a habitual reader will depend to a great extent on how much satisfaction and enjoyment he or she comes to expect from books.

There are several things a teacher needs to do to promote and encourage private reading. First, reading aloud to children is, as the earlier part of this chapter explained, one way in which children can be 'lured' into reading by themselves. Second, it is essential to have a wide range of books freely available in the classroom attractively displayed. This collection needs to contain both fiction and non-fiction, both prose and verse, and books at varying levels of reading difficulty, both to meet demand and to create it. Third, it is important to give children time for sustained independent reading, not just to fill in when other work is finished or when the teacher is marking the register or collecting dinner money. Classroom organisation must allow space both in terms of time and location for children to sit quietly and read when they wish and are ready to concentrate on reading.

There is, though, a tendency for reading to be restricted to short bursts. One way to overcome this tendency is to attempt to give children a period of uninterrupted, sustained, silent reading (USSR), otherwise known as ERIC (Everyone Reading in Class), or SQUIRT (Sustained, Quiet, Uninterrupted, Independent Reading Time). Remembering what was said earlier about the role of the teacher as a literacy model, during this time teachers should be reading silently their own choice of book. The Schools Council Project (Southgate et al., 1981) offered a model of how this practice might take place:

a) Set aside a particular period every day for personal reading – perhaps the end of the morning or afternoon.

b) See that every child has a personally selected book at a level which he is likely to be able to understand, and, if he has nearly completed reading it, a second one to hand.

c) Tell the children that they will be allowed, say, ten minutes to enjoy their chosen books without anyone interrupting them.

d) The teacher should sit . . . preferably also quietly reading and trying to avoid speaking, for example by merely catching the eye of any child who is not reading and perhaps raising an eyebrow.

e) Every effort should be made to establish that pattern that children neither talk nor leave their seats during this period.

f) A notice on the door might read: 'Class reading – please do not disturb'.

g) As children become accustomed to this procedure, gradually increase the period devoted to this personal, uninterrupted reading.

A word about silent reading may be appropriate here. Many children do not become capable of inaudible reading for some years. It is preferable during USSR sessions that children read as quietly as possible if they are not capable of completely silent reading, but this should not become a major concern. It is now understood that even the most able adult readers subvocalise. The crucial distinction is pointed out by Holdaway (1980). It is not between oral and silent reading, but between reading for personal understanding and satisfaction on the one hand, and reading for the understanding and satisfaction of an audience on the other. 'It is not important for children actually to suppress audible vocalisation in the early years of reading. The important thing is that they should *read to themselves*.'

SOCIAL CONTEXT

We need, finally, to look at one other key feature of traditional apprenticeship. It concerns the embedding social context in which learning takes place, a subject dealt with elsewhere in Chapter 6. Apprenticeship derives many of its characteristics from its embedding in a subculture in which most members are visible participants in the target skills. Apprentices have continual access to models of expertise in use. It is not uncommon for apprentices to have access to several masters and thus to a variety of models of expertise. Moreover, apprentices have the opportunity to observe other learners who have varying degrees of skill. Among other things this encourages them to view learning as an incremental staged process while providing them with benchmarks against which they can measure their own progress.

Margaret Donaldson's book *Children's Minds* (1978) is just one of the many inquiries which are helping us to understand the importance of the social context in all learning. Donaldson explains how thought and language depend upon the interpersonal contexts within which they develop. The apprenticeship approach to teaching reading recognises the significance of this aspect of learning by carrying with it a package of practical measures which help to create the embedding social context of apprenticeship in general. Some of these measures, such as USSR where readers are made very obviously aware that they are part of a community of readers, have been described earlier in this chapter. The importance of the shared experience of the teacher reading to the class, perhaps with copies available to the children to allow them to follow, has also been mentioned. The common sense of enjoyment and the resulting sense of being part of a reading community is a deeply educative process. There are other ways of ensuring that, within the school at least, children begin to feel part of what Frank Smith calls the 'literacy club'. For instance, many schools are adopting an approach which ensures that the child has access to more than one reading teacher by ensuring that parents play a crucial role in the reading 'life' of the child (see Chapter 8); some schools make arrangements for members of the local community to come regularly and share books with children; some schools adopt peer tutoring and paired-reading practices where older children within the school partner younger children, reading and talking about books together; or where friends within the classroom get together and share a book with the more competent reader taking the lead. In these ways children can play the role of both teacher and learner and thus begin to understand the nature of progress in reading by meeting and reading with other learners of varying degrees of skill. There are still other practices which can be promoted to create an appropriate social context:

- On occasions children might be asked to bring their favourite books from home. These are then spread around the room in a way which allows the class to browse before each child chooses one or two to take back to his or her desk to read for a set period.
- Children might be asked simply to 'share' books they have enjoyed by telling the class about them.
- The teacher might read to the class part of something he or she has enjoyed reading – a letter, an extract from a book, a newspaper or magazine article, etc.
- There might be a corner set up permanently in the classroom where children can go to listen on headphones to taped stories.
- Older children might write brief book reports, perhaps on a pro forma which are kept in a specified folder or file for other children to consult when they want to obtain recommendations from their peers about which books to read.
- The practice of buying multiple copies of the same book has died out and yet group reading, where five or six children take turns reading a book they are all confident with, offers many learning opportunities. Children can support each other's reading, offer each other information about the text, discuss, share jokes, share possible interpretations, etc.

These are simply a few suggestions. Experienced teachers will have many more, and there are many books which offer ideas for corporate activities (e.g. Holdaway, 1980, pp.60-3; Southgate, 1984, pp.92-3; Arnold, 1982, pp.97-8). Holdaway, for instance, suggests that every morning should start with a collecting together of reading experiences from the previous day, when small excerpts are read out by the teacher and children, and when what is read will be briefly discussed. Reading plans for the day are then proposed. So children will be reading out snippets that they have already prepared to an audience who are used to listening to each other and there is also the implication that reading may be brought from home for sharing.

The crucial element in all these practical measures is the intention to create a classroom subculture of shared reading experience which contains all the benefits of co-operative and social activities, one in which participants read together and together enjoy the reading experience.

But there is a further relevant aspect of the social context in which traditional apprenticeship takes place. It has to do with the economic bias in traditional apprenticeship. Apprentices are encouraged at an early stage to learn that they are useful and therefore meaningful within the social context of the workplace. Apprentices have the opportunity to realise the value, in concrete economic terms, of these skills: well-executed skills result in saleable products. Apprenticeship reading, as well as finding a way to create in the school a culture of expert practice for children to participate in and aspire to, must devise incentives for progress parallel to the economic incentives of traditional apprenticeship if it is to follow that model.

So how can apprentice readers realise the value of their developing skills? Well, primarily perhaps through the pleasure principle. The joy of reading good books can itself be the reward for increasing independence in reading. Moreover, reading fiction can, even for very young children, be an experience which, as Hall (1987) noted, helps extend an understanding of life and what it means to be human, and offers rewards in those terms. But it is also the case that reading is linked to work and instrumental effort. If this is to be recognised the classroom must provide a literacy environment and genuine literacy activities where children can 'cash in' their skills and begin to see the purpose of acquiring them for instrumental reasons too. Chapter 4 of this book, dealing as it does with the reading of non-fiction texts, explains one crucial way in which this can be done.

SUMMARY

If, when considering reading, we treat apprenticeship as a suggestive, rather than an exact analogy, there are useful insights to be drawn from traditional apprenticeship especially in regard to the business of 'hearing children read'. Two features particularly hold messages for how we help children learn to read.

First, the movement in traditional apprenticeship from observation, through coaching, to practice can act as a model for reading 'instruction'. It highlights, for instance, that a 'real books' approach is not *laissez-faire*, that coaching is required, but that coaching will be most effective if it is seen as a way of assisting performance, and as a way of making explicit to the learner processes which are usually internalised in skilled performance. The implications for teachers are radical. A number of traditional practices, such as hearing children read as a kind of ritual, almost a magical laying on of hands, require major revision. This is not a new point. It is continually being made by various commentators on the teaching of reading.

Second, a close look at traditional apprenticeship provides evidence for the importance of the social context in which learning takes place. Again, reading teachers can use the apprenticeship model to reflect on their own school/classroom practices to see whether they help create a culture of expert practice for instance, whether there is a genuine feeling of sharing reading, whether they offer the opportunity for learners to realise the value of their increasing skills.

I hope the theme of this chapter is clear. Good reading teaching is about assisting performance along a pathway through the zone of proximal development, to go together with children where at present they cannot go alone. There is a Chinese saying that: 'The best sort of leader is hardly noticed by people; the next best is honoured and praised; the next best is feared, and the next best is hated. But when the best sort of leader has finished, people say, "We did it ourselves".' Surely that's true of reading teachers too?

QUESTIONS FOR PERSONAL REFLECTION OR GROUP DISCUSSION

1 Do children in your class ever see you reading for enjoyment?
2 How much opportunity do you have to read aloud to

children ... as a group? On a one-to-one basis? Should this time be increased?

How far is it appropriate to talk with children about aspects of the text during these sessions?

Is your reading aloud to children confined to fiction or do children in your class get a chance to listen to an adult reading other types of material?

3 Do you ever offer children the opportunity to group? How might this be beneficial?

4 What do you see as the prime purpose of a child reading to you? Are there other important purposes which you don't normally take into consideration? How can you organise the class to allow you uninterrupted time with individual children during reading conferences?

Consider your coaching strategies when holding reading conferences with individual children. Compare your strategies with the list on page 114. What do you do which is not suggested here? Could you improve your practice by incorporating any of the suggestions into your normal practice?

5 How much time do children in your class get for sustained independent reading? Is this enough? If not, would it be feasible to organise your classroom in such a way as to allow space both in terms of time and location for a child to sit quietly and read?

6 What opportunities does a child have in your classroom to share a book with a more competent reader other than you? Would it be useful and possible to increase these opportunities?

7 Consider the list of suggestions for creating a reading community on page 122. Would it be worth while trying to adopt any in your classroom?

RECOMMENDED READINGS

Campbell, Robin (1990) *Reading Together*. Milton Keynes: Open University Press. This short book deals with story reading, shared reading, hearing children read and sustained silent reading. Throughout the book, the role of the teacher as a systematic, responsive adult who offers good models to learners is stressed. It is full of ideas to enliven and instruct on INSET days.

Wray, D., Bloom, W. and Hall, N. (1989) *Literacy in Action*. London: Falmer Press. *Literacy in Action* takes a contemporary view of the way children learn to be literate and suggests ways in which teachers can facilitate this learning. It is primarily a *teaching* book, in interactive format, which encourages observation in classrooms and reflection on these observations in the light of theory.

Donaldson, M. (1978) *Children's Minds*. London: Fontana. This book is now recognised as a classic inquiry into the way children think. It shows how thought and language originally depend on the interpersonal contexts within which they develop, and argues that the way in which reading is taught is even more important than we have supposed.

Waterland, L. (1989) *Apprenticeship in Action: Teachers Write About 'Read With Me'*. Stroud: Thimble Press. Waterland's first book, *Read With Me*, written by a practising teacher who was so obviously aware of the potential practical problems of a radical change in classroom practice in this area, found a wide and receptive audience. The first edition (1985) ran to seven reprints. *Apprenticeship in Action* is likely to be equally popular with teachers. It is described by the author as an informal resource book for people at various stages of understanding and practice in the apprenticeship approach to reading, and is the outcome of correspondence she has had with readers of *Read With Me*. These readers share their experiences and concerns about such things as parental involvement, record keeping and assessment, resources and unsympathetic colleagues. The many direct quotes from letters form an album in which the voices of teachers coping with the practical difficulties of teaching reading are heard very clearly.

Wood, D. (1988) *How Children Think and Learn*. Oxford: Blackwell. This book explores critically conflicting views about how children think and learn. In particular it compares Piaget's approach with those offered by Bruner and Vygotsky establishing areas of common ground. It then considers what contribution these researchers can make to current debates in education asking, among other questions, what is the value of literacy and why some children have such problems in reading and writing.

Graves, D. (1991) *Build a Literate Classroom*. Oxford: Heinemann. Graves's book, rich with specific approaches and suggestions, is a book for teachers about making reading/writing decisions in the classroom. Like *Literacy in Action* it has an interactive style which is intended to encourage readers to rethink their classroom practice and in particular to change their use of time in order to set children on the road to becoming lifelong readers and writers.

BIBLIOGRAPHY

Arnold, H. (1982) *Listening to Children Reading*. London: Hodder & Stoughton.

Bamberger, R. (1976) 'Literature and development'. In J. E. Merritt (ed.) *New Horizons in Reading*. International Reading Association.

Bruner, J. S.(1966) *Toward a Theory of Instruction*. Cambridge, Massachusetts: Harvard University Press.

Bruner, J. S. (1983) *Child's Talk: Learning to Use Language*. Oxford: Oxford University Press.

Bryant, P. and Bradley, L. (1985) *Children's Reading Problems*. Oxford: Blackwell.

Donaldson, M. (1978) *Children's Minds*. London: Fontana.

Hall, N. (1987) *The Emergence of Literacy*. London: Hodder & Stoughton.

Holdaway, D. (1979) *Foundations of Literacy*. Sydney: Ashton Scholastic.

Holdaway, D. (1980) *Independence in Reading*. Sydney: Ashton Scholastic.

Meek, M. (1982) *Learning to Read*. London: Bodley Head.

Meek, M. (1988) *How Texts Teach What Readers Learn*. Stroud: Thimble Press.

Minns, H. (1990) *Read It To Me Now*. London: Virago Press.

Southgate, V. (1972) *Beginning Reading*. London: University of London Press.

Southgate, V. (1984) *Reading: Teaching for Learning*. London: Macmillan.

Southgate, V. *et al.* (1981) *Extending Beginning Reading*. London: Heinemann Educational Books.

Vygotsky, L. S. (1978) *Mind In Society. The Development of Higher Psychological Processes*. Cambridge, MA: Harvard University Press.

Waterland, E. (1985) *Read With Me: An Apprenticeship Approach to Reading*. Stroud: Thimble Press.

6

STORIES AND THE LITERACY ENVIRONMENT OF THE CLASSROOM

Carol Fox

At first the term 'literacy environment' might conjure up a set of visible props – a cosy reading corner with cushions, plants, and a rug, good library facilities and display areas, tape recorders with story cassettes and earphones, poetry posters, message boards, big books, topic tables, alphabet friezes – I could go on. In many primary classrooms (though not so often in secondary ones) the careful and imaginative display of literacy materials has become almost axiomatic. It is very important that children associate reading with pleasure, comfort and relaxation, and that reading corners are attractive places which invite children into them. There is no shortage of good ideas from teachers on the *presentation* of literacy to children. Yet I have been in classrooms with many of the props I've listed above which I would not regard as very good literacy environments, and, conversely, there can be positive and helpful literacy environments with none of this bright packaging. Take some children's homes – my own when I was growing up after the Second World War will do. In a large family with few books of our own and even fewer rooms for private, solitary reading, our literacy environment was the kitchen. At any time two or three of us would be reading in the kitchen, and sometimes in the evenings all of us. We were a small community of readers, utterly dependent on the public library which was open six days a week and twelve hours a day. If reading is a mental activity, and it is, then perhaps a less superficial reading of the term 'literacy environment' would see it as largely a set of habits, attitudes, and reading behaviours which draw in the young and inexperienced. My parents were avid readers themselves who saw reading as a natural part of living and a major means of entertainment and enlightenment. It is interesting to see in Margaret Clark's *Young Fluent Readers* (1976), coming twenty-five years after my own initiation to literacy, that her precocious young readers also benefited more from the attitudes of their parents than from other more tangible kinds of literacy provision. Without wanting to belittle in any way the things teachers do to make reading an attractive and pleasant activity for their pupils, in this chapter I want to look at literacy environments in the broader sense, though from time to time I shall use the term more literally.

For many years now I have been conducting a rather detailed study of just what it is that young children gain from a wide experience of books and literacy before school. What I've discovered is taken from the evidence of 200 oral invented stories, tape recorded from five pre-school children who were chosen on the basis of their great familiarity with stories read aloud from books. These five children subsequently learned to read with ease and were well above average in reading attainment at age 7; they also became very good writers.

They seemed to give some support to Gordon Wells' (1980) finding that experience of books and literacy before school was the most significant factor in reading success at age 7. We all know that many children come to school at 5 without extensive book experience and that their introduction to reading will be very dependent on what the teacher can do to make a rich literacy environment in his or her classroom. Though these children may not have heard many stories read aloud at home, one thing we can be certain of is that they know what stories *are*, may have heard many fantasy stories *told* at home, and, if not, will still have encountered dozens of stories of great variety simply by watching television.

Not only can we be fairly sure of this in most cases, but the research evidence tells us that, regardless of book experience, children learn to tell stories at the same time as they learn to develop spoke ι language. All the large oral story collections taken from young children have been able to start with 2 year olds (Pitcher and Prelinger, 1963). We know several other things about the stories very young children make up for themselves. The stories are likely to be more 'realistic' at 2 and 3, and to move increasingly into fantasy at 4, 5 and 6. This is because the more secure children become in their knowledge of how things actually are, the safer they feel in moving into created, invented worlds of their own (Ames, 1966). Vygotsky (1978) has described for us the onset of imagination as a major development in young children's thinking through these early years, and he claimed that the early metaphorical representations of their pretend play are the basis of future literacy and abstract thought. Nursery and infant classrooms need to be storytelling environments, places where making up stories, retelling and changing stories, and acting out stories in role-play, are central activities.

Another finding of storytelling research (Ames, 1966) is that (in Europe and North America at least) violent themes predominate in young children's invented tales. Though children have story techniques for protecting themselves from violence and death in their fantasies – dead characters come back to life, evil and violent things only happen to 'baddies' or to characters other than the main protagonist – I nevertheless found these violent themes to be true of my own story material. A monster bird consumes everything in the world, bit by bit; God gets rid of Dracula by driving one of Dracula's own blood-sucking teeth right through his heart so that the tooth comes out at his back; a little girl is abandoned and left alone to live by herself in a small corner of her own home. These bizarre and very unpleasant events are typical of the stories of my five children. If some adults are shocked by this, perhaps they need to look again at traditional fairy tales and myths, or at the content of some of the best picture storybooks for young children.

Though the authors of these books present their material in humorous and enchanting and happy ways, nevertheless a baby is left on a doorstep in *Burglar Bill* to be found there by a common thief. In *Hansel and Gretel* two children are taken into the woods by their parents to die there of hunger. Even in the relatively anodyne *Topsy and Tim* stories children are invited to accommodate themselves to real fears – the school, the hospital, and so on. And in one of the most famous and influential picture books of all, Sendak's *Where The Wild Things Are*, a small child vents his rage in a wild rumpus with a set of grotesque monsters. These are not randomly chosen examples, for all these books made a very powerful impact on the stories in my study. They are retold, quoted from, transformed, or made use of to supply images and motifs for newly invented stories. Yet the children do not seem to tell stories with violent elements simply to relish cruelty, gore, and death from the warmth and safety of their sitting rooms, though there is something of that, rather in the way that we all enjoy thunderstorms when we are tucked up indoors. The children also try to work out, through their story metaphors, both those they read and those they tell, what the world is all about, how we came into it, what it is to be very powerful or very weak, how you defeat your enemies, what death and dying are. When 4 year old Justine has done with all the things her monster bird eats up, finishing with 'the whole world', she adds, as a coda to her story – 'God made us all in his tummy'. Perhaps she thought that if that is where we were all made then that is where we should all return. God and St Peter, in a series of stories by 5 year old Josh, try to kill Dracula three times (the tripling device of the oral tradition). They stab him with his own teeth, set fire to him, and even consider cutting him up into little tiny pieces. But Dracula always comes back to life, and, after a debate, the only solution to the Dracula question is for him to become God and St Peter's friend. Five year old Sundari in one story solves the problem of sibling rivalry, and the problem of wanting to be the oldest and youngest child simultaneously, by having her main character, the first born, die, then come back to life after all her brothers and sisters have been born. Justine's story ends by returning to God, Josh's ends with God, St Peter, Dracula, and a cast of heavenly servants all dancing in a circle to celebrate Dracula's friendship deal, and Sundari's ends with a birthday party for all the brothers and sisters. Destruction, evil, and jealousy are worked through and resolved in stories in ways that life itself does not make possible.

I received more than twenty stories of this sort from each of my five children. Some of them 'learned to read' in school on basal readers whose narratives so lacked any significant content that there must have been an enormous disjuncture between what these children thought books and stories were, and what they were being led to believe *reading* was. A reading environment which does not capitalise on children's natural propensity to make story metaphors for the fundamental aspects of their own living will surely be inadequate to persuade children that it is worth making the effort to understand (i.e. read) what the words on the page say. Making words 'say' in reading probably has more in common with joining in with the words, sounds, and rhythms of familiar catchy tunes than with plucking sounds off the page, letter by letter, word by word. The latter may be a logical process but it is incredibly tedious, because it takes so long and so much concentration to synthesise the sounds that all sense is lost. Children soon become bored and think that reading must be very difficult. Of course they need all kinds of careful help at the beginning – fewer and larger words on the page, support from the superb illustrative skills of good artists, plenty of repetition. But fewer words need not mean boring, colourless language. Illustrations ought to be another way of telling the story, and repetitions can follow the patterns of the oral tradition or of poems and verses. Texts to support beginning readers need not be constructed at the expense of the gripping stories children carry in their heads and tell themselves all the time; young readers should turn the page not to learn the 'new' word in the scheme but to find out what happens next. We may not be able to supply hundreds of books in our classrooms but, *especially if resources are limited*, the ones we choose should be powerful – powerful enough to offer strong competition to TV soaps, the daily news, or even video nasties. We do need a wide variety of books, as the National Curriculum urges, but we cannot afford to lose sight of the motivating force of really powerful stories.

Though I have taken the space here to make the point about the importance of powerful stories my intention is not to reiterate a very well-understood theme, one which is dealt with elsewhere in this book, but to tie that idea to other kinds of evidence which emerged from my study. Much of my work has involved the detailed analysis of the language of the children's stories. I want to talk about that language here, but also to see that language as a natural outgrowth of the power of the story material the children both heard and narrated themselves. Perhaps even 'outgrowth' does not really describe what I mean, for stories are made of words and sentences, so that the language is an integral part of the powerful meanings I think are so important; indeed language cannot be separated from those meanings. What I'm saying is that children acquire very advanced linguistic structures from their encounters with story material that is strong enough to engage them emotionally and intellectually. I've found that in their storytelling my five children were highly creative and extremely competent at every level of linguistic analysis - the word, the phrase, the sentence, and the narrative discourse itself. They show competencies which are surprisingly advanced - I say 'surprisingly' because I think we still know very little about language development after the early stages of acquisition.

The vocabularies of the five children are very striking not only for obviously 'literary' words ('perished', 'astonished', 'scolded', 'dismay', 'realised', 'evil', etc.), but also for the creative ways in which the children invent the language they need at any given time. We have a verb 'weared' from the adjective 'weary' from Sundari, and the noun phrase 'icicled snowball person' from Jimmy. In one of Josh's stories Robin Hood goes 'through the town snatching foolish money for poor people', and Sundari's narrator announces a 'nearly crying story, nearly, nearly, nearly'. One of Robert's 'baddie' characters 'wasted things', Sundari's witch 'collects' a 7 year old to put in her brew, and Josh's superheroes are out of action because 'Robin's got chest-ache and Batman's got flu'. Names are invented with amusing originality – Cletcher (a boy), a Choryda (a monster), Truggle and Mubble (witch's daughters). In unconventional but highly colourful usages like these the children show themselves ready to take risks with words, to use them when they think they *may* be appropriate, to use what makes the discourse sound like real stories sound, to use grammatical knowledge to coin new words out of old ones, and to get them occasionally wrong – 'It was humble in the sea' (Sundari); 'He looked through his kaleidoscope and what did he see? The English riding out to sea' (Josh). There is no doubt that books have been part of what has created these children's interest in and enjoyment of strange, unusual, colourful, and sonorous terms. Indeed some words are very unlikely indeed to have occurred anywhere but in a story from a book – 'As morning approached the little dewer man spread his dewdrops to meet the day' (Josh). It is hard to imagine a context for this sentence outside the pages of a children's storybook. This sort of thing is not parrot memorisation; Josh has not quoted verbatim from the original but made several changes. Their frequent encounters with book language which is strange or unusual have given these children an experimental and creative focus on words, and that focus is intimately bound up with the power of the stories the words tell.

I frequently hear from teachers, and see written into students' teaching practice schemes, the very understandable intention to 'broaden vocabulary' or 'enrich language', yet we know very little about how this actually works. I suspect that we learn new words when we need them to make new meanings *and* when we have the opportunity to use them, to try them out for the appropriate fit. Communication with others, including the physically absent authors of children's books, soon teaches us whether we are putting words in the right places or not. Yet learning language is a matter not only of learning the conventions, but also of learning to play with them, to change them, to recreate them or to make new ones, and writers and poets are particularly good teachers of invented, created languages. It seems obvious that if children frequently meet unconventional and original uses of language they will learn as a matter of course that that is the way language works, these are the things you can make it do. We have known since Chomsky that children do not learn language by copying adults or by adding on new words until they arrive at longer and longer sentences. They learn it by discovering under-lying regularities in contexts which are highly meaningful and situations where there is maximum feedback, and then they use those regularities to recreate words, phrases, and sentences for themselves. Literacy makes an enormous contribution to this process, for at 5 when they go to school children are still learning language in the ways they learned it at the beginning.

There are several implications for literacy environments. Adults need to be receptive to this kind of language themselves, not too rigidly tied to dictionary meanings and definitions and literal usages, but enjoying poetic uses of language enough themselves to notice them in children's speech, to give children plenty of opportunities for creative storytelling and the verbal arts, and to foster pleasure in language for its own sake in their choices of books for children to read. Unfortunately, whatever their other qualities of method, basal reading materials do not do well in this respect. That may not matter too much if children have many other sources of literary experience. But if they haven't, controlled vocabularies of 'common' or 'easy' or monosyllabic words will hardly demonstrate to them just what writing and literature can *do* with words and how they can do it themselves. I know that some readers will disagree with this, arguing that children need limited vocabularies in their reading materials in the beginning when they are learning how to take the words off the page for themselves, and that stories can be reserved for listening to or for later stages of reading indepen-dence. People who read to young children have told me hundreds of times how the child will not accept any alteration at all to the text of his or her favourite storybooks; indeed if adults try to do this the child will often get very angry and even cry. Why should this be? I think there are probably several reasons, but a major one must be that the story *is* the words and the words *are* the story, and if the words are changed the child knows he or she is getting something different. I have never heard anybody say that children do this with the texts of basal readers. Indeed these books are usually written with the aim of getting the child on to the *next* text as soon as possible, not for the child to savour, relish, and have repeated so often that the words stay in his or her head long after the story is over. To take the creativity out of the language of books for young readers is to waste a golden opportunity to fix the tunes of poetic language inside children's repertoires as the basis for their first independent reading. Children's malapropisms, their word coinages and experiments, need to be regarded positively by their teachers as manifestations of interest in and excitement about language.

The child who learns these lessons initially through encounters with strong, well-told stories will later be the child who takes on the specialised terminology of school subjects. We can already see that happening in some of the stories my five children tell. At the beginning, even before children can read themselves, stories are vessels which carry many different kinds of knowledge. Walter Ong (1982) tells us that the Homeric bards included in the *Odyssey* all the structures of knowledge of their times, from family trees to lists of ships in the Trojan wars. Stories have settings, and one of the first 'rules' of storytelling young children absorb is the orientation of the listener to the vital setting information which is required to make sense of the story events. They do this well before the age of 5. In Baum's (1900, 1904) stories *The Wizard of Oz* and *The Land of Oz*, which I read to Josh a chapter a night at around the time he was recording his stories, readers are introduced to whole terrains and landscapes - mountains, rocks, rivers, underground passageways, and so on. There is an enormously varied territory waiting to be explored by Dorothy and her friends in these books, just as there was in nineteenth-century America. All of this is picked up by Josh. Through his listening he learns to see stories as journeys whose stages define the story events - it is in fact the classical plot structure of early picaresque novels, and it is repeated in many excellent picture books for young readers; as I write, Michael Foreman's *Panda's Puzzle* springs to mind. But as Josh takes in this story structure he also absorbs a discourse which is about maps, journeys, and terrains:

> and then they made little passageways through the mountain just on the ground and they walked through them and looked for treasure David saw a necklace Joshua saw only a ring and then they walked through the tunnels the passageways then they made a passageway going under ground and when they came to the river they could do nothing about it so they got out (sic) of the river and swam and then they made another deep hole then right down and then it came up at their tree house then they went back to the starting again and did it even longer from there
>
> (Josh story 60, 5 years 9 months)

Here Josh shows that he has a mental map of a territory of mountains, caves, and underground rivers, and from it he constructs a circular 'tour' which fully reflects his understanding of the reversibility of journeys (Piagetians will notice that he *conserves* the beginning of his journey in its end). But his range of terms for the exploration of the inside of the mountain is extensive in such a small story space – passageway/tunnel/underground/deep hole. He can explore these concepts in his own story but first they have been encountered in the stories he has heard read aloud. Jimmy, at 4 years old, shows a similar interest in geological excavation:

> once in Highbury Fields we dug a hole right to the core of the earth and we saw the rocks moving
>
> (Jimmy story 16, 4 years 9 months)

This little sentence shows a remarkably specialised use of the term 'core', and Jimmy may have acquired it from looking at *adult* books or television programmes rather than children's books. Children don't need all their books to be tailored to children's level. They also need to be able to browse through what the grown-ups read, and good literacy environments keep some of these special adult's books for children to look at and thereby discover where the reading journey they are beginning can eventually lead them. I can still remember how, as a young child in the late 1940s, the reading I always wanted when I was ill in bed were some books of photographs about how people lived in London during the War, books which belonged to my parents and which were brought out as a special treat. All these years on I would give anything to look at those books again.

I could give many other examples of the ways in which young children explore concepts of number, shape, size, height, weight, geography, physics, *meta*physics, ethics, and much more, in the course of their storytelling (Fox, 1989).

Of course attaching the children's explorations to the names of formal disciplines has the effect of exaggerating the intellectual journeys the children make. The point is that it is their *play* – their sometimes rather serious play with language and narrative – which necessarily calls upon them to think in these ways – ways which in future will be more abstract and which perhaps will not require the story context to sustain them. We know that information books which give children a clear and interesting introduction to different fields of knowledge are essential to good literacy environments. The National Curriculum endorses this. Unfortunately good information books are desperately hard to find, and, in any case, as James Moffett (1968) pointed out long ago, for young children 'narrative must do for all', just as it had to for the Greeks in the oral culture which produced the great epic poems. We must of course see that children come to regard books as sources of information, but we also need to be aware that narrative discourse is the vital link between the natural discourses of everyday life and the formal discourses of school subjects. Even as I write this I have just read in today's *Guardian* (26 September 1991) a forceful indictment of modern history teaching by the historian Simon Schama, because, he claims, it has lost sight of the power of narrative literature to draw children into historical discourses. Those who have read *Citizens* (Schama, 1990) will know that it is possible to enjoy this 1,000 page analysis of the French Revolution because it is told as a *story* and the story is able to bear the weight of the historical sources and evidence that it inevitably has to carry. If stories are full of conceptual wealth for children, we ought to ask where the basal readers stand in relation to the acquisition of knowledge. Are the ones in use in so many classrooms vessels which will carry children on journeys, expand their mental maps, inform them about the world? Or are we separating learning how to lift the words off the page from the mental stimulation and knowledge to be had from books?

I also heard on this same day, as I write, of the death of Dr Seuss. Perhaps his books may strike some teachers as very close to the schematic in the ways that they try to structure children's progress through the intricacies of sound/spelling patterns in English. But I would argue that Seuss' work was much closer to play than that. His word coinages hilariously and cunningly match the unrhymable words in our language, his stories are utterly fantastic, bizarre, and original, and there is always a deeper structure which has to do with making metaphors for children's fears, passions, and conflicts as they grow up. You cannot afford to change the words of any of his books if you are reading them aloud, for their verses and rhythms are especially mnemonic and young readers soon know them by heart. His terrain is infinite – whole armies, tribes even, of invented creatures make mockery of mean, petty, and evil values in human life. Yet children read his books for *fun*; they enjoy his anarchic originality with language and the preposterous rhymes which cleverly give them the phonological awareness so helpful to inexperienced readers and writers.

If good literacy environments stem from the attitudes and orientations to literacy of literacy teachers, as I believe they do, then verbal play, all the zany, complex, crazy manifestations of it, needs to be really enjoyed and appreciated by teachers themselves. They can never discover children's understanding of phonologi-cal regularities, never mind teach them, unless rhymes, songs, jokes, puns, verses, and role-play are allowed to *naturalise* those regularities so that they become part of the capital we can draw on in learning to be literate. There is all the difference in the world between doing phonic blending exercises, divorced from all natural uses of language, and discovering phonological patterns because they happen to be part of something hugely enjoyable like tongue-twisters or jokes. Oral cultures (to which pre-literate children can be said to belong) all over the world have highly valued and skilled forms of verbal play, usually mastered and performed by adolescent boys after an induction of many years' duration. (Recently some female ethnographers are dis-covering that girls too have their different forms of verbal play.) Research from places as remote from one another as Turkey, Burundi, St Vincent, New York, and Tibet shows that verbal duelling, rapping, 'talking sweet', ritual insults and so on, are the linguistic mirrors for the values, status relations, and world view of whole communities. Not only are the most successful men of words *always* the leaders of their groups, but the verbal play forms themselves twist words and meanings about in very subversive and radical ways (Dundes *et al.*, 1972; Albert, 1972; Abrahams, 1972; Labov, 1972; Leach, 1964).

What has all this got to do with young children learning to read? Well, we need only to read the Opies' (1959) *Lore and Language of Schoolchildren*, or listen to the infants in the home corner, to realise that this is an almost universal phenomenon among children. Whether it takes the form of knock–knock jokes, or cheeky words to well-known hymns and popular songs, or skipping rhymes, and, later, rapping and playing the dozens, or even Pig-Latin or backslang, children of all ages love to play with language, to make it say dangerous things according to strict rules of rhyme, metre, and double entendre. The links with what we call literature are obvious, especially with much literature for young children. There has been an explosion in recent years of cheeky, funny, or 'silly' verse for kids – Michael Rosen, Roald Dahl, Brian Patten, Spike Milligan, and Allan Ahlberg are among many others who have tapped this tradition, written it down, and given it value, and their popularity with children is enormous. This is not to imply that such poets are not 'serious', but that they are serious in ways which children will perceive primarily as fun. Comics do it too, though sometimes in more limited ways. Children need to have hundreds of opportunities to enjoy these kinds of verbal play and to learn to master them themselves. Valuing the oral language skills which many children have, strangely enough, may provide a clear pathway to literacy once children find out that not only do books do this sort of thing very well, but that in books you can read and enjoy it again and again, and even have a source for getting the words right.

The children in my study showed that their exposure to verse, rhymes, and poetry led to some extraordinarily poetic passages in their stories:

> but the boy did play on his ice skates on
> the ice which was a puddle which was ice
> turned in ice

This complex syntactic structure from Sundari plays with grammatical rules (embedded subordinate clauses as in *This is the House That Jack Built*), with an understanding of the transformation of water into ice, and with repetition. It comes from a story which Sundari *sings*. If this seems a little odd we ought to remember that that is exactly what the bards of the oral tradition did. Brian Sutton-Smith (1981), in his large-scale study of children's invented stories, calls the stories of younger children 'verse stories' because he finds that they are usually structured on phonological and prosodic principles rather than on logical story events. And Walter Ong (1982) tells us that in the history of writing it is only with the rise of literacy that logical, complex plots appear in novels. In an imitation news broadcast recorded at age 6, Josh, in a plummy voice with a 'posh' accent, uses rhyme and rhythm to lampoon the news:

> On the News last night at Belfast a big pooh-pooh was dropped from Nonsenseland to Conscienceland at that Conscienceland Mr Reagan came out with a chimney for a nose and some daggers for a toes and really peculiar pet-dragon nose

These days most primary classrooms are full of funny poetry books but not so often full of the more lyrical and serious ones. I found that Josh and Sundari invented verses and lyrical passages in their stories which came straight from the poems they had heard. When he was 5 Josh thought poems had to be about the sea, needn't tell a story, and ought to be spoken in solemn dirge-like tones; those were the 'rules' he'd internalised for poems:

> the rocks and shore scatter upon the lighthouses some days storm breaks up ships and buildings get ship-wrecked under the water pirate ship-wreck has become the treasure under the sea

Though it probably does not do to look for clear meanings in this 'poem' (Josh's own word for it), it is apparent that this is intended to describe a scene in a lyrical way as though looking at it in the present, rather than recounting events in the past tense which characterised his stories. Sundari produces one of the most syntactically complex and poetically satisfying sentences in the whole study when she echoes, in an invented story, the lyricism of Joan Aitken's (1975) *A Necklace of Raindrops*:

> she liked doing things playing about at the beach on sunny

140

days when cool wind was blowing making sand-castles
playing with her little necklace with people on it and some
little rain-drops falling from the people and bags on it what
the teddy-bears were in what the people were holding

(Sundari story 12)

So far I've focused on the kinds of books we need to choose to
surround children with, read to them again and again, and,
where appropriate, help them to try for themselves. I've talked
about powerful, emotionally strong and sustaining stories, books
which use language in rich, innovative forms, adult books which
can whet children's appetite for knowledge, storybooks which
carry in them information and specialised discourses, poetry
books ranging from the loopy phonological patterning of Dr
Seuss stories and the modern anthologies of silly verse through to
more serious lyrical work. The quantity of books available to
children in classrooms will depend on resources of money. Books
are becoming very expensive and we cannot take their supply for
granted with the new local management of schools (LMS).
Determined teachers seem to be good at finding ways round these
resource problems. But really the richness of the books available
to children is more important than the number. The schemes
often fail to conceptualise that really meaningful, well-written
stories are returned to again and again. The best become 'transitional objects' like the teddy-bears or bits of blanket young
children cannot bear to be parted from. Children may learn more
from repeated visits to a text that is rich in the ways I have
described here than from the onwards and upwards progression
through a series of dull but structured 'readers'. Josh retold
Hansel and Gretel eight times in my study, transformed it into an
invented story many more times, and, for good measure, added a
retelling of an African *Hansel and Gretel* called *Fereyal and
Debbo-Engal the Witch*. He could not read for himself the
version he would retell – the language was sonorous, traditional,
and strange, and there were sections of the story he almost
certainly did not understand at the beginning. It is possible to
trace his developing comprehension of different parts of the story
from his early retellings to his later ones. His realisation that the
stepmother and the witch represent the same things, for example,
comes in his fifth retelling, while his understanding of the death
of the children's real mother and the woodcutter's subsequent

remarriage comes towards the end. For his independent reading there were simpler but equally powerful texts like *Burglar Bill* and *Where the Wild Things Are*. But his listening to texts that were full of strange words and poetic effects, and rather old-fashioned traditional fairy-tale prose structures, put into his head the language of writing and the complex meanings that writing is able to express. It taught him and the other children that writing is not speech written down but is in some ways a language which is 'other' than speech. An analysis of the sentence structures of the children's stories showed that their sentences in narrative are usually longer, more explicit, and more grammatically complex than the sentences which appear on the tapes as ordinary conversations with their parents at the periphery of the storytelling. Space does not permit me to report those findings here, but they are important evidence that the structures of written language are internalised by children who are familiar with book stories long before they become writers themselves.

There are other implications for the literacy environment that underlie what I've said so far. These have to do with talking and writing. We cannot have good classrooms for literacy if children are not enabled to become tellers and writers of their own stories, poems, and verses. To focus on reading alone is but to do half the job, for it needs to interact with talking and writing for the meanings taken from reading to be actively expressed. Many of the stories in my study would make excellent books for children to read. Or they might make very good starters for pieces of narrative writing if the child could listen to his or her own tape and attempt to write a story from it. Reading is not passive. Children actively seek out meanings and struggle for the words and structures to express them if we also allow them to talk about books, retell stories, make up oral stories, and write stories down. I think too that we should actively encourage them to borrow ideas and even words from the stories they have read – after all, that is what adult writers from Shakespeare onwards have done. Children make stories mean in accordance with their own structures of interest, their own past experiences, and their individual personalities and preferences. The wonderful thing about reading fiction is that we can make it mean in so many varying ways, both among readers and in the same reader on new and repeated readings. The kind of literacy environment

I envisage here will be a community rather than a set of props (desirable and helpful though those are). The community will be one of writers, talkers, storytellers, singers, actors, jokers, and poets, not a silent community of silent readers, though of course children reading for real will demand quiet spaces for reflection and private reading.

The tape recorder in my view is a vital part of a modern literacy environment. Its benefits extend well beyond its usefulness for recording role-play and storytelling, or even for teachers to use as a means of studying pupils' language in depth. The five children were very much at home with the tape recorder, regarding it, and the distant, absent listener in some future time, as the audience for the story. Sundari invents narrators to tell her stories, and they frequently come out of the narrating to speak directly to the listener:

> they're silly names aren't they?
> Did you say yes? Well if you did I'm pleased if you didn't
> I'm still pleased
>
> (Sundari story 4)

Sundari's narratives are full of interpolations of this kind. They are not addressed to her mother, who is sometimes present during storytelling and sometimes not, but to the imagined listener who one day will hear the tape. The audience for her story is a fiction, as much imagined by Sundari as her story events and characters. This does not imply that her audience is not 'real', more that it is an audience much like the reader of a book who will have to do without the presence of the author as he or she reads. There has been some confusion about 'real' audiences for writing in recent years, as though children must always be writing with an actual person or persons in mind, rather than a more distanced 'reader-ship' which has been imagined and fully catered for in the writer's mind and in the text the writer produces. It is a precondition for writing that children come to understand that they themselves will be absent at the point at which their text is read by somebody else (even if that somebody is the teacher). This lesson is learned easily and virtually unconsciously by children who have had plenty of practice in being listeners/readers before they learn to write. Of course imagining the audience means that the child becomes simultaneously author and narrator of, and listener to, his or her own tale, and this inevitably leads to great explicitness in the telling. The children are remarkably clear in their references to characters, story events, and phenomena that are part of the story setting. Indeed their stories are loaded with explanations of all kinds, anything from how it was possible for Dracula to come back to life with his teeth intact, to the workings of rainbows or the height of castle walls. The internalisation of an audience, the ability to see themselves as the listener to their own narrations at such an early age, must have helped them at a later stage to become the imagined readers of their own written texts. They became competent writers because they were accustomed to see the reader's view of what they had written.

The special facility of the tape recorder is that we can hear ourselves on it. All five children *always* listened to the story they had just told before going on to narrate another one. The metalinguistic and metanarrative benefits of this activity must be enormous, for now the children were not only the imagined audience for their own stories, but the actual ones. The children seemed to tell cycles of stories, repeating the same themes or structures in a series of stories told on the same day, or reworking the material over weeks and months. This is most evident in the data from Josh for he tells eighty-six stories in all. Sometimes I play one of his more successful stories to a group of teachers or students, and they are usually surprised by the intricacy of the structure and ideas in a spontaneous story made up at the whim of the storyteller. But this is really a false impression. The story has usually been 'rehearsed' in a whole series of previous storytellings, and the apparently magically well-structured narrative is really the result of successive retellings of his own story material, which in turn has often been transformed from stories he has heard. But it isn't just the story material which is reworked; continually telling stories and listening to them themselves offered the children the opportunity to develop the *telling* as well as the *told*. The literacy environment needs at least one tape recorder with built-in microphone so that children can easily record themselves. The background noise of the classroom can make tape recording difficult, and finding quiet places is not easy in many schools. However, we can really look and see if we are utilising what spaces there are to best advantage. I have seen tape recorders and computers set up in wide corridors, school libraries, medical rooms, and even large stock cupboards which are built into some classrooms. Ideally two or three tape recorders ought to be stationed in or near the reading corner so that children can listen to recordings of their favourite stories again and again. Background noise is not such a problem if earphones are supplied.

The children were very explicitly aware of what it means to be the teller of a tale, and the most self-conscious linguistic knowledge revealed by the story data is manifest in the remarks they make about kinds of story and about ways of narrating. I believe that listening to themselves, and constantly recycling their inventions, brings to the surface of consciousness the knowledge which is deeply subconscious during storytelling itself. Their knowledge of syntax is of course implicit and at no point in over 49,000 words of storytelling do they ever discuss sentence structure or syntactic rules. However, they do show that at other levels of linguistic structure, particularly the *word* and the *discourse*, they have unexpectedly high awareness of their own knowledge. This knowledge is relayed to the listener of their stories through a very heightened awareness of the narrator's role to inform, to direct the story material, to comment, to explain, and to evaluate the story during the telling or *as part of the telling*. The various functions of *narrating* have been categorised for us in great detail by Genette (1972) and when I used his categories to analyse my data I found that the two 5 year olds, Josh and Sundari, were aware of a whole range of narrating functions. Sundari often uses her first-person narrator to comment on both narrated and narrating:

> she couldn't tell everything she did so much nor can I it's nearly the end of this story 'cos it's not a long story it's a quick story not talking fast though talking slowly and wearily along
>
> (Sundari story 10)

Justine uses her conscious awareness of the narrator's power over the story to bring about an almost post-modern ending:

> and that is the end of the story but it's not really because I'm telling you it and there was a book once upon a time it's still same day I know I said it's the end of the story but I don't mean it's the end of the story
>
> (Justine story 22)

Knowing the difference between saying things and meaning

them is part of the children's explicit awareness that words are arbitrary signs whose meanings are only agreed by convention. Josh explains to his listeners in a retelling of an African folk-tale a term they may not know:

> and then (he – um) Fereyal nearly got his life cut off *'cut off' that's another word for getting his life cut down*
>
> (Josh story 75)

Sundari, on the other hand, has learned a convention of narrating which assumes knowledge on the part of the listener. This is the convention, common in children's literature, of starting sentences with 'as you know':

> now you know what 'annoyed' means

Defining terms is part of the storyteller's concern for the audience's understanding:

> Do you know why they were poor? Because they had no money
>
> (Josh story 19)
>
> and then a monster came to that road a huge monster it was called a hooligan and that is a dragon
>
> (Justine story 24)

The children show that they know stories belong to different genres although their categories tend to be invented, playful categories. Already they have learned that sets of story categories can be made fun of. Sundari's categories are *rubbish stories* ('all people called her was "Rubbish" 'cos this is really a rubbish story'), *rhyming stories* ('you know well this is a rhyming story'), *quick stories* ('so you've got to quickly talk as quickly as possible') and *nonsense stories* in the manner of Edward Lear ('all the words in here are funny aren't they?'). Robert, at age 3½, tells *tiny stories, little stories, horrible stories, joke stories,* and *secret stories.* Justine has a category called *stories for babies,* in which there is an opening and an ending but no action in between. Research by Pradl (1979) tells us that formal openings and endings are the first story conventions very young children learn; Justine instinctively knows what a very young child would know about storytelling. Sundari's rhyming stories, quick stories, and nonsense stories are defined in terms of the manner of telling. Robert's joke stories, tiny stories, and horrible stories are defined in terms of the story content. And Justine's stories for babies are defined in terms of the story structure.

For teachers to discover what their pupils' explicit knowledge of language might be, a rich talking and storytelling environment is required. The sort of discourse knowledge I have been sketching here (for there is much more of it than space allows me to discuss) is specifically contextualised within a set of literacy practices which include listening to stories read aloud, making up stories of one's own, taping them or writing them down, talking about them and role-playing the storyteller, and retelling the stories told or written by others. For teachers to manage these kinds of activities in large classes situated in small rooms is a major problem which can partly be solved by the active engagement of parents and other adults to assist both in and out of school. Probably these forms of literacy activity will be embedded in many other kinds of role-play, drama, and talk in the classroom. Knowing the language of books is obviously very important in learning to read and write, but children try out many other discourses in their pretend play – Mums and Dads, Doctors and Nurses, Teachers and Pupils, Shopkeepers and Customers, and so on. The processes are probably the same – the children rework what they have heard in imaginative form with their peers. Unfortunately this sort of creative activity often seems to belong more to the nursery than to the later years of infant and junior schools, where things become more formal and the discourses of play are pushed out to the playground and beyond. This can sometimes have serious consequences for children whose cultural background is not the mainstream British one, children whose parents have inherited rich oral traditions in their mother tongues, and the larger group of children whose spoken English has the phonological and metaphoric richness of non-standard dialects. If the competences of those children are squeezed out of the curriculum early on we burn the bridges to literacy that they bring with them to school.

I hope that throughout this chapter the quotations I have included from these young children's invented stories will offer convincing evidence of the linguistic and literacy gains to be made from doing a lot of listening to really strong, gripping narratives. I will close by summarising the implications for literacy environments. Good literacy environments will be communities of readers and listeners, storytellers and writers, role-players, actors and singers, circulators of jokes, puns, rhymes, and other forms of verbal trickery, linguistic explorers and creators, active seekers of knowledge, and exploiters of all the mother tongues and non-standard dialects to be found in the classroom and beyond it. The teachers who create these environments will find out as much as they can about children's language competences by listening to their pupils and learning to recognise and value what the children bring to school, and parents and other interested non-professionals will inevitably be drawn in so that the community extends beyond the classroom walls. Stories will not only be read and repeated when children want them, but other media for the experience of literary language will be used – tape recorders, gramophone records, and videos. Children's own stories will be included among the books on the shelves, and among the story tapes for listening to. In such an environment children will actively produce literacy for themselves as part of their real interaction with the environment. Building in to this environment notions of progression that will be helpful to beginners will be a matter of looking at reading development in accordance with criteria which have to do with the interests of the child, the meaningfulness of the text, and both the quantity and quality of the language of the text. Structure need not be a monopoly of the authors of scheme readers, but ought to grow out of the interaction between child, teacher, and text. Children whose narrations include sentences like 'they were really truly of their home and going to it' (Josh) and 'a Little-Bo-Peep story was a long time ago told by a little girl' (Sundari) did not acquire their literacy from the blank-faced tower blocks of published reading schemes but from the warm hearths of the houses of children's literature.

QUESTIONS FOR PERSONAL REFLECTION AND STAFF DISCUSSION

1 Is there a school policy for communicating the importance of storytelling and story reading at home and at school to parents?
2 Are there enough emotionally powerful stories in the book collection for each class? If you use a reading scheme are the stories in the scheme books sufficiently strong to be as

satisfying to young readers as some of the books mentioned in this chapter?

3 Do you have ways of observing and recording which stories are most meaningful to individual children? Have you thought about getting parents to help with this?

4 Are the children in your class getting enough repetitions of the stories they like most? Have you considered the introduction of extra readers into the classroom to read to children on a one-to-one basis or in small groups (e.g. parents and other relatives, older pupils from secondary schools, friends of the school, and so on)?

5 Are your pupils hearing enough book language which is rich, colourful, or unusual? Or do you worry that strange words will be outside the children's comprehension? What strategies can you use to introduce new words to children without destroying their pleasure in stories?

6 Do you have a small stock of special, more grown-up books, especially information or reference books, for the children to browse through? Can you think of any which would appeal to the children in your class?

7 Are poems, rhymes, jingles, verbal jokes and games an everyday part of oral language activity in your class? Can you compile a list of books which could be a central resource for you and your pupils (e.g. Allan Ahlberg's *Old Joke Book* or, for teachers, the Opies' *Lore and Language of Schoolchildren*)?

8 Do you regularly invite groups of children to change or expand on stories you have read to them? Can you think of any stories or picture books which particularly lend themselves to this kind of imaginative exploration?

9 Have you thought of making a collection of story tapes for children to listen to as they read the books themselves? Is it possible for a group of staff to make some tapes together, thereby getting a variety of voices and accents on the tapes?

10 Have you thought of inviting parents and grandparents to record autobiographical stories for your pupils to listen to?

RECOMMENDED READINGS

Applebee, A. (1978) *The Child's Concept of Story*. Chicago: University of Chicago Press. This book explains children's understanding of story structure using a model adapted from Vygotsky's developmental model of concepts.

Fox, C. (1989) 'Children thinking through story'. *English in Education*, vol. 23, no. 2. An article which relates the language of children's invented fantasies to the different discourses of school subjects. Shows how 'narrative must do for all' in the early years.

Meek, M. (1988) *On Being Literate*. London: Bodley Head. In her latest book Margaret Meek relates literacy to culture. This is the best available account of what membership of the literacy club actually looks like.

Meek, M. (1989) *How Texts Teach What Readers Learn*. Stroud: Thimble Press. A short but very dense booklet showing how the authors of really good children's books give readers lessons in reading. It takes the view that reading is much more than lifting words off the page and links literacy to literature. A reader who unpicked the references in the text would arrive at a very full understanding of Meek's arguments.

Sutton-Smith, B. (1981) *The Folk-Stories of Children*. Philadelphia, PA: University of Pennsylvania Press. The introduction gives an account of the nature of this very large collection of children's oral stories. The bulk of the book gives us the stories themselves, at every age and stage.

Vygotsky, L. (1978) *Mind in Society*. Cambridge, MA: Harvard University Press. Essential for 'The role of play in mental development' in which Vygotsky claims that play lays the foundations of future abstract mental operations.

BIBLIOGRAPHY

Abrahams, R. D. (1972) 'The training of the man of words in talking broad'. In T. Kochman (ed.) *Rappin and Stylin Out*. University of Illinois Press.

Adamson, J. and Adamson, G. (1982) *Topsy and Tim Go to Hospital*. Glasgow: Blackie.

Ahlberg, J. and Ahlberg, A. (1977) *Burglar Bill*. London: Heinemann.

Aitken, J. (1975) *A Necklace of Raindrops*. Harmondsworth: Penguin.

Albert, E. M. (1972) 'Culture patterning of speech behaviour in Burundi'. In Dell Hymes and J. J. Gumperz (eds) *Directions in Sociolinguistics*. New York: Holt, Rinehart & Winston.

Ames, L. B. (1966) *Children's Stories*. Genetic Psychology Monographs No. 7.

Ames, L. B. (1978) In *Mind in Society*. Cambridge, MA: Harvard University Press.

Arnott, K. (1962) 'Fereyal and Debbo-Engal the Witch'. In *African Myths and Legends*. Oxford: Oxford University Press.

Baum, L. F. (1904) *The Land of Oz*. Rand McNally.

Baum, L. F. (1900) *The Wizard of Oz*. Rand McNally.

Clark, M. (1976) *Young Fluent Readers*. London: Heinemann.

Dundes, A. *et al.* (1972) 'The strategy of Turkish boys' verbal duelling rhymes'. In Dell Hymes and J. J. Gumperz (eds) *Directions in Sociolinguistics*. New York: Holt, Rinehart & Winston.

Foreman, M. (1977) *Panda's Puzzle*. London: Hamish Hamilton.

Fox, C. (1989) 'Children thinking through story'. *English in Education*, vol. 23, no. 2.

Genette, G. (1972) *Narrative Discourse*. Oxford: Basil Blackwell.

Labov, W. (1972) 'Rules for ritual insults'. In *Language in the Inner City*. Oxford: Basil Blackwell.

Leach, E. (1964) 'Anthropological aspects of language: Animal categories and verbal abuse'. In E. H. Lenneburg (ed.) *New Directions in the Study of Language*. Cambridge, MA: MIT Press.

Moffett, J. (1968) *Teaching The Universe of Discourse*. London: Houghton Mifflin.

Ong, W. (1982) *Orality and Literacy*. London: Methuen.

Opie, I. and Opie, P. (1959) *The Lore and Language of Schoolchildren*. Oxford: Oxford University Press.

Pitcher, E. G. and Prelinger, E. (1963) *Children Tell Stories*. New York: International Universities Press.

Pradl, G. (1979) 'Learning how to begin and end a story'. *Language Arts*, vol. 56, no. 1.

Schama, S. (1990) *Citizens*. Harmondsworth: Penguin.

Schama, S. (1991) 'A room with no view'. *The Guardian*, 26 September, Review Section.

Sendak, M. (1970) *Where The Wild Things Are*. London: Bodley Head.

Sutton-Smith, B. (1981) *The Folk-Stories of Children*. Philadelphia, PA: University of Pennsylvania Press.

Vygotsky, L. (1978) *Mind In Society*. Cambridge, MA: Harvard University Press.

Wells, G. (1980) *Some Antecedents of Early Educational Attainment*. Centre for Study of Language and Communication, University of Bristol.

Williams-Ellis, A. (ed.) (1959) *Grimm's Fairy Tales*. Glasgow: Blackie.

Winnicott, D. W. (1971) *Playing and Reality*. Harmondsworth: Penguin.

7

CHILDREN'S EARLY EXCURSIONS INTO LITERACY

The need for a comprehensive account of the development of reading, writing and spelling

Eric Ashworth

In this chapter I shall focus on young, mainly pre-school, children. In doing so I shall put forward four propositions which I believe apply equally to the linguistic education of children of all ages. The first proposition is that before we consider reading we should consider literacy as a whole. This would include handwriting, written composition and spelling as well as reading. The second proposition is that we should find a model of reading within the wider notion of literacy that goes far beyond, while still including, word recognition or identification, that takes into account other facets of reading and recognises that there is a wide plurality of reading behaviours. The third proposition is that it makes no sense to isolate literacy, still less reading, from other language skills, that is from speaking and listening, because of the interdependence of all the language 'skills'. They need to be considered together because they feed and draw upon each other in significant but different ways at different stages. The fourth proposition is that when we are considering the place of good books (I prefer 'good' to 'real') we should do so in relation to language as a whole and not just to reading. When I have sketched the cases for the first three of these propositions I shall look briefly at what we can call literacy events, and then at the development of early writing. Finally, I shall return to the fourth proposition concerning the place of good books and to a very brief consideration of the implications of all this for schools, teachers and researchers.

PROPOSITION 1: THAT WE SHOULD CONSIDER LITERACY AS A WHOLE - NOT JUST READING BUT WRITING TOO

Reading and writing have much in common. Both deal with the written mode of language which differs from the spoken mode in several respects. It is made of different substance - graphic rather than phonic. It has a word stock that is similar but not identical to that of spoken language. Its grammar is different, though there is much overlap. Each mode has its own resources which users can treat as stores of information on the way to meaning. For example, speech has its intonation patterns - the 'tunes' which help speakers to envelope their language in overall patterns of sound and which are themselves meaningful to the experienced listener. Writing contains no such thing but has its own characteristic resources in spelling and punctuation. Also, it typically lends itself to some uses and not to others. It is not, for instance, conversational. Physically, it is arranged (in English) in a certain way on the line and upon the page and pages themselves are arranged in a certain sequence. It exists in the dimension of space whereas speech exists in time.

Both reading and writing have to deal with and in the written mode of language and in our case with the English writing system - alphabetic in spelling but including also numerals, punctuation marks and complex layout rules. Both have to cope with words, not enveloped in a possibly undivided stream of sound but existing on the page with spaces around. Both reading and writing require a basic understanding of the writing system.

What they have in common constitute some of the reasons why the notion of 'emergent literacy' is becoming widespread. This is an idea vastly superior to what it replaces, including the accompanying paraphernalia of pre-reading and 'reading readiness'. However, although there is common ground between reading and writing there is also a fundamental difference which is what we may call a process difference. It is not true that, whatever the process of reading is, the process of writing is simply the same in reverse. Margaret Peters put the point well in relation to spelling. It is not, she said, the 'flip side' of reading. Both young children and adults can sometimes read what they cannot write and young children frequently can write what they cannot read (Bryant and Bradley, 1980; Frith, 1980).

PROPOSITION 2: THAT WE SHOULD MOVE TOWARDS A DEEPER AND WIDER MODEL OF READING

It is a major error to regard reading as being mainly the recognition of words (through look and say) or their identification (through sounding out or phonics). What we actually read is language, which is made up of more than words and which is organised into texts, which may be of any length. Look and say and phonics are both word bound. Neither alone nor together can they serve as a model of reading behaviour, first because they ignore so much of language and, second, because they do not deal with the achievement of meaning and response.

A better model of reading would be one which acknowledges that it is language that we read (Ashworth, 1988). So, in addition to words as vocabulary there would be grammar to cope with. Here I use 'grammar' to mean an array of structures and systems which, among other uses, help to order what is written and which are indispensable devices when a reader tries to achieve meaning. I am referring, that is, to certain linguistic resources and neither to grammatical analysis of a sort once done in certain schools nor to grammar as a description of aspects of a language.

There is space enough only to indicate very briefly what these structures and systems are. Structures comprise words, parts of words (morphemes) – the preservation of some of which, incidentally, will become important in more advanced spelling – phrases, clauses, sentences and structures above the level of a sentence, including story structure. These structures package the language, so to speak, order it and, incidentally, allow the reader to make certain predictions.

The grammatical systems are even more various. They include ways of indicating whether nouns, pronouns and verbs are singular or plural, ways of making relative time references through the use of tenses, ways of asking questions, of making statements and commands, and include systems with markers such as 'may' which puts us into a sort of hypothetical world of possibility and 'if' which moves us into conditions. These are examples of a longer series of systematic resources. Their importance is that they allow us to get well beyond bald labelling statements of name or 'fact' and to make more complex meanings. One other system, which is most important, is the set of

154

rules which are used to put words in order. Much, probably most, of this grammar is learned at an implicit rather than an explicit level: it remains tacit.

So much for the extension of the concern with words into a concern with language. However, a viable model of reading needs to spread wider and deeper still. If we take it as obvious that the goal is the construction, or reconstruction or creation of meaning – and let us beg this question by referring only to the 'achieving' of meaning – and with it the engendering of response, it is clear that there is more to reading than just the language on the page. There is also the child's previous knowledge of language and his or her knowledge of the world.

A model of reading would try to show how readers would use information that is picked up from the page, previous knowledge of language and how it works, and previous worldly knowledge and treat it all as being available in the process of achieving meaning. These resources are, especially with more sophisticated readers, sometimes alternatives – if one uses some one does not need others and therefore there is redundancy. The same is true of stores of language and of worldly knowledge. Together they allow expectations to be built about both local and global meanings and permit inferences to be made when appropriate. Reading, as it proceeds towards meaning and response, is always a matter of language and it is always a matter of more than language.

There are, I suggest, four main criteria for a model of reading beyond the obvious one that it should be useful for whatever purpose is in hand. It should take into account development. Perhaps this might mean that not just one model but successive models are necessary, for the beginning reader does not read exactly like the expert reader but relies on different resources and employs different strategies. This brings us to the second criterion: a reading model should be dynamic. That is, it should not deal with a static structure so much as with a process. Third, it should be interactive – some of the dynamism is in moving between different strategies and alternative sources of information on the page and elsewhere, with each liable in principle to affect whether or to what degree use is made of the others. So the model will be complicated and only in exceptional cases will processing show a simple, straight, linear pattern. A fourth criterion is that it should allow for variation and variety. One person's strategies may legitimately differ from another's even when both are reading the same text; and the same person may use different strategies as he or she encounters different sorts of texts or reads for different purposes. A viable model or set of models would allow the reader to go well beyond the information on the page – it would take account of the ability to hypothesise and build expectations, to make inferences and to monitor and self-correct at different levels and to behave as much like a creative artist as a communicator (Smith, 1985).

From our present point of view it is vital that the reader of any text should have prior experience of written language – its grammar, organisation, style and distinctive use of vocabulary, its redundancies and the ways it packages information. The principle applies equally to the beginning reader and to the university graduate. The question is: where should this knowledge come from? Part of the answer is that it should come mainly from being read to and from the reader's own previous reading. That is why good books, which are linguistically resourceful books, are important.

PROPOSITION 3: THAT LITERACY SHOULD BE TREATED AS PART OF A WIDER LANGUAGE PROGRAMME

I suppose that there are two grand routes into literacy. The first is from within the child, a creative rather than a copying venture, when the child may invent or reconstruct literacy, or a version of it, for him or herself. The second, which concerns us now, is the move from speaking and listening into reading and writing.

Even old-fashioned class readers (particularly the early books among such sets) worked on the assumption that the words in them were already known to the reader. Phonics and look and say enabled them to identify them. Somewhat newer approaches, also assuming previous knowledge, are what we might call idiolectal: that is, they are based on the language – not just the vocabulary – that the child already possesses. The Language Experience Approach (Goddard, 1974) is an instance of this. It has the merit of extending, or at least identifying, experiences – for example, a shopping expedition – and then of using them to make a text. Children would talk about the experience and with the teacher's help refine the language which he or she would then write down. This text would then be used as a basis for reading. As with the second example, the approach has the inestimable advantage for early readers that they would know what the text 'meant' before they actually read it. The second example is Breakthrough to Literacy (Mackay *et al.*, 1978). Here the child who cannot necessarily handwrite (i.e. in the conventional way) or spell (again in the conventional way) is helped by materials and by the teacher to find a written version for what has been said and to acquire gradually increasing independence of the teacher as this takes place. This written version is the text for the child's early reading. Both the Language Experience Approach and Breakthrough – and they are not exclusive alternatives – have much to commend them still. Both are literacy approaches not just reading methods and both are rooted in the experiences of children.

If we return again to our question: where does a child's familiarity with written language come from? I would suggest three sources. First there is the child's previous knowledge of spoken language together with all the referencing, meaning, ordering, shaping for purpose and dips into vocabulary, sound patterns and grammar that this entails. Some of this will be simply transmuted into a written form; some will be used to process print for meaning.

Then there is the direct knowledge of written language which will have come from being read to and later from the child's own reading. Reading aloud always involves the reader in utilising the devices of pitch, pauses and stress and of chunking information to help the listener and so makes texts accessible that otherwise would not be. It allows the listener to gain an expanding knowledge of written language. It also provides opportunities to discuss the text and the act of reading.

The third source is really a subset of this. It is language gained in revisiting the same book. Worthwhile books in which a child is interested are worth visiting time and again. Sometimes children themselves demand such repetition. These encounters are worth while quite apart from their usefulness in preparing the child for reading. A revisit is almost never identical to an earlier encounter. Different matters come up. The rhythm is different. Meaning and the process of achieving meaning can be tackled in greater depth. Discussion tends to focus on different places or on different matters. Probes for meaning tend to go deeper.

In all this book quality is a major factor. It is what makes the book worth revisiting. It may be the pictures, the language, or the movement into metaphor and away from the literal. It may be its efficacy in prompting talk, its ability to interest, engage or enthral, its ability to create feelings of suspense, excitement and curiosity, and so on. Whatever the particular nature, it is the quality that makes the activity worth while, though we should note that it may also require a willing and compliant adult.

Thus speaking and listening, including being read to and talking about books, are important ingredients of work towards literacy.

Before I come to the fourth proposition I want to turn to what have been called literacy events, to the place in them of young children's early efforts to read, to write and spell, then to a more detailed look at early writing.

LITERACY EVENTS

Literacy events are encounters in which a person comes across printed or written language, or sees other people reading or writing, or tries to read or write him or herself. They occur over the whole of life and they are broadly analogous to and some-times overlap with speech events in which the individual encounters instances of speaking and listening. In the child's early years they provide opportunities to learn a great deal that lies deep at the heart of the writing system and thus of reading and writing. He or she can learn how print is arranged and how it takes a typical order inside books, how the horizontal and directional principles work, what a word is and how it is made up of letters, what the alphabet is, what writing is used for, and so on. These are all matters of intellectual endeavour and it takes years before the successive hypotheses that are made come into line with adult conventions. When children are read to as part of these events, they learn, too, about how language can be ordered into texts and how information can be structured to give shape to a text. They take in literary forms in grammar, literary uses of vocabulary, and literary style, much of it well before they can themselves read in conventional senses of that term.

Further, literacy events exemplify the ways in which literacy is woven into the fabric of the lives around a child. They are valued activities. They themselves constitute a norm; they shape attitudes and they motivate.

Within the spectrum of literacy events much has been made of the importance of environmental print – the print on packets, labels, hoardings, television and so on. No doubt it is a very important element (Goodman and Altwerger, 1981). But too much can be made of it. There is, for example, a great distance between appreciating the significance of such print and the rather odd claim that, because of it, reading is 'natural', for there is another ingredient that should not be overlooked. When we examine successful readers and look particularly at early readers (Clark, 1976; Durkin, 1966; Van Lierop, 1985; Sutton 1985) we usually find, even among claims that they are self-taught, that close at hand has been an interested, supportive adult or sibling, ready and willing to answer questions. Even independent children need support, information, models and feedback, and these come from interactions with others within literacy events. What has frequently been noted among early successful readers, however, whether they are 'self-taught' or not, is the initiatives they show. They often take the lead. Very often, I believe, this itself may depend on adults and others who support and validate, sometimes by little more than being an approving presence, sometimes by more active participation, the children's literacy activities and the initiatives they feel they can take. Independent initiative, in other words, is itself often derived from other people's support. There is thus a social or interpersonal aspect to literacy. While it is not 'natural' to learn to read and write, it is common and relatively easy in a literate and supportive culture.

On the way to literacy children will hopefully come across hundreds of examples which are instances of what we can call 'modelling', and as they get closer to a text so they will become more aware of what adults and other practitioners actually do when they read and write; literacy events not only shape attitudes and interests, they give children chances to learn techniques.

The potency of literacy events and of what takes place within them is illustrated, I think, by cultural differences. There is plenty of documentation which shows not only their powerfulness but that they differ with different cultures. Ron Scollon (Scollon and Scollon, 1981) has shown how his daughter was 'orientated' towards literacy by the time she was 2 and how she differed from the Athabaskan children in Fort Chipewyan who had a radically different regard for books and reading. Similarly, Brice Heath in an exhaustive study of language events and literacy events among three communities in the Carolinas – black industrial, white industrial and white 'mainstream' – has shown substantive differences in the kinds and totals of literacy-relevant learning that occur in the pre-school years (Brice Heath, 1983).

Finally, let us note the scale of literacy events. Teale (1986) studied a group of low-income children aged between 2.8 and 3.8 years in San Diego. His data gives an impressive picture of the incidence of such events over a period of a year. He looked at both the frequency and the duration of literacy events and found that the frequency ranged from 0.34 to 4.06 per hour and that the minutes spent in each encounter ranged from 3.09 to 34.72 per hour. Teale estimated that, as children were awake about 13 hours per day, they experienced reading and writing from approximately 5 to 53 times per day and spent on average between about 40 minutes and 7.5 hours per day on such activities. Even a child who experienced literacy less frequently than others would encounter reading or writing over 2,000 times and for almost 500 hours in the course of a year. Within the data there was a considerable range but every child in the sample 'was somehow involved with reading and writing during the course of everyday home experiences.'

Of course, the data does not in itself reveal the quality of the encounters. Some of it will be intense, one-to-one interaction, some of it will be more diffuse. Nevertheless, it would be instructive to compare these figures with those of the times spent related to literacy in schools. Literacy events are massively important. Unfortunately, because of the range in frequency and quality, some children are less favoured than others.

CHILDREN'S EARLY WRITING

Vygotsky (1978) saw writing as developing from gesture. Scribble was gesture on the page and that was the earliest 'writing'. (In this respect we can note in passing and also encourage parents to agree that a child needs to enjoy a long career as a scribbler and maker of marks – preferably with different sorts of instruments on different sorts of surface – as a preparation for handwriting.)

Writing had, according to Vygotsky, another root. This was in pretend-play. Such play, when something 'stood for' something else, was a notable instance of symbolic activity and as time went on this developing idea of the symbol had somehow to marry the gesture and its descendants to make writing which had an abstract quality – that is, which represented something, namely speech and what lay beyond speech.

So we have a wide range of outcomes in children's early writing. There is writing that is more or less spontaneous, writing that is a broad emulation of what the child sees around him or her, writing that takes on a symbolic or representative character, writing that more closely resembles that of adult convention in being truly alphabetic, and so on. As with the rest of writing, including spelling and even handwriting, there is a strong conceptual basis to early learning. Learning to write, whatever else it is, is basically a cognitive exercise. It is founded on various understandings which may change gradually or untidily over a period of time. It is some of these that I want to discuss next.

As I do I must mention two adjacent ideas put forward by Vernon (1967) and by Downing (1973) about reading, not writing, but relevant to our concerns. Vernon believed that one of the causes that disabled children from reading was that they suffered from 'cognitive confusion'. They had no clear idea of what they should do when they read and so they could not do it. Downing took the same tack and called for 'cognitive clarity'. Both may have misunderstood the true nature of children's early efforts to read, for the 'confusion' that they detected was in reality highly principled. Here we can outline some of the many concepts that children may entertain as they move towards an 'adult' or conventional understanding of the nature of writing. It would be wrong to call these misconceptions. Although they are not conventionally 'correct' they are for the most part triumphs of reasonableness and sheer good sense, evidence of cognitive activity, persistent, typically reshaping understandings under the pressure of contrary evidence.

Investigations by Clay, by Ferreiro, by Gundlach and colleagues, among others, have shown that children read and write (according to the model that they possess at that particular moment) in ways that are interesting but which do not immediately result in 'real' reading and writing. This, I believe, is in addition to the pretend play at reading and writing which may or may not incorporate such models.

The early history of literacy in the individual is therefore of encounters with prints and books, of seemingly endogenous attempts to read and write which apparently owe much to inner momentum and are part of overall semiotic development, and of the activation of succeeding schemata which operate to cause writing behaviour and which gradually come to terms with the essentials of conventional reading and writing of English.

The concept of 'word' provides an instance. It would be a mistake to suppose that, simply because children use words in speaking, or because they understand words addressed to them as part of someone else's speech, they understand what a word is or that they grasp that speech can in principle be segmented down into words. Still less may they understand that all words in a message must be written down, or that the length of a word is in general (with the exception of many plurals) unrelated to the quantity, size or any other quality of its referents, but that a general but not exclusive principle prevails that the word when written is linked alphabetically to the sound of that word when spoken.

The following instances are no more than a peep into the conceptual learning that is necessary before the children come to this sort of sophisticated understanding.

The 'undifferentiated signs and squiggles' that Vygotsky noted frequently begin to take on certain characteristics. They may proceed roughly from left to right. They may incorporate odd letters and letter-like forms. Clay (1975) noted a 'sign' concept which she saw as a reaching out towards mature writing, and also a 'message' concept when the child understands that messages can be written down but when there is still no real correspondence between the message and what is written. Another important understanding is what Clay calls the 'recurring' principle when the child incorporates elements again and again in his or her writing. As yet the child is far from understanding the alphabetic principle but the alphabet is the key to the recurring that he or she is now aware of. Also the child becomes aware of a contrary or supplementary principle – the 'flexibility' principle which allows variation in what is put down. Clay, in fact, was among the first to systematise these early understandings.

Ferreiro (Ferreiro, 1985; Ferreiro and Teberosky, 1982) has also shed much light on early literacy. She has tracked children's understandings from beginning through the 'syllabic hypothesis' to acceptance and utilisation of the alphabetic principle. She has investigated the ability of children to recognise (not yet read) print and to discriminate it from other markings including random marks, pictures, numerals and punctuation marks. She has done fascinating work within a Piagetian framework on children's notions of the length of words. She has demonstrated that some children at various points in their early development will use the same number of letters as there are in the group that is being written about. Thus four stars would have 'stars', or whatever stood for stars at this time, with four 'letters', and three bears would have 'bears' with only three. Sometimes the 'letters' are written large for big objects and small for little objects. Important objects and people may be given more letters. Ferreiro also investigated what her children understood as constituting a word. She found that many children believed that what was written could not be a word unless it contained a minimum number of letters, three being the usual number.

It is important to note, first, that the development of writing is not just a matter of executive ability. Underlying it is greater understanding at a conceptual level. Second, this conceptual basis is the basis for literacy, not just for reading or writing alone. Therefore the deepening of understanding revealed in writing will also show itself in reading. In particular we can note the understanding of the equivalence of the spoken and the written word, the use of the alphabet and, pedagogically, the practical partnership between teacher and child which encourages and shapes the child's spontaneous efforts.

In writing, time and again we find the same story as we found in reading. Children who develop well before school and who thus are the best prepared for schools as they exist usually come from a background in which literacy is valued and where encouragement and approval - direct through personal inter-actions or indirect through the provision of materials and opportunities - are common. Books, environmental print and supportive adults and siblings all have a role to play.

PROPOSITION 4: THAT THE CASE FOR 'REAL' BOOKS IS FOUNDED IN RELATION TO LANGUAGE DEVELOPMENT AS A WHOLE

We can now finally summarise the case for good books under several headings. Some of these pertain to reading, others apply to other parts of the language spectrum. As I have tried to show, the language skills of reading, writing, speaking and listening are mutually constitutive, though in different ways at different points in development, so that, for example, the use of good books to bring on speaking and listening will have an indirect effect on literacy.

Speaking and listening

When children are read to they practise sustained listening. Further, a book, whether it is a picture book or one with written text, provides a sort of changing focus for talk. There are different matters on the page, different parts of a picture, a range of characters and incidents all of which are grist for possible discussion. Talk about books tends to be very rich. It changes too with successive visits, providing that the book is of sufficient quality and interest, provided, that is to say, that it is a good book. Snow and Ferguson (1977) found that the mother's talk in encounters with picture books was richer than in free play with toys. One probable reason is that the book provides the topic or in grammatical terms, the subject, and what remains is to elaborate this and to add comment.

Actually, using real books itself may include a wide range of activities: looking, pointing, reading, discussing content, linking content to experience, rereading, using as a basis for further play, revisiting, answering questions which themselves will act as a scaffold for future activity, retelling the story, extending ranges of interests, collecting and storing books, learning a metalanguage, and so on. Many such activities insinuate themselves into the regular routines and rituals of family and later of school life. For example, Ninio and Bruner (1978) found that speaking behaviour was routinised in the sense that encounters were typically made up of a series of small units each with only a few utterances. One partner would try to get the other to focus attention. Then one would try to get the other to label. If this was done the first would provide the other with feedback. If not, the first participant would provide the label. We can note that it was usually the mother who provided the source of stability in these rich and productive sequences.

Writing

It seems clear that a crucial phase in the child's development as a writer is the achievement of an 'adult' (i.e. conventional) understanding of what a word is. The importance of constant presentations of print in the environment and in books is therefore obvious. Words cease to be 'transparent' and become opaque. The advantage of good books is that, being intrinsically resourceful, they are potentially interesting and so will allow and even demand this sort of commerce.

As writers children need access to the grammar of writing. This they get, *par excellence*, through good books - fictional and factual. The grammar that they use as writers diverges from that of their speaking and especially from their conversation. They need a store on which to draw. At this point we should not forget the importance of the way information can be structured, the sequencing or other organisation of events, the ways in which a writer deals with the presumptions that are made about what a reader knows and needs to be told. Closely linked with this is what has been called story grammar - the ways in which stories typically begin with the introduction of the main characters and set the scene and period in the very first sentences, progressing through familiar patterns until the final resolution. Story grammar does not perhaps have the exactness that is characteristic of other grammars but it is very powerful all the same. Almost certainly the story grammar learned from good books is useful in three respects - in remembering when it provides a structure, in reading when it enables one to 'know' what is likely to come next and in writing where it provides the writer with a sort of plan of action that becomes so familiar that it seems to be part of the furniture of the mind.

Finally, as far as writing is concerned, we can turn briefly to spelling. When real spelling emerges after various conceptual excursions, the child looks for ways to handle the correspondences between sounds and letters. (Visual strategies seem to be secondary or lacking in importance at this early stage.) The child

165

tries various ploys – one sound one letter, one syllable one letter, straight correspondences with articulatory units and so on. There are at least two indispensable needs for the child who can be counted as a competent speller at this stage. The first is an acquaintance with a wide range of vocabulary. The second is the clear articulation of that vocabulary. A child spells as he or she articulates (Read, 1975) but the articulation is influenced by what has been heard. Having good books read to a child meets both needs.

Reading

When we turn back to reading we must stress two matters. The first is that good books are not homogeneous. Picture books with little or no text can be very important. By what other means will a child grasp the vital distinction between picture and text? On the other hand a central criterion of the text of a good book is its employment of linguistic resources – grammar, vocabulary, style, structure and its use of metaphor and other tropes. Different sorts of good books offer different sorts of opportunities and the same book may offer new opportunities when it is revisited. This is another way of saying that good books are important at each successive stage, or with each succeeding model, of the reading process.

The second point is that there is a strong and continuing place for a range of supportive activities from adults or other experts from near passivity to the most active and detailed participation. This support can supply the flywheel of gentle discipline as well as the scaffolding for tackling texts.

In dealing with reading one is always conscious of metacognitive and metalinguistic values. The objective sight of a word upon the page, one which can be understood to correspond to a word spoken, is probably fundamental to a child's reading development and overspills into literacy generally.

From books a child learns that print has purpose and that it works in certain ways. Here we are thinking of the 'figural', the directionality and horizontality of the line, the ways lines succeed each other. But we go beyond this to literary matters, to how information is organised and sequenced, and to the understanding that all that can be read has a writer.

This brings us to the central matter. Even a non-literate child is used to processing language for meaning. Spoken language is, or rather seems to be, natural in a culture and so when children speak they are hardly conscious of what they are doing. But with print it is different. Embedded sentences, hierarchical processing (when one has to return to part of a text after one has gone further), the possible abundance of non-literal language – which seems to mean something different from what it says – are difficult matters which may call for conscious or self-conscious treatment. The point is that texts must be rich enough to present such features. Hence the importance of support. Hence, too, the importance of gaining background knowledge from books, from being read to and from elsewhere that we have characterised as crucial.

Again we come back to the notion of being read to from quality books. The idea is that being read to while one follows the print is one very good road into reading. This is discussed by Pugh (1978) and elsewhere by the present author (Ashworth, 1988, Chapter 4). And whenever a story is revisited this offers a chance to do what the Language Experience Approach and Breakthrough to Literacy both allow – the opportunity to fit the meaning (which one already knows) to the text. It seems to go without saying that if there is to be such reacquaintance, there ought to be real quality in the book.

QUESTIONS FOR PERSONAL REFLECTION OR GROUP DISCUSSION

1 Does your school have a comprehensive language and literacy policy? Where is reading located within that?
2 Teachers should work towards the creation of their own personal model of reading. What is yours?
3 There is a difference between a model of reading and a model of the teaching or fostering of reading, though the latter may incorporate the former. What is your model for the teaching of reading?
4 Teachers recognise that between one child and another in a reception class there may be a difference of thousands of hours of experience of literacy or literacy-mediated events. What are the implications of this fact for your own practice?

RECOMMENDED READINGS

Among the books referred to above, the following complement the present chapter by extending the argument and relating it to other examples of good practice.

Ashworth, E. (1988) *Language Policy in the Primary School: Content and Management.* London: Croom Helm.
Clay, M. M. (1972) *Reading: The Patterning of Complex Behaviour.* Auckland: Heinemann Educational.
Ferreiro, E. and Teberosky, A. (1982) *Literacy before Schooling.* London: Heinemann Educational.
Heath, S. B. (1983) *Ways with Words: Language, Life and Work in Communities and Classrooms.* Cambridge: Cambridge University Press.

BIBLIOGRAPHY

Ashworth, E. (1988) *Language Policy in the Primary School: Content and Management.* London: Croom Helm.
Bryant, P. E. and Bradley, L. (1980) 'Why young children sometimes write words they do not read'. In U. Frith (ed.) *Cognitive Processes in Spelling.* London: Academic Press.
Clark, M. M. (1976) *Young Fluent Readers.* London: Heinemann Educational.
Clay, M. M. (1972) *Reading: The Patterning of Complex Behaviour.* Auckland: Heinemann Educational.
Clay, M. M. (1975) *What Did I Write?.* Auckland: Heinemann Educational.
Downing, J. (1973) 'The cognitive clarity theory of learning to read'. *Reading*, 7, 63–70.
Durkin, D. (1966) *Children who Read Early.* New York: Teachers College Press.
Ferreiro, E. (1985) 'Literacy development: a psychogenetic perspective'. In D. R. Olson, N. Torrance and A. Hildyard (eds) *Literacy, Language and Learning.* Cambridge: Cambridge University Press.
Ferreiro, E. and Teberosky, A., (1982) *Literacy before Schooling.* London: Heinemann Educational.
Frith, U. (1980) 'Unexpected spelling problems'. In U. Frith, (ed.) *Cognitive Processes in Spelling.* London: Academic Press.
Goddard, N. (1974) 'The language experience approach'. In N. Goddard (ed.) *Literacy: Language Experience Approaches.* London: Macmillan.
Goodman, Y. and Altwerger, B. (1981) 'Print awareness in preschool children'. *Program in Language and Literacy.* Arizona Center for Research and Development, College of Education, Tucson.
Gundlach, R., McLane, J. B., Stott, F. M. and McNamee, G. D. (1985) 'The social foundations of children's early writing development'. In

M. Farr (ed.) *Children's Early Writing Development*. Norwood, NJ: Ablex Publishing Company.

Heath, S. B. (1983) *Ways with Words: Language, Life and Work in Communities and Classrooms*. Cambridge: Cambridge University Press.

Mackay, D., Thompson, B. and Schaub, P. (1978) *Breakthrough to Literacy Teacher's Manual* (2nd edn). London: Longman for Schools Council.

Ninio, A. and Bruner, J.S. (1978) 'The achievement and antecedents of labelling'. *Journal of Child Language*, 5, 1-14.

Pugh, A. K. (1978) *Silent Reading: an Introduction to its Study and Teaching*. London: Heinemann Educational.

Read, C. (1975) *Children's Categorization of Speech Sounds in English*. Urbana, IL: NCTE.

Scollon, R. and Scollon, S. (1981) *Narrative, Literacy and Face in Social Contexts*. Norwood, NJ: Ablex Publishing Company.

Smith, F. (1985) 'A metaphor for literacy'. In D. Olson, N. Torrance and A. Hildyard (eds) *Literacy, Language and Learning*. Cambridge: Cambridge University Press.

Snow, C. E. and Ferguson, C. A. (eds) (1977) *Talking to Children: Language Input and Acquisition*. Cambridge: Cambridge University Press.

Sutton, W. (1985) 'Some factors in preschool children of relevance to learning to read'. In M. M. Clark (ed.) *New Directions in the Study of Reading*. London: Falmer Press.

Teale, W. H. (1986) 'Home background and children's literacy development'. In W. H. Teale and E. Sulzby (eds) *Emergent Literacy: Writing and Reading*. Norwood, NJ. Ablex Publishing Company.

Van Lierop, M. (1985) 'Predisposing factors in early literacy: a case study'. In M. M. Clark (ed.) *New Directions in the Study of Reading*. London: Falmer Press.

Vernon, M. D. (1967) *Backwardness in Reading*. Cambridge: Cambridge University Press.

Vygotsky, L. S. (1978) 'Mind in Society: The development of higher psychological processes'. Trans. M. Cole, V. John-Steiner, S. Scribner and E. Souberman. Cambridge, MA: Harvard University Press.

8

PARENTS AND READING

Keith Topping

'Parental Involvement' has been a fashionable catch phrase in education for over a decade now. Why pursue this bandwagon? The answer lies in the effects – parental involvement is not only fashionable, it can also raise the basic attainments of the children concerned and improve motivation. Additionally, as market forces come ever more into play in the world of education, those schools who successfully involve parents will enjoy the popularity needed to maintain large numbers of children on roll.

The involvement of parents in their children's education on any widespread basis is a relatively new phenomenon. The late eighteenth century and the early nineteenth century saw increasing 'professionalisation' among teachers, with all the defensiveness and the erecting of barriers of mystique that this usually implies. The net result was to 'de-skill' parents, who of course still continued to try to help their children at home, but now did so in a state of confusion and with a great lack of confidence, uncertain whether they were helping or hindering what was happening at school.

With the development of an era of relative prosperity, more parents had the time and energy to pursue their interest in what was being done to or for their children at school. Schools began to have more open evenings, although these can still be characterised by very brief contact between teacher and parents, and the exchange of polite euphemisms and bland generalisations. An increasing number of schools developed arrangements for contact with parents prior to a child's admittal. Parents began to be invited into school, and now most schools make use of parent helpers on outside visits, while a majority of schools would claim to use volunteer parent helpers with art and craft, sewing and baking activities within school hours. However, a smaller proportion of schools involve trusted volunteer parents in other, more cognitive, aspects of the curriculum, and even fewer regularly and consistently encourage and support *all* parents as direct educators of their own natural children.

Evaluative research on the effect of parental involvement in day-to-day activity in school on pupil achievement in nursery schools and classes is encouraging. Controlled studies show good results, including maintenance of gains at six months' follow-up. The situation is less clear for primary schools, where many studies have failed to 'partial' out the effect of the parental involvement component. Nevertheless, there is generalised evidence that schools developing parental involvement tend to produce high standards of learning, but of course the causative linkages may be multiple. Deploying parents as teaching aides certainly raises skill levels in a curriculum-specific manner, independent of the effect of 'extra attention'. Unfortunately there is very little evidence that secondary schools are successfully involving parents in anything like the same way. A summary of the research evidence is available in Topping (1986a).

However, the most potent thrust of the parental involvement movement has certainly been the expansion of work to encourage parents to assume the role of direct educators with their own natural children in the home setting. It is here that we move from the notion of 'parental involvement in school' to the much wider concept of 'Parents as Partners' – parents and school as equal partners in the total education of the child.

For years many ordinary primary schools claimed to have a policy of sending reading books home, so that children could be 'heard read' by their parents. In fact, surveys indicate that practices even within one school are often very various according to which class teacher a child happens to have. Often, little guidance might be given to parents as to why the child was reading what he or she was reading, and what they were actually expected to do at home in interaction with the child and the book.

The Haringey research led to both quantitative and qualitative changes in practice. In 1980, Jenny Hewison and Jack Tizard reported research on a disadvantaged area of inner London which demonstrated clearly that one of the largest factors in children's reading attainment in school was whether they read with their parents at home, irrespective of whether the school operated a formal parental involvement scheme. This was followed up by a direct intervention, and in 1982 Jack Tizard, Bill Schofield and Jenny Hewison were able to report on a project wherein teachers had encouraged parents to hear their children read at home, given a little additional guidance and the support of home visits. The attainment of the project children rose substantially, in comparison to a control group and children who had received extra small-group help from qualified teachers. Hewison subsequently reported that these differentials had been maintained at long-term follow-up (Hewison, 1988). Suddenly it had become clear that it was actually more cost-effective for a teacher to spend some time encouraging and organising the involvement of parents in their own children's reading development, rather than spend all his or her time on the direct classroom teaching of reading.

The early 1980s then saw a rapid expansion in activity in involving parents in their children's reading development. The PACT (Parents and Children and Teachers) scheme grew in inner London, the CAPER (Children and Parents Enjoy Reading) project expanded in South Wales, and many other initiatives burgeoned. More structured approaches for parents grew in popularity, most notably Paired Reading, with Pause, Prompt and Praise gaining some followers later. In a very short time, a whole host of methods and approaches were in use around the country, and some teachers were rapidly becoming confused about the interaction of different techniques and modes of organisation.

THEORETICAL FOUNDATIONS

Yet what could parents offer that teachers could not? The first of these factors was extra practice – children who read at home regularly simply get more practice at reading than those who do not. It is well established that practice consolidates a skill, promotes fluency and minimises forgetting. However, it is important that the practice is *positive* – i.e. is practice at reading *successfully*. Teachers have traditionally tried to keep error rates during reading in check by using carefully structured and graded reading schemes. But with close support from parents, it became possible for error rates to be kept low by the deployment of much more supportive tuition techniques, coupled with carefully articulated correction procedures.

In a busy classroom, children receive relevant feedback about the correctness of their attempts to decode a particular word or deduce the semantic implications of a section of text rather late and often in a less than clear manner. In the luxury of a one-to-one situation with a parent, feedback can be immediate, preventing the compounding of error upon error. Of course, immediate feedback will only be advantageous if it is supportive and positive in nature. Certainly, detailed guidance about the nature of parental feedback, particularly at the point of an error, is essential to incorporate in all parental involvement in reading projects.

Weak readers by definition experience little success – they generate few opportunities for the teacher meaningfully to offer them praise. Teachers do not praise children as often as they would like to think they do, and the evidence suggests that natural rates of parental praise for children are a little lower than those of teachers, but not greatly so. In a parental involvement project, great attention is usually given to the development and application of parental praise. Parental praise has the big advantage of being offered by someone who is a very major and important figure in the child's life – certainly far more important than the teacher. A teacher figures in a child's life for less than a year, but parents are there more or less permanently, and have the advantage of association with tangible rewards! So the social reinforcement a parent dispenses for success in reading can be more powerful than the teacher's attempts in the same direction, and can be given more frequently and regularly (if required) than a teacher can manage.

The fourth crucial advantage that a parent has as a reading tutor at home is much greater scope for modelling or demonstration of the required behaviour. Many children want to 'be like' grown-ups, particularly the most significant grown-ups in their life, their parents. Thus where parents can demonstrate enthusiasm for books and appropriate and mature reading behaviour, the effect on the child is likely to be considerably more profound than that of innumerable verbal urgings in the classroom. Modelling is likely to be more powerful the more the child feels emotionally involved with, and wants to be like, the model. It follows that the father's role can be particularly crucial for boys, and one might assume that the greater incidence of reading failure in boys is partially a result of the majority of primary teachers being female, although the research evidence is equivocal on this point.

Thus, compared to teacher input, parental modelling is more powerful, parental reinforcement is more valuable, parental feedback is more immediate, and practice is more regular.

VARIETIES OF PRACTICE

As the parental involvement in reading movement has developed, a variety of particular techniques for parents to use have been articulated, which show varying degrees of structure.

Perhaps the simplest technique could be termed 'Parent Listening'. Projects using this somewhat more sophisticated extension of traditional practice have consisted largely of co-ordinated attempts to encourage parents to 'hear their children read', sometimes from reading scheme books which are chosen by teachers to be within the child's independent readability level but sometimes from readability-banded 'real books', sometimes with a list of 'do's and don'ts', and occasionally with a demonstration of good practice. Launch meetings are usual, books are commonly supplied and a simple recording system is likely to be used. The work at Belfield in Rochdale (now well known) followed this model. Subsequent projects (e.g. Swinson, reported in Topping and Wolfendale, 1985) attempted to make the advice for parents more specific, detailing clearly what parents were expected to *do* in terms which were realisable.

Paired Reading is a specific supported reading technique which was invented by Roger Morgan in the mid 1970s. Children choose books of high interest irrespective of readability, often 'real' books both fiction and non-fiction, and are supported through high-readability texts by both parent and child Reading Together. Synchrony is achieved with practice, and associated discussion and frequent praise are emphasised. A very simple word supply and repeat correction procedure is incorporated. On easier texts, the child signals the parent to be silent and Reads Alone, continuing to receive praise, until an error is made. At a hesitation or minor error, parents allow five seconds for self-correction before intervening, then if necessary apply the correction procedure and return to Reading Together.

A number of variants on the original Paired Reading technique have been developed (see Topping, 1986b), and it is important for professional workers to be very clear as to what they are talking about in this area of endeavour, since confusion easily ensues otherwise. These variants are much less well researched than the pure form of Paired Reading.

Even more complex is the situation with respect to 'Shared Reading', under which label a number of totally different techniques can be found. There is a class-based technique for teaching beginning readers originated by Don Holdaway, using giant books for large-group reading tuition which are associated with smaller versions of the same book used independently by children for extension practice and repetition. However, this scheme was designed for use specifically by professional teachers, not by parents. Alternatively, some teachers are inclined to use the expression 'Shared Reading' in relation to almost anything that parents and children do together in interaction with a book – they are 'sharing' the book. Unfortunately what the parent is actually expected to *do* is often left very fuzzy, and parents who are lacking confidence and/or skills can become very confused. This notion of 'shared reading' owes much to the concept of 'reading apprenticeship' promulgated by Liz Waterland, and although this may be fine in the hands of teachers and confident and imaginative parents, other parents are likely to need clearer training and support.

However, there are two further meanings of the expression 'Shared Reading'. In Cleveland in the north of England, a great deal of work has been done on a version of 'Shared Reading' which consists of parent and child reading the book simultaneously, without the specification of any particular correction procedure – mistakes are more or less ignored. As in the Reading Together aspect of Paired Reading, a wide range of books of unrestricted readability is used. Shared Reading in this version is simpler than Paired Reading, and perhaps particularly suitable for younger children needing strong support with the reading material in play, although its promulgators have also used it in junior schools and high schools and have researched its effectiveness. The final version of 'Shared Reading' is the South Wales technique, quite different again, which consists of the parent reading a book to the child, followed by the parent reading a book to the child but stopping occasionally for the child to supply a contextually relevant word unaided, with the parent supplying the word if the child cannot. Evaluation research here is very limited.

The 'Pause, Prompt and Praise' technique is another detailed and structured technique which originates from New Zealand. It consists of the child reading aloud to the parent from texts of carefully controlled readability (which could nevertheless be real books), with the parent pausing at error words to allow the child to self-correct. In the absence of self-correction, the parent gives a discriminatory prompt related to the nature of the error (semantic, visual or contextual). Praise is much emphasised. This technique is specifically conceived as suitable for children with reading difficulty. It has been utilised and researched successfully in Australia and New Zealand as well as the United Kingdom.

The 'Workshop' approach typically involves parents in a series of meetings in school, where information is given about the school reading curriculum, with advice about helping at home, perhaps coupled with activities such as making and using reading games. Parents might make such games, observe demonstrations of these in use, and borrow them for practice at home with their own child. In addition, there could be further 'modules' in the workshop 'curriculum' which might include specific advice on reading to and with children and hearing children read. There is no reason why any of the other methods or techniques here described could not be incorporated in the workshop curriculum, but often reading games, 'storying' and 'parent listening' are the major features.

A number of other procedures for parent use have been deployed with children with reading difficulty, and these are often highly structured with limited usage of 'real' books within the prescribed structure, although the Precision Teaching system (for instance) can be used with any book given some preparation beforehand.

A variety of other approaches to parental involvement in reading can be identified. In some areas, 'Family Reading Groups' have been established, more orientated to heightening appreciation of literature than to specifically developing reading skills, in which parents and children meet regularly to discuss and mutually review books that they have read. Favourites are recommended to others and written reviews may be produced. Many commercial publishers now include a 'Parental Involvement' component in their primary-level reading material. Early examples of series targeted solely on parents were the 'Puddle Lane' series and the Cambridge University Press 'Read Along Stories'.

Of course, it is possible to use a combination of methods with a particular child, or to use different methods with the same child at different ages and stages in the child's reading development. It is to be hoped that eventually all teachers will be familiar with a range of parental involvement techniques, and able to deploy them sensitively and discriminately to meet effectively the individual needs of all children.

DEMANDS ON BOOK RESOURCES

A ubiquitous feature of parental involvement in reading projects is that the children's enthusiasm for reading increases greatly, possibly to an extent sufficient to embarrass even schools who previously thought their book stocks were perfectly adequate. If using Paired Reading, this is further complicated by children having free choice. It is necessary to review current resources in school carefully, from the point of view of volume, type, current location, frequency of child access and the existing policy on which books from which sources are allowed to go home. The existing record-keeping system for noting who possesses which book will also need to be reviewed, as some may be insufficiently informative while others will be far too complex and time consuming.

Some schools differentiate between books according to internal organisation pressures, but the children will find it hard to understand such discrimination, and in any event they are unlikely to lose or damage books that they are very interested in reading. A decision must be made about where any 'reading scheme' books stand in relation to the project – are they to be the only books to go home, the only books *not* to go home, or treated just like any other book? The latter option becomes particularly appropriate where individualised reading via colour-coded levels of reading difficulty based on a wide collection of different types of book is the approach adopted by the school. It may be desirable to make a special collection of books in the school for the project children, which serves to raise the status of their participation, or it may be possible to arrange for a special loan of carefully chosen books.

The school bookshop may get a boost in the context of a project, or the opportunity may be taken to operate a secondhand swap shop for books. Visits to the local public library are usually welcomed by all concerned, and parents can be given details of mobile library availability. Special funding to increase book stocks may be sought from the local education authority or from the Parent–Teacher Association, or a relevant fund-raising event such as a 'sponsored read' considered.

EVALUATION RESEARCH

For teachers interested in this area, it is not enough to know what is fashionable nor indeed to have a perception of what seems beguiling and attractive to oneself – it is also necessary to be clear about what has been demonstrated to **work**. This is not necessarily the same as what has been widely publicised.

Descriptions of the impact of 'Family Reading Groups' and 'Workshops' emphasise high take-up rates and participant enthusiasm, but more objective evidence is hard to find. In the case of the Fox Hill workshops, subjective ratings by parents, teachers and children concerned indicated improvements in attitude, less widespread improvements in child reading skill and good communication between parents and teachers (Weinberger, 1983).

The 'Parent Listening' or 'Hearing' approach generates variable outcomes on reading tests. Some well-known projects, such as Belfield, have produced disappointing test results. Aggregating the test outcomes from fourteen 'Hearing' studies (Topping and Lindsay, 1992) shows that rates of gain in reading accuracy are on average about 2.5 times normal rates during the intensive period of parental involvement (assuming normal progress to be one month of reading age in one calendar month). There is solid evaluative evidence from control group studies, and while there is no doubt that this approach can work well, it is clear that not everybody has made it work well.

Paired Reading in its more or less original form has now been very widely disseminated, and has been the subject of a great deal of research. The general picture from these reports (Topping and

Lindsay, 1992) is that Paired Readers progress at about 4.2 times 'normal' rates in reading accuracy on test during the initial period of commitment. Nor are these results confined to isolated research projects, as in the Kirklees LEA the technique has been used widely by a large number of schools, and in a sample of 2,372 children in 155 projects run by many different schools, average test gains of 3.3 normal rates in reading accuracy and 4.4 times normal rates in reading comprehension were found. These results were supported by baseline and control group data. At follow-up the gains of Paired Readers had not 'washed out' (Topping, 1992).

The Pause, Prompt and Praise technique has so far been almost exclusively used with children with reading difficulties. The gains in reading accuracy quoted by different studies do vary considerably, but PPP has registered very few poor results and the overall average gain is roughly equivalent to 2.5 times normal progress. On the other hand, there is as yet little research evidence from more widespread and less controlled dissemination, and it will be interesting to see to what extent effectiveness is sustained should the approach percolate into the fabric of everyday school life.

The only type of 'Shared Reading' to be adequately evaluated in terms of reading attainment gain is the Cleveland version embodying continuous synchronous reading – small-scale results here are most encouraging. Other forms of 'Shared Reading' have been the subject of descriptive, anecdotal accounts.

Some studies, usually of small scale, have attempted to compare the relative effectiveness of different varieties of practice, usually in terms of outcomes on reading tests. Given the small numbers involved in many studies, the finding of statistically significant differences is rare. However, Paired Reading tends to outperform simple Listening/Reading Aloud, and in seven out of eighteen studies this difference attained statistical significance, although in the majority with peers as tutors rather than parents (Topping and Lindsay, 1992). In comparative studies PPP tends to yield similar outcomes to Paired Reading although its application is intended to be narrower.

Naturally, parental involvement projects aim to yield many benefits other than gains in reading skill as measured by reading tests. Many studies report high levels of enthusiasm, improved attitudes to reading and better generalised communication between home and school as outcomes of projects, but often in terms of subjective description and selective anecdote. Unsurprisingly, it proves difficult to aggregate, meta-analyse or otherwise summarise the incidence of these other benefits, some of which are quite idiosyncratic. The largest-scale survey of attitudinal change in participants, albeit based only on questionnaire returns, is that of Topping and Whiteley (1990) in the context of the Kirklees Paired Reading Project.

The responses of over 1,000 parents showed approximately 70 per cent of responding parents considered that their child was now reading more accurately, more fluently and with better comprehension. A slightly smaller proportion were reported to be reading more expressively and demonstrating a more positive attitude to reading. Sixty-seven per cent of parents reported their child to be reading more in absolute volume and 73 per cent were reading more widely. Sixty-five per cent of parents reported their child was now more willing to read and 62 per cent reported more interest in reading, while 73 per cent felt their child was enjoying reading more. Perhaps the most striking outcome was that 78 per cent of parents reported that their children were now more confident in reading. The finding of increased confidence is supported by studies of changes in reading style following Paired Reading, the general trend being towards fewer refusals, increased self-correction and greater use of the context as well as fewer errors and better use of phonic skills (Topping and Lindsay, 1992).

Class teachers submitted their subjective assessment of the change in reading response in the classroom in a similar format for almost 500 children. On most items of the questionnaire the teachers were also extremely positive, suggesting generalisation of effects of Paired Reading at home to reading in the classroom. Areas in which teacher observations were more than a few percentage points below those of parents included: Reading More Widely (53 per cent), More Willing to Read (48 per cent), Enjoying Reading More (57 per cent), More Fluent (64 per cent) and More Expressive (38 per cent) – some of these differences possibly reflecting the different demands and purposes of classroom reading.

The participant children themselves offered their observations in almost 700 cases. Ninety-two per cent reported they now liked reading better and 95 per cent felt they were more competent as readers, while 70 per cent wished to go on doing Paired Reading at home.

PRE-SCHOOL INITIATIVES

We have already noted the encouraging research on the effects of involving some parents in activity in nursery schools. Conscious of the power of parents as partner educators, and aware of the need to lay firm foundations in pre-reading and reading skills and positive attitudes at the earliest possible age, some nursery units and schools have developed wider initiatives including more parents, often encouraged by the book by Tizard *et al.* (1981). These are often based upon a parent–child loan library, including wordless picture books for parents and children to talk about, stories for parents to read *to* young children, and other relevant material. Some nurseries have programmed meetings with parents to develop a dialogue about ways of learning at home and at nursery in preparation for school entry (e.g. Weinberger, 1989).

However, many children do not attend nursery, and a workshop programme specifically targeted on pre-school children who had no nursery place is described by Currie and Bowes (1988). More recently, in the context of the Sheffield Early Literacy Project, Hannon *et al.* (1991) contrasted the impact of home-based and centre-based support for parents of children mainly aged 2 to 3 years, evaluating on a case-study basis. Some parents only attended group meetings based in the local school and were provided with literacy materials on one home visit, while others also had a further six home visits. Both methods had an impact on the parents' approach to their children's pre-school literacy experiences, but home visiting appeared to promote more book borrowing and sharing. However, home visiting is obviously more costly in resources.

This area is certainly under-researched, and further controlled longitudinal follow-up studies are necessary to ascertain the extent to which the promotion of pre-school literacy experiences at home advantages children in the long term, after school entry. Background cross-sectional studies meanwhile give us cause to be optimistic.

PARENTS, READING AND REAL BOOKS

To what extent, then, does the notion of parental partnership in reading development relate to the debate regarding 'real' versus 'other' books?

Certainly there is little evidence that a 'real book' as distinct from a 'reading scheme' approach in school is of itself likely to result in any lowering of reading standards. Indeed, a review of forty research studies by Tunnell and Jacobs (1989) reported the opposite – that in twenty-four studies the outcomes favoured the 'real books' approach, in only one study did the outcome favour the reading scheme, and in the remaining studies there was no significant difference. Of course, there is a great deal more to the 'real books' approach than merely the books involved, and arguably this approach puts greater demands on the organisational skill and awareness of the teacher than does proceeding through a pre-structured reading scheme. This may make the 'real books' approach less durable in the hands of inadequate, stressed or demoralised teachers than other approaches, and thus the research findings may not truly reflect current day-to-day reality in schools across the nation.

Of the varieties of practice for promoting parental involvement in reading described above, many have strong implications for widening children's reading experience and increasing their desire to seek out books for themselves. Family Reading Groups and Paired Reading are perhaps particularly likely to have this effect, although increased exposure to 'real books' can be built into Listening and Workshop projects. This is not to say that the children will end up reading material which conforms to a middle-class conception of 'good literature'. The purpose of education is to impart skills and motivation and belief in your ability to deploy those to achieve your *own* goals.

Education is empowerment. It follows that it is for the individual child to decide whether any book is 'real' or not. Teaching mechanical reading skills to children is of limited use without also heightening their motivation to use those skills for their own purposes, and equally, flooding children with high-quality 'real books' is pointless in the absence of a well-structured programme of skills tuition to enable them to access those books. In-school teaching thus needs to be eclectic, well organised within the classroom and well co-ordinated across the school irrespective of the reading materials used. Parental involvement to raise standards should never be pursued without the closest initial scrutiny of the adequacy of the professional teaching within school. Good organisation **remains** crucial as you begin to plan your parental involvement initiative.

As there is more widespread usage of existing methods, it is important that the organisation of implementation improves. As techniques become more widely talked about, there is a grave danger of increasing vagueness in nomenclature, accompanied by dilution. Even the most effective parental involvement in reading technique will not survive a ramshackle attempt to deliver it, wherein no one teacher takes full responsibility for co-ordination and the meeting of planned objectives in terms of both major issues (such as type and frequency of follow-up) and minor issues (such as whether the television is working). Carefully planned and executed service delivery is essential if the effectiveness of an initiative is to be sustained in the long term.

QUESTIONS FOR PERSONAL REFLECTION OR GROUP DISCUSSION

1 How much parental involvement is there:
    (a) in your class?
    (b) in the school as a whole?
2 Existing parental involvement:
    (a) what percentage of parents are involved?
    (b) parents of what type of child?
    Is your current practice on parental involvement:
    (a) offering equal opportunities?
    (b) reducing or increasing relative disadvantages?
3 Existing parental involvement – is it a few parents in school or are *all* parents encouraged, guided and supported to be partners in improving their children's reading skills and attitudes at home?
4 So what are you (and your colleagues) going to **DO** about it? Write down one small first step.

RECOMMENDED READINGS

Parent listening
Branston, P. and Provis, M. (1986) *Children and Parents Enjoying*

Reading: a Handbook for Teachers. London: Hodder & Stoughton (paperback).
Partners in Reading (1984) (colour video, 23 minutes) Chiltern Consortium, Wall Hall, Aldenham, Watford WD2 8AT.

Workshops

Smith, H. and Marsh, M. *Have You a Minute? The Fox Hill Reading Project* from Fox Hill First & Nursery School, Keats Road, Sheffield S6 1AZ.
Baker, C. (1980) *Reading through Play.* London: MacDonald Education.

Paired reading

The Kirklees Paired Reading Training Pack contains both written and video material, available separately or together, and covers peer as well as parent tutoring. Details from: Paired Learning Project, Oastler Centre, 103 New Street, Huddersfield HD1 2UA.
Also see: Morgan, R. (1986) *Helping Children Read: the Paired Reading Handbook.* London: Methuen.

Pause, Prompt and Praise

Video, professional handbook and parent handbook available from Positive Products, P.O. Box 45, Cheltenham, Gloucestershire.

Family reading groups

Obrist, C. (1978) *How to Run Family Reading Groups.* Edge Hill College, Ormskirk: United Kingdom Reading Association.

General

Topping, K. and Wolfendale, S. W. (eds) (1985) *Parental Involvement in Children's Reading.* London: Croom Helm and New York: Nichols. Covers issues of organisation.
Pearce, L. (1989) *Partners in Literacy.* Wisbech, Cambridgeshire: Learning Development Aids. Includes video, teachers' handbook and reproducible parent booklets.

BIBLIOGRAPHY

Currie, L. and Bowes, A. (1988) 'A head start to learning: Involving parents of children just about to start school'. *Support for Learning*, 3, 4, 196-200.

Hannon, P., Weinberger, J. and Nutbrown, C. (1991) 'A study of work with parents to promote early literacy development'. *Research Papers in Education,* 6, 2, 77-97.

Hewison, J. (1988) 'The long term effectiveness of parental involvement in reading: a follow-up to the Haringey Reading Project'. *British Journal of Educational Psychology,* 58, 184-90.

Hewison, J. and Tizard, J. (1980) 'Parental involvement and reading attainment'. *British Journal of Educational Psychology,* 50, 209-15.

Tizard, B., Mortimore, J. and Burchell, B. (1981) *Involving Parents in Nursery and Infant School.* London: Grant McIntyre.

Tizard, J., Schofield, W. N. and Hewison, J. (1982) 'Collaboration between teachers and parents in assisting children's reading'. *British Journal of Educational Psychology,* 52, 1-15.

Topping, K. J. (1986a) *Parents as Educators: Training Parents to Teach their Children.* London: Croom Helm and Cambridge, Massachusetts: Brookline Books.

Topping, K. J. (1986b) 'WHICH parental involvement in reading scheme? A guide for practitioners'. *Reading (UKRA),* 20, 3, 148-56.

Topping, K. J. (1992) 'Short- and long-term follow-up of parental involvement in reading projects'. *British Educational Research Journal,* 18, 4.

Topping, K. J. and Lindsay, G. A. (1992) 'Paired reading: a review of the literature'. *Research Papers in Education,* 7, 3.

Topping, K. J. and Whiteley, M. (1990) 'Participant evaluation of parent-tutored and peer-tutored projects in reading'. *Educational Research,* 32, 1, 14-32.

Topping, K. J. and Wolfendale, S. (eds) (1985) *Parental Involvement in Children's Reading.* London: Croom Helm and New York: Nichols.

Tunnell, M. O. and Jacobs, J. S. (1989) 'Using "real" books: Research findings on literature based instruction'. *The Reading Teacher,* 42, 7, 470-7.

Weinberger, J. (1983) *Fox Hill Reading Workshop.* London: Family Service Units.

Weinberger, J. (1989) 'Talking about education: Increasing the dialogue between parents and nursery'. *Education 3-13,* 17, 2, 49-53.

9

ASSESSMENT AND RECORD KEEPING

Diana Bentley

THE NEED FOR TEACHING AND ASSESSMENT TO BE INTERRELATED

Teaching, learning and assessment are inter-related . . .
teacher assessment should become an integral part of the
teaching and learning process.

> (*A Guide to Teacher Assessment in the*
> *National Curriculum*, SEAC, 1991)

As our understanding of the complexity of the reading process
deepens, so it is essential that our assessment procedures reflect
this knowledge. It is no longer acceptable to administer a reading
test once a year in order to monitor a pupil's progress in reading
and to believe that this gives anything like an adequate picture of
that child as a reader.

The major problem that faces teachers is that attempting to
keep fuller and more informative records does take up an
inordinate amount of time. However, if new record-keeping
approaches do inform our teaching and we are able to build
upon such knowledge then this time must be found. Traditionally, the assessment of reading progress was accomplished
through the administration of published standardised tests,
possibly linked to the teacher's own observation of how the
children were managing in the classroom. The test results were
kept and this information relayed to the appropriate authority:
head teacher, local authority, or the DES. Rarely were parents
given any indication as to how their child had performed, nor
were parents considered in any discussion as to how they might
contribute or support their child's development. Recently, as

Keith Topping emphasises in his chapter in this volume, this has begun to change. Parents now have the right to see the school records and since the publication of the TGAT Report (Black *et al.*, 1988) assessment has begun to change in emphasis. In this report, which was commissioned to set a theoretical framework for assessment in the National Curriculum in England and Wales, the observations and reflections of the teacher, parent and pupil are recognised as just as important as more formal assessment procedures, as the following extract shows:

> The assessment process itself should not determine what is to be taught and learned. It should be the servant and not the master of the curriculum. Yet it should not simply be a bolt-on addition at the end. Rather it should be an integral part of the educational process, continually providing both 'feedback' and 'feedforward'. It therefore needs to be incorporated systematically into teaching strategies and practices at all levels. Since the results of assessment can serve a number of different purposes, these purposes have to be kept in mind when the arrangements for assessment are designed.
>
> (Black *et al.*, 1988)

WHAT FORMS OF ASSESSMENT SHOULD SCHOOLS CONSIDER WHEN FORMULATING A SCHOOL POLICY?

Assessment and record keeping have to play a central role in a school's reading policy, and careful consideration needs to be given to the weighting that the different forms of assessment receive. Traditional standardised tests are no longer regarded as adequate on their own and many schools have become more critical of tests which do not reflect the way in which the school is teaching reading. However, standardised tests still form a significant part in the overall assessment of a child's progress in many schools and teachers need to be able to assess the information they provide, especially as parents often adamantly request the 'reading ages' of their children as displayed by such tests. It seems sensible therefore to look at the different kinds of tests on the market and to consider their strengths, their limitations and the contribution they may make to the overall understanding of a pupil's progress.

187

WHAT ARE STANDARDISED READING TESTS?

A test is standardised by testing large numbers of children of a specific age and then determining the average standard of the group. This means that when a standardised test is administered it is possible to see how a child or group of children compare to the population on which the test was standardised. These tests generally fall into two kinds: norm-referenced tests and criterion-referenced tests. The National Curriculum has emphasised that it is the latter type that is seen as having the greater value. The term *norm* is often a synonym for the average performance in a standardised test. A norm-referenced test aims to give an indication of how a child performs on that test in relation to the average of those tested when the test was developed. The information it provides, if it is accurate, gives an indication of overall performance; it is rare for such a test to give diagnostic information. Traditional intelligence tests, for example, were generally norm referenced, with the average set at a score of 100, within one population. Norm-referenced reading tests tended to be related to the scores of children at particular ages, and an average given as a 'reading age'. This concept was criticised by some commentators, who suggested that the concept may mask great differences between readers of different chronological ages who happen to share the same score on a reading test, and therefore the same 'reading age'.

A criterion-referenced test aims to show what the person who takes the test can achieve in relation to a particular target, or criterion. A criterion or mastery level is set and the results show how far certain skills have been attained. It is possible for the same test to be both norm referenced or criterion referenced. For example, a child who swims a certain distance could be awarded a badge for achieving that criterion. Alternatively, his or her time could be compared with that of others who have swum the same distance, and the performance related to that normative data.

IS THERE A PLACE FOR THE STANDARDISED TEST?

It has been argued by some researchers that standardised tests can be more reliable than teachers' judgements. In the Extending Beginning Reading project (Southgate, 1981), 1,638 children were assessed using the Southgate Reading Test and these results were compared to the estimates of 134 teachers. Thirty-six per cent of the teachers were correct to within three months, while 64 per cent underestimated or overestimated their pupils' reading ability. Even if one accepts that a three-month target for accuracy was rather stringent, and that no test is perfect, this research did suggest that there may be problems in relying solely on global teacher assessment. It is possible for a teacher to recognise that a child is suddenly making progress but to overestimate this progress. Similarly, children who are making very slow progress compared to their peers may be thought to have made no progress. Another perspective on the child's reading progress may therefore be potentially valuable.

The standardised test may alert teachers to aspects of reading which they had overlooked. The Edinburgh Reading Test attempts to examine performance in a number of different areas. For example, one version contains a section which has to be read within a certain time, and another which includes many inferential comprehension questions. When schools looked carefully at the results of the different sections of the test many children did not perform well on these two areas. The teachers recognised that these were areas of the reading curriculum which they had overlooked. Standardised tests do aim to be economic (both with time and cost) and reliable guides to the reading performance of individual pupils. Tests are used on the assumption, in Bridie Raban's words, 'that their results can stand in place of lengthy observations of each pupil's reading behaviour. Because of this, tests can offer teachers a greater opportunity for monitoring pupils' progress in a regular and systematic way' (Raban, 1983).

However, as Raban points out, the danger which becomes associated with the test materials is that their content is assumed to give guidelines for teaching. For example, Schonell, whose Graded Word Reading Test first appeared in 1945, believed that rapid recognition of sight words and the ability to decode print are correlates of being a 'good reader', but his test resulted in a greater emphasis on flash-cards presented in isolation in an attempt to teach sight word recognition. Such teaching, as Colin Harrison argued in Chapter 1 of this book, may well be counter-productive. Teaching to the test has always been a cause for concern and it is essential that teachers are fully aware of what skill a test is testing and to see this as only an indication of how the child is performing on that skill at that time. Standardised tests have not yet been devised which cover all the very complex processes involved in reading. There is a danger, inherent in all these tests, that the results they give are seen as far more important and significant than is justified. However, if the tests are recognised as contributing towards a global picture of the child as a reader then they may have an important part to play.

Before deciding on which of the many tests on the market to administer a school should take into consideration the following points.

- Does the test reflect the philosophy of the school's approach to teaching reading?
- What does the test claim to measure? Is this something the school considers of value?
- Can you relate the information provided by the test to the school's responses to the demands of the National Curriculum?
- Is the content of the test interesting and relevant to the pupils? Does it take into consideration the multi-ethnic make-up of today's society?
- How is the test scored? Does it allow for a range of possible answers?
- Do the items in the test look appropriate for what the test claims to measure?
- Is the text of sufficient length to allow the reader to make use of a meaningful context?
- Can the test be used to measure the child's progress over a number of years, or is it part of a graded series of tests which may do this?
- Are the items within the test clearly understandable and unambiguous?
- Does the language reflect today's usage, or is the child expected to read words such as *wireless*?
- Will the test help the teacher to teach reading more effectively?
- Does the test treat reading as an accumulation of a set of skills, or does it allow for reflection and response to texts?
- Is a detailed, simple, informative manual provided?
- Is the test worth while in terms of the likely cost in both time and money?

This is by no means an exhaustive list, but if teachers are hoping to use a standardised test then these questions need to be addressed.

THE PLACE OF INFORMAL ASSESSMENT

In any matter of assessment, it is important to consider the purpose of collecting the information. If the need is for global information concerning reading attainment then there may be a case for using a standardised test. If the purpose is to assist in the development of the individual, then other methods may be much more appropriate. Although the standardised test was once seen as a vital component of assessment, today, more and more teachers, if given the choice, would opt to abandon formal tests and increase their use of informal methods. We should perhaps stress again at this point, however, that the terms we use to describe tests, such as 'formal' versus 'informal', or 'summative' versus 'formative', are related to how we use an instrument, and not just to the test itself. The National Curriculum in English for England and Wales, for example, offers many assessment opportunities, and the results can be collapsed into levels and used in school league tables, but they could also be used for diagnosis, and to inform practice in relation to individuals.

MISCUE ANALYSIS

As informal methods of assessment gained currency, the most popular and well known was miscue analysis. This approach is based on the notion of recording how a reader reads aloud, and it seeks to value the constructive and intelligent use of partial information and guessing which all beginning readers use to some extent, and in doing so avoids wherever possible the term 'error'. In 1972, Goodman and Burke published 'The Reading Miscue Inventory', in which they examined a reader's miscues (i.e. unexpected oral reading responses that did not match the text) and proposed that these gave an insight into the strategies a reader uses when reading aloud. They specified that the materials chosen had to be of sufficient difficulty to ensure that the reader produced miscues. These miscues were then categorised under such headings as omissions, insertions, mispronunciations and self-corrections. The miscues fell under two broad headings – those that did not apparently interfere with the meaning of the texts and those that did. Finally, the teacher would ask the reader about the passage in order to check that the child had read with understanding. The teacher could then examine what the reader had done and link his or her teaching to the apparent needs of the children. Miscue analysis has been valued by many teachers, although it can take a great deal of time to conduct for individual children, especially if the teacher wants to avoid potentially unreliable results by analysing the child's reading using a range of passages.

CLOZE PROCEDURE

Another approach to informal assessment has been to present readers with 'cloze' passages. Here selected words are deleted and the readers are asked to complete the passage by putting in their own choice of words. The words to be deleted are chosen in one of two ways: either on a regular basis, in which every *n*th word is deleted, which means that the reader is likely to have to replace a random selection of word classes, such as nouns, verbs, adjectives, etc.; or on the basis of selecting specifically chosen words or word classes, for example words which act as cohesive ties (such as pronouns or conjunctions). The theory behind using cloze procedure is that readers who can replace the missing words successfully must be both reading for meaning and using context intelligently.

However, unless clear guidance is given to the readers, many children select words they can spell, at the expense of attempting more adventurous language, and some readers can think of so many alternative words that they begin to lose the sense of the passage while they make their selection. These children often do not complete the passage within the given time. Finally calibrating such passages is both difficult and time consuming and the results can only be taken as one indication of a reader's ability.

INFORMAL READING INVENTORIES

Informal Reading Inventories (IRIs) built upon the research into miscue analysis and cloze, but began to extend the information recorded. The IRI is usually based upon the child's reading of a series of relatively short prose extracts which are read aloud, and on which questions are subsequently put, to be answered orally.

There are various ways of scoring the answers, including errors of word identification and in comprehension. The score is sometimes used to determine whether a reader is at the 'independent', 'instructional' or 'frustration' level in relation to a particular text, and such information can thus help to identify the degree of help that a child might need to achieve meaning (Holdaway, 1979). It may be that the greatest value of the IRI, which it shares with cloze procedure and miscue analysis, is that it permits the teacher to explore the techniques that the child is using, and, if discussion allows, the concepts that may underlie the reader's behaviour.

Accordingly, it may be best from the point of view of enhancing the child's reading to combine the use of an inventory with the procedure that has come to be known as the reading conference. Normally the conference should have one or both of two larger purposes. The first is to discuss the particular text that a child is reading; the second is to discuss the reading itself (see Ashworth, 1988, for a fuller account of how this might be done). Such a conference might go well beyond the reading of a single set of passages.

THE READING CONFERENCE

What should be recorded in a reading conference? First, we would argue that a child should keep a log of all the books that he or she has read. Some schools offer a form on which this can be done, and later in the present chapter, in the section on pupil self-assessment, details are given of what might be recorded in a log. The teacher might help the child to fill in the log, discussing recent reading and acting as an audience for the child's views. In many schools, conferences take place in the time that used to be given to hearing children reading, although the teacher might still listen to the child read from time to time. On occasion, though, the teacher might read aloud for part of the conference, in order to provide a model, or to introduce a particular book or author.

In the teacher's records, it can be useful to consider keeping details under each of the following headings: *books read, attitudes, concepts* and *techniques*. Knowing what a child has read in terms of reading level is no substitute for knowing what subjects or types of text are valued and enjoyed by that child, and

WHAT DO YOU READ?

Name _____

Class _____

Date _____

1. What book are you reading now?
   (a) at home
   (b) at school

2. What is the best book you have read recently at home or at school?

3. What is the best book you have ever read or heard?

4. What kind of reading do you prefer? Score these kinds of books out of ten: finding out, poems, stories, comics, magazines, newspapers

5. Do you go to the library to borrow books?
   No sometimes often every week

6. How many books of your own do you have at home?
   A few about twenty more than twenty

7. Do you prefer to read at home or at school?
   Can you give a reason?

8. Do you read with anyone at home? Who do you read with?

9. What do you read at home apart from books?
   (a) comics. Which one?
   (b) magazines. Which ones?
   (c) newspapers. Which ones?
       Which parts do you read?
   (d) *Radio* and *TV Times*?

Figure 9.1

this can be vital information to pass on to another teacher. So perhaps a teacher might fill out a brief questionnaire with each child during that time normally used to 'hear children read', such as the checklist in Figure 9.1 (taken from Bloom, 1987).

In the area of attitude, there should be a place for recording details of motivation, the willingness and ability to persist, and whether these have been observed to grow or diminish. During the conference and perhaps at other times such as story-time, the teacher builds up a knowledge of the child's conceptual knowledge of print. Young children only gradually come to grasp such notions as *word*, and to see a correspondence between the written and spoken version. It takes time for a child to learn that to read a story is not the same as to tell a story, that print is arranged horizontally, that you can interpret a picture but not read it in the same way that you can read a sentence. The child's emergent awareness of all these merits inclusion in the teacher's records.

Finally, but very importantly, there should be a place for details of the child's reading techniques. These might involve comment on the child's phonemic awareness (as described in Chapter 1), which is the ability to hear and segment words, and which is a vital component in word building and in the subsequent ability to make use of analogies. Equally important in a beginning reader is the willingness to read on in order to gain meaning in a difficult passage. It is also sometimes important to go back within a text to recheck meaning and re-examine tentative hypotheses which were inaccurate. All these are strategies which fluent readers use when the passage is difficult, and to which beginning readers need to be introduced. If the strategies of a fluent reader are modelled, discussed and valued in a reading conference the child can take them on with much more clarity and confidence than if they have to be deduced and inferred tacitly. Learning how to be a reader can be much simpler if it is externalised and discussed.

The content of records is a whole-school policy matter, partly defined by National Curriculum legislation. However, the sort of assessment which helps readers to develop may be on a much finer level of analysis than that required by law, and some schools will want to develop it more than others. The important principle is that the demands of national or standardised assessment may serve the information needs of politicians, but could be inadequate for the needs of young learners. The detailed needs of young readers are best served by a policy which devises assessment systems and records that keep the reader in sharp focus, and are part of an ongoing interaction between the teacher and the reader.

RUNNING RECORDS

Running records are another approach to capturing the strategies of individual readers. The approach is popular with some teachers who feel that it is quicker and simpler to use than those described above. Marie Clay devised these records and further details can be found in her book *The Early Detection of Reading Difficulties* (1985). She suggested that before making the running record a book was chosen which was familiar to the child and a copy of the text was made on which the teacher could record the 'miscues' of the reader. The teacher ticked each correct word as the child read and then marked any deviation in the following ways:

Substitute words were written over the top of the correct word:

road

e.g.   The little girl ran down the path

Any word that was omitted was circled:

e.g.   She came to the edge of a (dark) wood

Self-corrections were marked as though for a substitution and then had the letters SC written beside them:

SC that

e.g.   The girl stopped and wondered what to do

Words 'sounded out' were marked with the 'sounds' written above the text:

f..f..frightened

e.g.   She was frightened of the tall trees

The teacher then analyses the text to try to discover what cues and strategies the child is using when reading.

Unlike the criterion-referenced test score these criteria are not judged to be absolute, but rather are seen as a rough guide as to how a reader performs on a certain selected text. The technique does enable a teacher to offer a wide range of text types that are not easily found in the standardised tests. In order to keep a more thorough record on the reader's progress it is useful to tape a child at regular (though not frequent) times during the school year. This could be early in the first term, using a book chosen by the child, and then once or twice later in the school year.

This 'oral record' often demonstrates the progress that even the weakest of readers has made. It enables a teacher to compare how a child has performed over a year and to share the progress with the parents. By taping a child it is easy to hear the strategies that child is using at the beginning of the school year and to check to see if these have changed over time. For example, a child who relies on 'sounding out' unfamiliar words as heard on the first recording may be using a more effective strategy later in the year. The main criticism that can be laid at this form of record keeping is that it does require an 'oral' read and as children move rapidly into silent reading and this becomes the more natural situation, then taping may be seen as less valuable. Indeed these readers may make more reading 'miscues' than normal as they know that they are being judged on the speed, intonation and production of the text and they could be concentrating on these skills at the cost of reading for meaning. However, there is no reason why they should not be allowed to read through the text beforehand in order to read the passage for its content and the teacher would still be able to pick up valuable information from hearing them read.

OBSERVATION

This section is complementary to others in this book, notably those on aspects of the teacher's role in the chapters by Martin Coles and Eric Ashworth. Both formal and informal testing procedures should have a place in a school's assessment programme but with the increased acknowledgement that reading must be of importance to the reader, teachers have begun to observe more closely the reading behaviours of children in the class during normal lesson time. The attitude and enthusiasm of the reader are now recognised to be of equal importance to the skills needed for decoding the text.

As Henrietta Dombey says so shrewdly (1991) about observation:

> The formative assessment it permits is essential to teaching that engages children at the most appropriate level, in the most appropriate way. Unless you know where children are, what they have done, what they can do, how they go about it, what they think they can do, what they want to do next, and what they find difficult but can do with your help, you risk expecting too much of them, under-challenging them or taking them along too narrow or alien a path.

When should teachers observe? Continuous observation during normal classroom activities is essential. Setting aside a specific time will only provide very limited information as the situation is likely to be the same each time. Teachers need to jot down what a child is doing at odd moments during the week and in this way it is possible to compile a reading profile that forms a whole picture of the child as a reader. It is essential that the teacher records what a child has done rather than simply interpret why they think the child has acted in a specific way. This is not to say that inferences are not important but that by observing and recording what has taken place the final profile is more likely to be reliable.

What should we focus on during observation? The following suggestions are not definitive or exclusive. The final decision should be the result of consultation with the whole staff but this is likely to contain some of the following:

- Is the child confident about choosing a book to read?
- Does the child select a wide range of reading material, e.g. poetry, non-fiction, fiction?
- Does the child willingly and regularly take books home?
- Does the child appear to enjoy reading to the teacher?
- Does the child choose to read in odd moments during the day?
- Does the child talk about the book s/he is reading?
- Does the child obviously enjoy rereading some books?
- Does the child talk about favourite authors/illustrators?
- Does the child make associations between books?
- Does the child analogise after reading about some situations?
- Does the child self-correct when reading aloud?
- Does the child want to share some texts with peers/adults?
- Does the child turn to books for information and enjoyment?

A checklist such as the one above will enable you to build a detailed reading profile with this information and that contained in the child's reading log. If you are a teacher of 7 year olds or 11 year olds in England or Wales you will of course administer the National Curriculum Standard Assessment Tasks on an annual basis and these should also provide you with information about individual children which you might use to feed into your teaching of reading.

It is the case, though, that teachers of young children are informally assessing a child's growth in reading all the time, for instance when they become aware of the influence of a particular story on a child's writing; when they note that a child is choosing to read silently; when they watch a child choosing a book; and more particularly, when they initiate a reading conference with a child in order to listen to a child read aloud or perhaps share a book with a child discussing that child's response to the book.

Sometimes, perhaps once a term, it might be useful to formalise this last kind of assessment by gathering specific information about a child's reading to place in the reading profile with the other information and the scores from any standardised tests that have been administered. Such information might be recorded using the kind of form devised by Wendy

Name _____

Class _____

Teacher _____

Author
Code/Level/Stage

1. Reads with interest and enjoyment

2. *Miscues.* Specify
   (a) same beginning but nonsense
   (b) no likeness but same class and meaning
   (c) reversal
   (d) refusal
   (e) omission? alters sense

3. *Tries to guess words*
   Using (a) first sound
   (b) first letter
   (c) first blend
   (d) phonic breakdown/synthesis
   (e) syllables
   (f) illustrations
   (g) looking on
   (h) looking back
   (i) miscues, then alters rest of sentence to match
   (j) other

4. Corrects miscues without prompting
   Corrects miscues with prompting

5. Can predict what might happen
   Can recount story

6. Reads in
   (a) words
   (b) lines
   (c) phrases
   (d) sentences

7. Uses finger/card

8. Can make inferences
   Can appreciate/evaluate

9. *Any other observations*
   Reading time, settles quickly?
   Choosing books, concentration
   One book or many?

Figure 9.2

Bloom (1987), which is shown as Figure 9.2. It implies that either a running record or a miscue analysis is carried out, that there is discussion about the text a child is reading (i.e. to answer question 8) and that a teacher gives some time to simply observing children reading to discover whether for instance they are becoming more discriminating in their choice of books, can sustain silent reading for longer periods, are choosing longer texts rather than several short ones (question 9). Other questions that might be answered by observation have already been listed.

Some schools have devised their own record-keeping systems which take account of the wide range of information which it is useful to collect in order to ensure that children are making progress in their reading development, and in order that teachers can pay attention to the individual needs of children. Examples of such forms, drawn from Waterland (1989), are given below, in Figures 9.3 and 9.4. The 'reading wheel' from Kingsbridge Primary School (Figure 9.3) is particularly effective in illustrating the fact that reading development does not necessarily occur in a linear way. The 'Reading Experience Record' from Waterbeach School (Figure 9.4) also includes some interesting perspectives on development; it has a very wide range of points, including some connected with attitude as well as others connected with response to reading a range of texts.

PUPIL SELF-ASSESSMENT

This kind of information should also be shared with the child either by giving the child his or her own list of headings or discussing the observations on a more informal basis. Children do enjoy keeping their own records and this should be more than just a list of what they have read and what they thought about. Allowing them to see and discuss what the teacher feels is important may help them to refine their own attitudes and clarify their goals, and this important point is stressed in the National Curriculum Assessment Document:

> Self assessment by pupils themselves, even at the primary stage, has a part to play by encouraging a clear understanding of what is expected of them, motivation to reach it, a sense of pride in the positive achievements and a realistic appraisal of weaknesses that need to be tackled. It should be

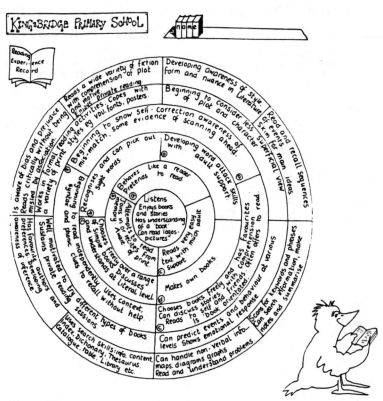

Figure 9.3

given due weight as part of the evidence towards the
teachers' internal assessment.

(DES, 1988)

We have already referred to the possibility of a child keeping a
reading log. Through it, a child comes to take on some of the
responsibility in the matter of assessment and record keeping. A
reading log, kept by the child, is one way in which these
responsibilities can be examined and developed. Details in such a
log might include:

- The date a book was started
- The date finished (or abandoned!)
- Title and author
- Whether it was enjoyed, and how much

201

READING EXPERIENCE RECORD

	1st week	1st term	1st year	2nd year	3rd year
Enjoys looking at books					
listening to stories					
Has a wide experience of books at home					
school					
Behaves like a reader					
Pretends to read					
Follows text with adult support					
Shadow Reading					
Chooses books carefully					
Attempts to read known text					
Chats about story					
Shows understanding					
Beginning to predict					
Finger pointing					
Reads known words					
Attempts unknown words					
Can read familiar text with little help					
Uses contextual clues					
Uses phonic clues					
Recognizes and can pick out sight words					
in known text					
Enjoys rhyming books					
Beginning to read independently					
Can predict events					
Reading shows self-correction					
Able to scan ahead					
Can sustain private reading sessions					
Confident with books					
Not confident with books					
Has favourite book					
Can discuss stories with comprehension					
Is 'book' orientated					
Reads fluently aloud					
Enjoys fiction/non-fiction					
Enjoys reading poetry					
Can use reference books					
Has extra help with reading					
Has specific reading problems					

Figure 9.4 Waterbeach Reading Experience Record

- Space for the teacher's or parents' comments on what has been written
- Space for child to comment on these.

Such a log would provide an overview of the kinds of books chosen and read; it would record a child's response to each book, and would give some indication of the amount of reading; and provide a basis for discussion during a reading conference.

In conclusion there is no one form of assessment that will provide a 'whole' picture of the child as a reader. The teacher needs continually to revise and change his or her opinion in the light of new evidence from all forms of assessment procedures. Assessment must be formative, it should emphasise what has been achieved and identify those areas which need further development, it has to be concerned with the process as well as the product and it needs to be negotiated with the learners so that they too become responsible for their learning.

QUESTIONS FOR PERSONAL REFLECTION OR GROUP DISCUSSION

The following questions are standard questions one might ask in any assessment situation. They are potentially very revealing when asked in relation to current assessment practices and very useful when planning to carry out some assessment.

1 What do I want to assess? Why?
2 Precisely, what do I want to assess?
3 What evidence can the children give me of what I want to assess?
4 What am I going to give them to do so that they can provide the evidence?
5 Do I need to set up special conditions?
6 Am I going to use a standard for comparison? If so, which one?
7 Am I going to make judgements against particular criteria? If so, which ones?
8 How will I record the information?

RECOMMENDED READINGS

Barrs, M., Ellis, S., Hester, H. and Thomas, A. (1988) *The Primary Language Record: A Handbook for Teachers.* Centre for Language in Primary Education, ILEA. This very useful booklet describes a language record for primary schools developed by working parties of teachers and other ILEA staff over a two-year period and extensively trialled in schools. This handbook gives an account of the thinking about children's language and literacy development from 3 to 13 which underlies the assessment and record-keeping system. It has detailed instructions about how to carry out miscue analysis, explanations to do with running records, and suggested procedures for informal assessment.

Barrs, M., Ellis, S., Hester, H. and Thomas, A. (1990) *Patterns of Learning: The Primary Language Record and the National Curriculum.* Centre for Language in Primary Education, ILEA. This book looks at the role that record keeping will play in the internal assessment of the National Curriculum. It has descriptions of classroom contexts and activities that support children's language development and shows teachers using the Primary Language Record to keep track of children's progress and development, and to gather evidence which will be the basis of internal assessment. There is also very useful discussion of equal opportunities and the National Curriculum with sections on bilingualism, Standard English, gender, special educational needs, and the early years.

Other books particularly recommended for their practical advice are those by Marie Clay, Don Holdaway and Cliff Moon, detailed in the Bibliography.

BIBLIOGRAPHY

Arnold, H. (1982) *Listening to Children Reading.* London: Hodder & Stoughton.

Ashworth, E. (1988) *Language Policy in the Primary School: Content and Management.* London: Croom Helm.

Barrs, M., Ellis, S., Hester, H. and Thomas, A. (1988) *The Primary Language Record: A Handbook for Teachers.* London: ILEA.

Bentley, D. (1988) *The How and Why of Reading Assessment.* Reading and Language Information Centre, University of Reading.

Black, P. *et al.* (1988) *National Curriculum Task Group on Assessment and Testing: A Report.* London: HMSO.

Bloom, W. (1987) 'Monitoring and assessing children's reading without using tests'. *New Childhood,* Spring.

Clay, M. (1985) *The Early Detection of Reading Difficulties* (3rd edn). London: Heinemann.

DES (1988) *National Curriculum Report of Task Group on Assessment and Testing.* London: HMSO.

Dombey, M. (1991) 'The sattable and the unsattable: giving children the assessment in literacy they deserve'. In C. Harrison and E. Ashworth (eds) *Celebrating Literacy: Defending Literacy.* Oxford: Basil Blackwell.

Goodman, Y. and Burke, C.L. (1972) *The Reading Miscue Inventory Manual: Procedures for Diagnosis and Evaluation.* London: Macmillan.

Holdaway, D. (1979) *The Foundations of Literacy.* New York: Scholastic.

Moon, C. (1990) *Assessing Reading Strategies at Key Stage 1.* Reading and Language Information Centre, University of Reading.

NATE (1989) *Assessing Language Development and English.* Sheffield: National Association for the Teaching of English.

Raban, B. (1983) *Guides to Assessment in Education: Reading.* London: Macmillan Education.

SEAC (1991) *A Guide to Teacher Assessment*. Oxford: Heinemann.
Southgate, V. (1981) *Extending Beginning Reading*. London: Heinemann.
Waterland, L. (1989) *Apprenticeship in Action*. Stroud: Thimble Press.

10

SUPPORTING READERS FOR WHOM ENGLISH IS A SECOND LANGUAGE

Guy Merchant

I started to learn English from the age of five. I am all right at speaking it alone in my mind. I hate reading it aloud. I started to speak Bengali from the age of two. I still have lessons at Palfrey School on Saturday and Sunday. I can read Arabic from the age of six. I started to take lessons off my mum. Now I can read Arabic well. I can understand Hindi – I picked it up from the films.

(Azizul Islam)[1]

At the age of 9 Azizul Islam was asked to write his own language profile. The picture that emerges is one of a child who is familiar with four quite distinct language systems. Azizul is literate in three of these languages. This extract from his profile is a powerful reminder of how the social and cultural world that children inhabit influences both their knowledge about language and their uses of it. Azizul's feelings about the languages around him are also important. They help to shape his view of himself as a language user – take for instance his lack of confidence in reading aloud in English and how this contrasts with his ability to read Arabic. Of course these attitudes are not necessarily fixed. We would all, I think, hope that his confidence in reading English might increase in future: but not at the expense of those other languages in his repertoire.

Azizul's story is by no means unusual. Impressive though it is, his experience as a language user is similar to that of children in many parts of the country. Nevertheless learning to read and write in more than one language is a significant achievement. It is the fruit of much hard work and learning and represents a versatility to be proud of. In a wider sense it enables an individual to participate in a variety of social and cultural practices and as such it is of central importance in a pluralist society.

Biliteracy for Azizul means a great deal. Not only does it have immediate and tangible benefits as he interacts with his family and friends, but it also links him with a wider community with its own distinct customs and history. He is undoubtedly fortunate in possessing a rich and varied knowledge of language. But Azizul is fortunate in a more down to earth sense. He is a part of a strong family which engages in and cherishes acts of literacy. They are already members of what Frank Smith calls the 'literacy club' (Smith, 1988). For Azizul and children like him from many different language backgrounds, maintaining a level of biliteracy and providing support for its development are important social and educational tasks.

Others may not share Azizul's good fortune. Literacy may not be an established part of the home experience, the family may be isolated or community networks may be difficult to organise. Those opportunities for learning to read and write the home or community language that have so clearly enriched Azizul's life may not, for one reason or another, be sufficiently developed.

Bilingual children in British schools have varying levels of proficiency in their home, community or religious languages. This variation is attributable to differences in linguistic background as well as differences in individual circumstances. With something in the region of 200 distinct language groups now forming a significant part of the school population of England and Wales a reappraisal of much of what constitutes language education is well overdue (Merchant, 1990).

An acknowledgement of the linguistic diversity of the school population would, in an ideal world, lead to changes in education policy and provision. Unfortunately the wide-ranging changes in provision ushered in through the Education Reform Act (1988) offer relatively little practical support for linguistic diversity. Instead they have resulted in a core curriculum which, while recognising the cultural diversity of our society, avoids any serious consideration of the issues this raises for language education (Savva, 1990). At best we find statements such as this one from the Cox Report:

Work should start from the pupils' own linguistic competence. Many pupils are bilingual and sometimes biliterate, and quite often literally know more about language than their teachers, at least in some respects.

(DES, 1988)

How can we build on this knowledge and experience of other languages? And how will it inform the decisions we take on the road to literacy? Before exploring these questions it will be useful to look at what is already known about biliteracy in the British context.

BILITERACY AND BRITISH SCHOOLCHILDREN

The DES-funded Linguistic Minorities Project (LMP), set up in 1979, remains the single most reliable source of information on patterns of language use in multilingual Britain. In the survey sample the project team found that:

Literacy in the minority language was never much less than 50 per cent . . . literacy rates range from over 80 per cent of the Polish- and Ukrainian-speaking respondents, through notably high proportions of the Gujerati, Turkish and Bengali speakers.

(LMP, 1985)

These findings suggest that the majority of bilingual children in British classrooms are likely to experience either formal or informal instruction in the written form of a community language. Such instruction will in most cases take place in voluntary schools or at home and not as part of their compulsory schooling. This will certainly be the case for all primary-age children in England.

A significant part of the debate on 'mother-tongue teaching' in the early 1980s focused on the importance of maintaining and developing levels of literacy in ethnic minority community languages. As Mahendra Verma emphasises:

A language is fostered, cultivated and preserved through reading and writing, not simply speaking. . . . Biliteracy is a prerequisite to sustained and stable bilingualism.

(Verma, 1984)

Despite pressure from ethnic minority groups for the provision of community language teaching in mainstream schools the emphasis has remained on transitional bilingualism in the primary school (DES, 1985) using the spoken language of home only until communicative English has been established. Ethnic minority languages can, however, be included as modern language options in secondary schools.

Although teachers may work hard to recognise community languages in the primary school (see Houlton, 1985) it is likely that children's most influential experiences of another language will take place outside of compulsory schooling. As the LMP survey (1985) suggests, the majority of bilingual children will receive some instruction in the written form of their community language. In most cases then, bilingualism will include biliteracy.

A basic definition of biliteracy would be concerned with the ability to understand and communicate through the written form of two distinct language systems. As with the wider term bilingualism, a more precise description would need to take into account variations in individual proficiency as well as the purposes for which the two languages are used. We would then need to have some insight into the social use of those languages.

The work of the Linguistic Minorities Project (LMP, 1985) draws our attention to some of the issues involved in looking at language repertoire and social use. The perceived aims of community-organised provision for minority language teaching are one such issue. For example, many voluntary schools organised by minority groups associate literacy quite closely with religious instruction. Polish Saturday schools, Welsh language Sunday schools as well as classes held in mosques, temples and gurdwaras perform this function.

Children's accounts of learning to read two languages do not, however, tend to dwell on justifications or purpose. Instead they more typically refer to the age they learnt to read, the environment in which they learnt and the approach of their teachers. They may make comparisons but these are rarely evaluative in character.

Nine-year-old Benares comments in this fashion:

I went to Mosque from 7 years old. My dad took me and

then I started learning it. I read English too. I'm learning to
read good. You know at Mosque this big man he – this big
man he give us Kaida (a primer). You go and read to him
and he tells you the word if you don't know. I learned
English in the infants. Mrs. Richardson said 'Read your
reading book and then you can play in the Lego.'

(Benares)[2]

Differences between 'the big man' who teaches reading by group
recitation from the Kaida and Mrs Richardson who listens to you
each in turn as you read your 'reading book' may well be
understated in this account.

Teaching and learning styles will obviously vary quite considerably between cultural groups as well as within cultural
groups. The proximity between methods of instruction in literacy in voluntary and state schools will inevitably be influenced
by this. Another child's account suggests a rather different
pedagogy:

I go to reading at 5 o'clock; this lady teaches me. She writes
them and I have to say them. It's hard because she writes
them joined up. I want to be a teacher. The lady who
teaches us shouts at us and we have to stand in the corner.
She used to have a stick. We read her the book. If we don't
know she tells us. Sometimes we go on to the next page.

(Shaheen Begum)[2]

In general such differences of approach are regarded by children
as 'normal' and do not constitute a problem. As the fascinating
case studies of Hilary Minns (1990) illustrate, literacy in a
culturally diverse setting includes a wide variety of experiences.
As a result we are led to consider new dimensions of literacy and
to ask more detailed questions. For instance, in a multicultural
setting we need to take into account the different status of the
languages of literacy and what it means to be a reader in different
cultural contexts. There is little detailed research with British
schoolchildren that addresses these and other aspects of biliteracy.

Despite a growing awareness of minority community
languages we are still relatively ill-informed about literacy and
bilingual children. Verma's observation still holds true:

In the present climate of muted support of minority languages there is a general tendency to adopt a narrow view of literacy as the ability to read and write English.

(Verma, 1984)

APPROACHES TO LANGUAGE TEACHING AND LEARNING TO READ ENGLISH

So far I have implied that an understanding of developing literacy in bilingual children has to take into account experiences of both reading and writing in a variety of different social contexts. Children's language repertoire may vary from emergent literacy in one language to fluency in two or more languages. Although schools continue to recognise the benefits of supporting community languages both in their spoken and written forms this is not done to the exclusion of English language teaching. Not only is English essential for progression through the school curriculum, it is also vital in achieving social and political rights. The importance of the majority language is clearly stated by Wallace:

While literacy in the mother tongue helps to ensure participation in the contexts of home and family, literacy in the standard language (English) is one necessary condition for access to the institutions of power in the wider society.

(Wallace, 1988)

Although we might predict a slightly wider domain of use for community languages than that described by Wallace, she is certainly right in emphasising the importance of literacy in English for ethnic minority pupils.

Learning to read in English is an essential task in the multilingual classroom – just as it is in other contexts. But are there any significant differences in teaching and learning approaches?

We have already observed that knowledge about literacy may be quite varied in the multilingual classroom. Children's experiences outside the school setting may have provided them with different versions of what it means to be a reader and how to go about learning to read. These experiences will be as diverse as the communities that the school serves and as a result it is very

211

difficult to generalise about bilingual children's experiences of literacy. However, the sort of detailed profiling encouraged through the Primary Language Record (Barrs *et al.*, 1988) shows how we can begin to gain more insight into the child as language learner.

Effective teaching will need to be based on an understanding of what the learner reader brings to the task. But beyond this it is likely to be informed by the teacher's views about how language develops. This is particularly true when we consider bilingual learners. Teachers working with bilingual readers are likely to build their practice on what they know about how pupils develop their use of spoken English.

Broadly speaking, English language teaching approaches are likely to fall into two distinct categories (Levine, 1990). The first approach is a structural–situationalist pedagogy in which English language input and output are controlled by the teacher with an emphasis on achieving accuracy. The second is a functional–communicative approach which encourages greater pupil interaction and stresses meaning rather than accuracy.

There are of course clear parallels between these two approaches and competing ideologies in the teaching of English as a mother tongue. It is hardly surprising then that professional practice in the teaching of reading to bilingual children has addressed some very familiar issues. Advocates of the structural–situationalist approach have argued that texts with a carefully selected and familiar grammatical structure and a controlled vocabulary will be the most helpful for non-native speakers. The structural–situationalists tend to favour a graded language scheme with a controlled vocabulary as a means of teaching spoken English. It comes as no surprise then to find that the structural–situationalists tend to advocate following a published reading scheme – or use teacher-made resources that support their approach to oral language teaching.

In contrast the functional–communicative approach lends itself more naturally to reading for meaning and interest. Reading schemes tend to be used in a more flexible way and pupils will be encouraged to use and enjoy a wide range of children's literature. Here reading is rightly seen as enriching the whole language of bilingual learners. The Real Reading Project described in the following section shows this sort of approach in action.

WORKING WITH BILINGUAL LEARNER READERS

It is probably true to say that the general lack of development work on reading with bilingual children in the British context has contributed to considerable confusion in practice. For instance, some teachers believe that there is a need to establish a fairly high degree of oral fluency in English before beginning reading: others claim that the oral fluency of young children can be improved through early encounters with print. With little published guidance on such matters schools have tended to seek their own solutions, and have met with varying degrees of success.

The work of a group of teachers in Sheffield[2] shows how school-based development can begin to address the needs of bilingual readers. The teachers started from the observation that children showed little interest in or enthusiasm for the reading material used in the school. Although basic decoding skills were efficiently taught and most children achieved a level of reading competence judged to be appropriate to their age, books were not generally regarded as a source of pleasure and enjoyment. This was seen primarily as a resource problem. A succession of cuts in education budgets had meant that the school had been unable to update its stock of reading materials. The books, the majority of which came from reading schemes, were often uninspiring in content and unattractive in appearance.

The teachers drew up a list of reading activities and experiences that they wished to promote. These are as follows:

- make reading easy and enjoyable
- use interesting and appropriate material (good stories with a multicultural or anti-racist content)
- encourage storytelling and reading from illustrations
- set aside time and space for enjoying books
- use high-quality dual-language texts
- make own reading materials
- share an enthusiasm for stories – talk about them!
- read the books aloud (remove the distinction between class stories and reading books)
- hear children read a whole book or allow them to choose a stopping place
- set up reading partnerships

213

- allow mistakes so long as they do not change the meaning of the text
- teach work-attack skills after initial confidence is built up

Initially, books brought in by the teachers themselves were used to resource this new development. This quite quickly had the effect of improving the quality of reading and influenced the children's enthusiasm for new stories. Bilingual children who had previously struggled to make sense from their reading were now able to enjoy such books as *Bringing the Rain to Kapiti Plain* and *Cops and Robbers*. Teachers began to feel that the rather stilted language of some scheme books, which often seemed confusing to those who spoke English as a mother tongue, had actually caused further problems for bilingual learners. As one teacher commented, 'It seems as if some of these reading books were written for no one in particular by no one in particular.'

Teachers were beginning to use material that they were enthusiastic about; and this enthusiasm was contagious. Books bought by teachers, often from their own pockets, were chosen for a reason – because they were 'good', 'interesting' or 'well illustrated'. Discussions with bilingual children tended to focus on the reasons for choosing a particular book, its presentation and favourite excerpts. Even with a relatively small collection of storybooks children were keen to read and reread the new materials.

Home-made books were used to supplement this growing resource. A series of such books were produced, based on amusing incidents that happened to members of staff in the school. These were illustrated with photographs, and captions were translated into various community languages. This material proved to be extremely popular with the children. More book-making projects are planned for the future.

Emerging from this work in Sheffield is the impression that building a stimulating reading environment in which good stories are created, appreciated and discussed is as important for bilingual learners as it is for monolinguals. The additional benefits of bringing an active multilingual element to this reading environment are beginning to inspire a growing number of both teachers and children.

Developments in the Linguistic Diversity Project in the West

214

Midlands (WMBEC, 1989 and 1990) pick up this theme of celebrating children's biliteracy. In one school[3] a class of Y5 children were involved in producing a series of dual-language storybooks suitable for sharing with younger children in the nursery and infant departments. Stories were written in Punjabi and Gujarati (checked by parents) and then shared with the younger children. This involved planning, drafting and redrafting – always working in two languages – and an insight into the processes of book production. Although time consuming the project was extremely well received.

It would seem that most bilingual learners will learn to read English quickly and fluently in a supportive environment. Development work with bilingual children has emphasised the importance of:

- recognising and valuing children's knowledge of other languages
- providing an exciting and rich reading environment
- emphasising reading for meaning and enjoyment
- using and developing appropriate materials

BILINGUAL CHILDREN AND ENGLISH TEXTS

In the last section I suggested that good practice in the teaching of reading will have the same benefits for bilingual children as it does for their monolingual counterparts. Previously I drew attention to some areas of difference in teaching and learning styles which bilingual children may have experienced. I also outlined the enriching contribution that biliteracy can make in schools and classrooms.

Bilingual learners will approach the task of reading in much the same way that monolinguals do. They will learn to draw on the same strategies for making meaning. However, their experience of another language system and their developing competence in English may influence the way they use these strategies. Goodman's work on cue systems (Goodman, 1964) and Halliday's theory of text and context (Halliday and Hasan, 1985) provide useful frameworks for looking at the ways in which bilingual readers approach English texts.

Difficulties in reading English can occur at a number of levels. These include different understandings of the *cultural context* of particular texts, problems with the *semantic system*, unfamiliar *syntactic structures*, and difficulties with the *grapho-phonemic representation* of the English language. By using miscue analysis (Goodman, 1964) the strategies that children employ as well as the problems that they experience in reading can be identified. Bilingual children may experience specific difficulties at each of the following levels.

Cultural context

Halliday has demonstrated how the understanding of texts is dependent upon a knowledge of the culture in which they are located (Halliday and Hasan, 1985). Our familiarity with the cultural context is often taken for granted in the process of reading. It is nevertheless true that a successful reader draws on a kind of cultural competence in order to construct meaning from a text. As Wallace suggests:

> Our cultural competence is a very complex package of beliefs, knowledge, feelings, attitudes and behaviours. . . . In terms of reading, the term might be used to refer to the ability to recognise, interpret and predict certain kinds of phenomena or behaviour described in texts.
>
> (Wallace, 1988)

Bilingual learners will have a repertoire of cultural competences and differing degrees of familiarity with aspects of British culture. It would be useful to ensure that reading resources embody a similar variety of cultural perspectives. Material written by bilingual writers set in a British context can be used to 'match' the experience of young bilinguals and to broaden the reading diet of monolingual children. More work such as that undertaken by Jenny Ingham in the Reading Materials for Minority Groups Project will be useful in this respect.

Semantic system

Successful reading involves making meaning by drawing on a prior knowledge of how texts 'work'. Our previous experiences of stories, books and other written material help us to recognise the significance of the events, phrases and words that we read. This experience enables us to organise our reading comprehension, to understand the text's underlying structure and to make reasonable predictions. Bilingual learners may not always be familiar with the vocabulary that they encounter in reading. Reading with a limited vocabulary can mean that children are not always familiar with the semantic alternatives (such as collocations) that authors use. However, it should be recognised that learner-readers can get words 'wrong' and still get meaning from what they read.

Syntactic structure

Our knowledge about words and how they are ordered in the clause and sentence structure of the English language helps us to read in a way that makes grammatical sense. Children in the early stages of learning English will only have a partial understanding of the syntactic structure of the language. They will show varying degrees of proficiency in judging how grammatically 'complete' or 'correct' their reading is.

Although other languages use different syntactic structures, interference is not likely to be a major problem. Speakers of those South Asian languages which commonly use the subject–object–verb (SOV) clause pattern (for instance, Punjabi or Urdu) rarely encounter more than minor difficulties in the early stages of learning English, where the SVO structure is used. Research evidence suggests that bilinguals are able to keep their language systems separate from quite an early age (Cummins, 1979).

The syntactical accuracy of bilingual learner–readers will become greater as their oral fluency develops. Brightmore and Ross (1990) illustrate this through their work with young bilingual readers. They show how through successive readings of a text a young bilingual progresses towards an accurate rendering. The text is Pat Hutchins's *Titch*:

Text	First Reading	Second Reading	Third Reading
Titch was	Little is	Little Titch	Tich was
little	Titch	was	little

(From Brightmore and Ross, 1990)

The authors also offer evidence that suggests that children in the early stages of learning English experiment with syntax as they

217

read and develop an ability to use the structures of story language through regular reading.

Grapho-phonemic system

The correspondence between sounds and words and the written symbols that are used to represent them is important for accurate reading and writing. Our understanding of the grapho-phonemic system of the English language is used to complement the other aspects of linguistic knowledge we use in the act of reading. With an alphabet of twenty-six letters representing about forty-six distinct sound features and comparatively complex spelling patterns, English has a grapho-phonemic system which is difficult to master. Bilingual children who are already familiar with the script of another language may observe some contrasts.

However, most languages use an alphabetic system of writing. In some cases (e.g. Italian and Finnish) the correspondence between sound and symbol is particularly close (Gelb, 1952). Bilingual children from such a language background may be surprised by the difficulty of using print cues in English. Although alphabetic writing systems are relatively common, some language groups, such as Chinese, use a single symbol to represent a whole word. However, there seems to be little evidence to suggest that children of Chinese origin experience specific difficulties with English as a result of differences in the writing system.

Similar observations can be made about other script-related language differences such as directionality. Some difficulties may be experienced in the early stages of learning English – and these are frequently reported – but lasting confusion or more persistent language interference is rare.

Through this brief discussion of the knowledge of cultural context and cue systems, I have looked at the strategies that bilingual children use to make sense of their reading. I have suggested that these same strategies will be used by both mono-lingual and bilingual readers. I have also tried to show how the home or community language and children's oral proficiency in English may influence how they read. These factors do not, however, suggest that the school reading experience of bilingual children should be any different in character. There is no evidence to suggest that specially designed language and reading programmes are any more effective than the best of good practice. I will conclude by looking at aspects of current practice that seem to be particularly appropriate to bilingual learners.

TOWARDS A READING POLICY FOR BILINGUAL LEARNERS

Here I consider the reader, reading resources, an audience for reading, reader response and the reading environment. It is intended that these points will be useful in developing reading policies for bilingual children.

The reader

- by identifying and valuing languages other than English the school is able to respond positively to the language skills of bilingual pupils;
- children's experience of literacy in a home or community language can be discussed and used in school;
- children who are already literate in a language other than English will have the advantage of knowing about the reading process;
- some children may have different ideas of what reading behaviour is like and how reading is taught or learnt;
- the motivation to read, to make meaning and to enjoy English language texts is important for bilingual learners;
- reading and listening to stories in both English and community languages will help to develop children's oral fluency in English;
- careful profiling of children's literacy development should include information about all their languages.

Resources

- bilingual children can be encouraged to listen, to retell and to read stories in their own language (or languages);
- good-quality dual-language texts and books set in a multicultural context are important materials to use;
- experience of a wide range of texts, both fiction and non-fiction, is essential;

- the enjoyment of listening to stories told by adults or other children should be developed – commercially produced or home-made tapes can be used to increase this experience;
- interesting stories that are lively and rhythmical can be read and reread;
- the repetitive structure of some contemporary children's literature as well as traditional rhymes and folk-tales will support English language development;
- retelling stories using drama, puppets or story maps will help to develop the language of story;
- children can compose and read their own stories – these can be written in several languages.

The reading environment

- good and enjoyable reading material should be available;
- children need to have access to this material with as few restrictions as possible;
- children should be encouraged to choose what they read as well as when and where they read it;
- an attractive and comfortable reading area is likely to encourage frequent and undirected use;
- opportunities should be created for extended independent reading.

Reading response

- children can be encouraged to talk both formally and informally about stories they have enjoyed – this will be particularly beneficial for children who are in the early stages of learning English;
- good stories can be used as a starting point for other classroom activities – this will help to deepen bilingual children's understanding of vocabulary and story structure;
- reading and rereading favourite stories and episodes from stories will provide the kind of repetition that bilingual learners need.

QUESTIONS FOR PERSONAL REFLECTION OR GROUP DISCUSSION

1 What are children's experiences of literacy in community languages and what are the sources of information about these?

2 What sort of relationship can be established between the mainstream and community schools?

3 How might the school's approach to reading development be communicated to the parents of ethnic minority pupils?

4 How can the school involve ethnic minority parents in the school's reading programme?

5 How can teachers create an environment in which children's reading ability in community languages can be valued and used?

6 How can we give bilingual children access to the literature of the majority culture without devaluing that of their own culture?

7 What are the specific difficulties that bilingual children face in reading English texts?

8 What sort of reading materials and resources are appropriate in multilingual settings?

9 How can more experienced bilingual readers, both within the school and the wider community, be encouraged to support beginning readers?

10 How can school policy on reading reflect the linguistic diversity of contemporary society?

RECOMMENDED READINGS

The Primary Language Record (Barrs *et al.*, 1988). These materials have been developed to assist teachers in profiling the language development of all pupils. Careful attention has been given to the experience of bilingual children. For instance, in considering the assessment of literacy development practical suggestions on how to include information about community languages is included. Examples of *The Primary Language Record* in use include extracts from the profiles of young bilinguals.

A Rich Resource – Writing and language diversity (National Writing Project, 1990). Like other publications from this project, *A Rich Resource* includes a wealth of case-study material. Here the emphasis is placed on the use of languages other than English in the classroom. While focusing on the development of writing, many references to children's reading ability in community languages are made. All the work included suggests practical approaches to valuing children's languages and in particular their developing biliteracy.

Read it to Me Now! (Minns, 1990). This very readable account of the literacy development of a group of primary schoolchildren in the Midlands gives us insight into the varied experiences of children in a multicultural and multilingual setting. Descriptions of learning to read in English and community languages are used to make practical recommendations for whole-school language policies.

All our languages (Houlton, 1985). A handbook for teachers showing how to recognise and use children's knowledge of language diversity in the classroom. Work on valuing the experience of children learning to read and write in community languages is included. *All Our Languages* provides practical suggestions for creating a school ethos in which bilingualism is seen as an advantage.

ACKNOWLEDGEMENTS

1 Graham Morgan of the Equal Opportunities Unit, Walsall, for case-study material on the language biography of Azizul.
2 Sue McDonagh, Mary Green and the children from Abbeydale Nursery First School, Sheffield, for their comments and reflections on the Real Books Project.
3 St Giles C of E Junior, Middle, Infant and Nursery School, Walsall, for their work on bilingual stories.

BIBLIOGRAPHY

Barrs, M., Ellis, S., Hester, H. and Thomas, A. (1988) *The Primary Language Record – Handbook for teachers*. London: Centre for Language in Primary Education (CLPE).

Brightmore, R. and Ross, M. (1990) 'Bilingual children and their infant schooling'. In J. Levine (ed.) *Bilingual Learners in the Mainstream Curriculum*. London: Taylor & Francis.

Cummins, J. (1979) 'Linguistic interdependence and the education development of bilingual children. *Review of Education Research*, 4, 9, 2, 221–51.

Department of Education and Science (1985) *Education for All* (Swann Report). London: HMSO.

Department of Education and Science (1988) *National Curriculum Proposals for English for Ages 5 to 11* (The Cox Committee Report Part 1). London: HMSO.

Gelb, I. J. (1952) *A Study of Writing*. Chicago: University of Chicago Press.

Goodman, K. S. (1964) 'A linguistic study of cues and miscues in reading'. In F. V. Gollasch (ed.) *Language and Literacy: the Collected Writing of Kenneth S. Goodman, vol. 1: Process, Theory, Research*. London: Routledge.

Halliday, M. A. K. and Hasan, R. (1985) *Language, Context and Text*. London: Oxford University Press.

Houlton, D. (1985) *All Our Languages: a Handbook for Teachers*. London: Edward Arnold.

Levine, J. (1990) *Bilingual Learners in the Mainstream Curriculum*. London: Taylor & Francis.

Linguistic Minorities Project (1985) *The Other Languages of England*. London: Routledge and Kegan Paul.

Merchant, G. (1990) 'Teachers' perceptions of linguistic diversity'. In C. James and Garrett (eds) *Language Awareness in the Classroom*. London: Longman.

Minns. H. (1990) *Read it to Me Now! Learning at Home and School*. London: Virago Press.

Savva, H. (1990) 'The multilingual classroom'. In J. Harris and J. Wilkinson (eds) *In the Know – a Guide to English Language in the National Curriculum*. Cheltenham: Stanley Thornes.

Smith, F. (1988) *Joining the Literacy Club – Further Essays into Education*. London: Heinemann.

Verma, M. (1984) *Papers on Biliteracy and Bilingualism*. London: National Council for Mother Tongue Teaching (NCMTT).

Wallace, C. (1988) *Learning to Read in a Multicultural Society: the Social Context of Second Language Literacy*. Hemel Hempstead: Prentice Hall.

Walsall Metropolitan Borough Education Committee (1989) *Linguistic Diversity Project 1987–88*. Education Development Centre, Walsall.

Walsall Metropolitan Borough Education Committee (1990) *Linguistic Diversity Project 1989–90*. Education Development Centre, Walsall.

11

READING DELAYS

Jean Hudson

SUPPORTING THE LESS EXPERIENCED READER

Slow Reader
I-am-in-the-slow
read-ers-group-my-broth
er-is-in-the-foot
ball-team-my-sis-ter
is-a-ser-ver-my
lit-tle-broth-er-was
a-wise-man-in-the
in-fants-christ-mas-play
I-am-in-the-slow
read-ers-group-that-is
all-I-am-in-I
hate-it.

(in Ahlberg, 1983)

The ILEA Primary Language Record (1988) encourages teachers to consider reading success as gradual development from dependence to independence. The handbook suggests that children move along a continuum from their initial complete dependence on the adult reader interpreting the printed text for them to complete independence in tackling familiar and then unfamiliar text for themselves. For the majority of children, this development takes place during the first six or seven years of their lives, but there are some children who do not 'get going' with reading as quickly as other children. Early in their school careers it becomes evident that they are not learning to read as well or as easily as other children in their class. It is particularly important that these children continue to get enjoyment from and to see purpose in their reading experiences. Above all, every effort must be made to prevent them from seeing themselves as 'failures' or their teachers seeing them as 'reading problems' at this very young age. The heartache caused to young children (and their parents) when they find reading difficult has often been seriously underestimated.

The previous chapters in this book have outlined many aspects of 'the reading for real approach' to the promotion of early reading success. What are the implications of this approach for children whose progress from dependence to independence in reading is slower than their peers'?

The focus of this chapter is on strategies and resources for helping children for whom the development of the ability to 'read a range of materials with some independence, fluency, accuracy and understanding' (English in the National Curriculum, DES, 1990) may take more time and need additional adult support and encouragement. It is important to emphasise from the beginning that the nature of this adult support is not essentially different from the support given to all beginning readers. The basic qualities of 'good reading teaching' are the same for all learners whether they be children who become fluent readers even before they enter the school situation, or children whose reading progress is delayed during their early school years. There may well be different emphases in the nature of the adult support and the approaches used at different stages of children's reading development, but it is essential that the 'apprenticeship model' (Waterland, 1985) is maintained. Children learn to read like they learn any other activity – by regular involvement with and support from people who already can do, and enjoy doing, the activity.

It is also important to stress that the nature of the reading process does not change. All readers whatever their stage of development are involved in a 'quest for meaning' (Cox, 1989). Reading is an active and creative process. It involves generating meaning from written language and does not mean simply saying the words correctly. Allen in a definition recorded in the first Cox report (1988) suggests that 'reading is active, creative, hypothesising, weighing the evidence, an individual construction and influenced by meanings available in the culture' (p.19). All these aspects of reading are just as true for the struggling reader as they are for the most able reader and should be reflected in the reading curriculum provided for all children. Indeed it is even more important that more dependent readers be given support and encouragement to interpret written text and bring their own individual responses to it. One young struggling reader when relating the text to his own personal experience wrote to John Burningham to suggest that the ending of *Mr. Gumpy's Outing* (1970) didn't really make much sense. 'How could all the characters go for a ride on another day if the boat had been sunk?' John Burningham responded promptly and explained that the boat had sunk near the shore so that there was an opportunity to refloat it and to mend it! Such response to text is a far more significant sign of 'becoming a reader' than the hesitant and accurate reciting of the words that is exemplified in the sad poem at the beginning of this chapter.

It is this emphasis on meaning and personal response in the early stages of reading development that helps young readers maintain their interest in reading and their motivation to learn to read for themselves. Research (Stanovitch, 1980) has shown that their efforts to 'make sense from the text' help them to predict the words and they then use a variety of cues to confirm their predictions. Stanovitch indicates that 'word recognition during reading can be facilitated by expectancies based on the prior sentence context' (p.64) and that such knowledge appears to be particularly important for poor readers. Particularly helpful meaning cues will be available to them if they have already heard the text read orally, and discussed it with an interested adult. The delightful illustrations provided in all good books for children are also a very useful cue as young readers begin to match their knowledge of the content of the book to the printed words of the text. It is crucial that the slower reader be encouraged to make maximum use of the illustrations to extend the story in the text and to help in the identification of the words. In addition, developing readers need to be helped to acquire an extensive sight vocabulary and also encouraged to transfer their great knowledge of the syntax of oral language and the language of the books that they have heard read aloud to help them recognise many words on the page. With increasing experience of written text, young readers also become more aware of the structure of words and the relationships between sounds and letters. Adult support for less able readers needs to be concentrated on all these

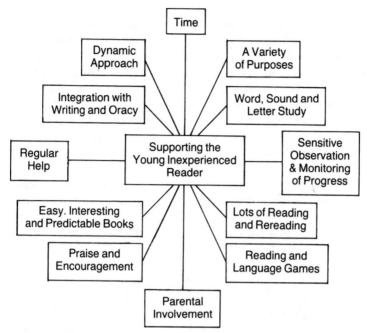

Figure 11.1

available cues and not focused on any one in isolation. The either/or debates in relation to the importance of specific cues are completely irrelevant. Children need to be encouraged to make use of every available cue in their efforts to make sense of the text.

The aim of the remainder of this chapter is to provide guidelines for formulating an integrated reading programme for young inexperienced readers. Figure 11.1 summarises some of the key teaching/learning strategies in such a programme.

PURPOSE, PLEASURE AND PRACTICE

Purpose, pleasure and practice have often been identified as key elements in a successful reading programme. These aspects certainly need major consideration when planning the curriculum for less experienced readers. The many purposes for reading at school, home and in the wider community need to be continually demonstrated to them through the use of a wide range of relevant and realistic reading activities. There is a need for constant reinforcement of *why* we read to help them to see reading as an essential part of life and to build their confidence that they are able to read and are getting more efficient every day. Reading to bake, to make a model, to play a game, to feed the hamster, to find out what is for lunch, to get information for a project and many many more similar purposes can be an integral part of the ongoing activities. Teachers, parents and other adults who are more experienced readers should also be continually demonstrating to inexperienced readers that reading fulfils many purposes in their lives, and also gives them great pleasure. Practice is important too, and persistence might also be added as a fourth P. Developing readers need a wide breadth of interesting and varied reading materials to maintain this constant practice and time and encouragement to use them. It could be suggested that just 'doubling the amount of reading' that less able readers do would have a very positive impact on their reading success. Indeed, Clay (1979) suggests that if we simply manipulated twice as much time for the slow children as for the good readers, we might be doing quite a lot for the prevention of reading failure. Practice in oral reading is important, but opportunities for sustained silent reading from an early age are also very necessary.

The role of parents

The importance of parents (yet another P) in their children's reading development is highlighted in another chapter of this book. However, their role does need special mention in relation to the child who needs additional help towards achieving independence in reading. The phrase 'children and parents who read together succeed together' has become a well-known cliché but it is nonetheless true. Parents have more time than teachers to provide the practice that is so essential for reading success, and to discuss the books and to encourage personal response to them. Grandmas, granddads, older siblings and adult friends and relatives also make an important contribution to children's reading progress when they share their own reading interests and enthusiasms with them, and become involved in the shared reading of many different kinds of texts. Parents and others may make young readers more aware of print in the environment, and create varied reasons for literacy through such activities as reading and writing letters, sending birthday cards, responding to advertisements, and reading instructions for many tasks around the home. Many schools now have carefully planned programmes and written materials to encourage parental involvement in their children's reading development. The parents of children whose progress towards independence in reading is at a slower rate than many of their peers need to be assured at a very early stage that the school has a well-devised and carefully planned curriculum for promoting their children's reading success, and that they have an important part to play in its implementation. With support and advice, they can work effectively with their child and his/her teacher to develop skills in using all the necessary reading cues identified in the National Curriculum documents.

Resources

In the HMI Report (1990) attractiveness of provision and access to books were highlighted as one of the first positive influences on reading standards in all primary schools. This provision has been made easier in recent years because of the great improvement in the quality and format of children's books. Lack of finance must now be the only excuse for not supplying all young readers with a wide selection of all kinds of books and other printed materials from which they can choose those that are interesting and relevant to them. This opportunity for self-selection of reading materials is as essential for less fluent readers as it is for the most successful. When children's personal response and enjoyment from text is recognised as the first vital ingredient of reading success, children do not choose texts that are too difficult for them to read. It is when initial reading success is mainly judged by the amount and complexity of the words in the book that children come to see reading success as merely climbing the rungs of a ladder and they tend to choose inappropriate books in order to impress others.

The more dependent readers need many good books with only one or two sentences per page. They need books that make sense, that tell a good story and that enable them to bring their own experiences and background knowledge to their reading. The difficulty of the book for these young children is more aptly decided by the amount of print on the page than a consideration of the actual words or the complexity of the sentences. Many simple easy-to-read caption books can be included with a multitude of good stories and information books. The need for a good supply of easy-to-read information books has often been neglected in the selection of beginning reading resources. Books like those in the Bookshelf series (1986–1991) contain some very interesting, well-illustrated content and have a minimum amount of print. Titles vary from *Growing Radishes and Carrots* to *Lorries, Caterpillars*, and *How to Cook Scones*. Such books can be particularly motivating to less able readers. They may provide real purposes for their reading through answering their many questions, and because of the children's interest and relevant background knowledge may actually be easier for them to read than some storybooks.

The key point is that we need to end the artificial division that has been created between books that children learn to read with, and the books that they like to read. The main criteria for book selection must be related to books that we like ourselves and books that children will enjoy. Joke books, books of riddles, stories told in simple plays and puzzle books may be especially relevant and encouraging to the young struggling reader. School-made (and home-made) books created from children's own language and experiences are often their special favourites among the wide range of interesting resources provided for them. Experienced teachers begin by sharing these books (and many of them are to be found among recently published reading schemes) with the children who then approach their own independent reading of the books with knowledge of their content and expectations of meaning.

A MULTI-CUE APPROACH

What then should be the structure of the programme for the young child who is making slow progress towards independent reading? What support and encouragement are needed to help him or her to find enjoyment, create meaning from text and also read with increasing accuracy the wide range of available resources? The programme of study for reading in the National Curriculum for English (1990) suggests that children should be guided 'to use the available cues such as pictures, context, phonic cues, word shapes and the meaning of a passage to decipher new words' (p.30). How can this guidance be provided? What additional support do less able readers need if they are to become proficient in the use of all these cues?

Meaning cues

Marie Clay (1985), whose work with young inexperienced readers is discussed in more detail later in this chapter, confirms that meaning cues must always be placed first because 'the message embodied in the print is the highest priority'. Young, inexperienced readers should never be asked to read texts that they haven't already heard read. Meaning must come before the recognition of words and it is the reader's knowledge of the meaning of the text that promotes early word recognition development. Clay (1985) emphasises that all readers from the 5 year old on his or her first book to the efficient adult reader use the sense and sentence structure of the text before they resort to word analysis and the left-to-right sounding out of letters. Books need to be read *to* children, *with* children and *by* children in that order. They need to be read and reread many times and the match between the reader's language and the words on the page will get closer at each reading. (Both Clay (1972) and Holdaway (1979) provide interesting examples of the development of this reading-like behaviour.) It is therefore essential that the written language materials that we provide for young readers are full of meaning, interest and relevance so that they merit this repeated rereading. It could be said that some of our traditional early reading materials do not merit a first reading, let alone second, third and fourth readings. All parents of young children know that good books provoke many rereading requests. If schools provide and share the right books, children will spontaneously select these familiar books and experience the constant practice that is so necessary for their increasing success in the recognition of words. Taped copies of their favourites may also be bought or made, and these tapes will provide another opportunity for shared reading practice and the development of more fluent reading.

The use of many big books (Holdaway, 1979) provides a context for reading, rereading and discussing books with a small group of children. It also provides an excellent context for modelling what real readers do. The children can be encouraged to use the illustrations to interpret the story and to recognise the words, and through techniques such as masking (covering up words), they are encouraged to use meaning and language cues to predict the hidden words, and what will happen next in the story. Pointing to the words as part of this shared reading experience demonstrates aspects of how written language works and helps young readers to focus on the individual words, elements of their structure and sound/letter correspondences. Readers may also be given additional support towards independent reading by having many opportunities to extend the stories through drama, art work and musical activities. If previous familiarity with the content is an essential ingredient of early independent reading, then children who have dramatised the major events in a story, or painted and sequenced them in picture form, have acquired increased meaning cues to aid their precise recognition of the words. The words of songs that they love to sing, or poems and rhymes that they know by heart, are also excellent sources of early reading material.

Language cues

Even before the publication of the Breakthrough to Literacy materials (1970), the 'Language Experience Approach' to reading development was recognised and used as an important part of adult support for early reading and writing development. It has also been found very useful with adults who find reading difficult (Walker, 1974). This approach is based on the link between children's oral language and their literacy development and promotes the retelling and recording of their experiences in written language which they then read, reread, share and analyse. This technique is especially useful for children who are making a slower start in reading. Lots of very readable material can be created for them through their dictation of their own significant experiences (grandma's visit, a new baby brother or even their favourite food). School activities, their individual hobbies and interests, and their retelling of well-known and well-loved stories can all be scribed to provide additional predictable reading resources for them. In one classroom Sam, the gerbil, became the centre of many ongoing literacy activities. The children composed many notes to him regarding school activities, school rules, happenings at home and also asked him many questions. These notes were always 'answered' at length and provided many opportunities for reading, writing and talking as well as extend-

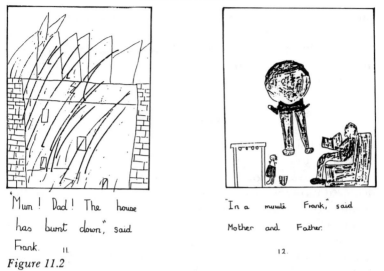

"Mum! Dad! The house has burnt down," said Frank. 11.

"In a minute Frank," said Mother and Father. 12.

Figure 11.2

ing the children's thinking skills. Young readers may also use the model of caption books, or simple stories that they have read to create parallel versions about themselves or their interests. One group of young less independent readers created 'In a Minute, Frank' (see Figure 11.2) as their delightful response to the well-known story, *Not Now, Bernard* (McKee, 1980).

I recently read a lovely bird story, 'Out of the Nest, Tweet, Tweet', that a group of young readers had created after reading a mouse story beginning 'Out of his hole, creep, creep' in the Story Chest Reading Scheme (Melser and Cowley, 1981). 'Things I Like' or 'Things I Can Do' are common parallel versions of caption books that can be made. Fitting their own story language to books with picture sequences or photographs is another helpful early learning experience.

The Breakthrough to Literacy materials (Mackay *et al.*, 1970) may provide an additional useful device for helping individual children or groups of children to transcribe their own oral language in spite of their limited spelling and handwriting skills. Again, this recording of their relevant text provides many opportunities to demonstrate how written language works and to talk about the structure of individual words. Long words, short words, words that begin or end the same or rhyming words can all be discussed and learned in this context.

Many teachers find the word processor a very useful device for providing reading resources based on the child's own language and experiences. With support, young children can become very proficient in using it for themselves, and their motivation to read and reread the writing on the computer screen and the print-out provides more much needed reading practice.

Visual cues

Many published reading schemes have concentrated on the need for young readers to acquire a large sight vocabulary (words that they instantly recognise in any context). This has often been achieved through the use of books with a very strictly controlled vocabulary where the author's main criterion in writing the book was repetition of the same words many times. Such writing has resulted in a sort of 'primerese language' which is spoken or written by no one except the authors of beginning reading books and it is certainly not predictable for beginning readers to read. In our justified negative reactions to these badly written and boring books, we must not forget that an important aspect of success for developing readers is an ever increasing bank of sight words that they recognise easily and quickly in any reading situation. Children's many rereadings of well-loved texts will provide much of the repetition that is necessary for promoting this instant visual recognition of many words. The word-rich environment in which they all live and the saturated literacy environments of their own schools and classrooms will also help. However, the children on whom this chapter is focusing may also need extra support. The format of any child's game can be made into a reading game. A squared board can be turned into a football field where goals are scored for the reading of words, phrases and sentences. In the same way, a reading 'Snakes and Ladders' or 'Sorry' game can be constructed and additional variety can come from word bingo, dominoes with words, Kim's game, pairs and many others. McNicholas and McEntree (1986) and Root (1982) have written two of many useful publications that suggest a variety of formats for constructing games to support reading development, and particularly the acquisition of a larger sight vocabulary. Children can also be encouraged to collect words and make their own individual lists of interesting and relevant words. Additional simple worksheets presenting key words in an interesting context might also be used sparingly.

These techniques will also be helpful to the organisation of a busy reading classroom.

Children who have difficulty in remembering core words may be helped if special attention is given to the link between reading and writing, and variations of Fernald's kinaesthetic approach (in Pumfrey, 1991) may be helpful. In this approach, young readers are encouraged to trace the word shape with their fingers at the same time as they pronounce it orally. Writing the word in the air or in the sand, or the use of felt or sandpaper letters, are also useful supports for the young reader's acquisition of an ever increasing sight vocabulary.

Phonics and word structure cues

The relationship between real reading and phonemic awareness is discussed in detail in another chapter of this book. Bryant's and Bradley's researches (1985, 1989) have confirmed the correlation between sensitivity to rhyme and alliteration and early reading success and have also suggested that weaknesses in phonological awareness are common among older children experiencing reading difficulties. Clark's (1976) young fluent readers appeared to experience no problems with auditory discrimination compared to the many problems of the unselected group of children. More recently, Goswami and Bryant (1990) have found evidence of a 'causal connection between children's phonological skills and their success (or lack of it) in reading and spelling' (p.94). This evidence is not conclusive but it does suggest that weaknesses in phonological awareness may well be a factor in delayed reading development. However, phonological awareness also increases as children become more fluent and independent readers.

Many traditional remedial reading schemes have been built on the premise that less successful readers need an increased 'dose of phonics' to support their reading development. Indeed, this component has often been the main one in the reading curriculum provided for them. HMI (1990) suggest that it is often seen as a last resort 'when all else has failed'.

For most children, the ability to use phonic and word structure cues appears to be an important aspect of their growth towards independence in reading. These cues provide one strategy among several which help the developing reader in the recognition of unknown words. Increasing ability to make use of these cues comes with more and more reading experience. Slower starters may need more explicit support to learn rhymes and jingles, to listen to repetitive sounds, to recognise little words in big words, and to relate speech sounds to letter symbols. However, they do not need such training in complete isolation from the meaningful act of real reading, and they do not need tedious phonic drills and exercises. The sharing of nursery rhymes in their printed form provides an excellent context for encouraging children's awareness of sound, their sensitivity to rhyme and alliteration and for beginning the development of their knowledge of sound/letter correspondences. Many good books for children are written in verse form and all the good books with which the children are involved will provide opportunities for drawing their attention to the structure of words and help them to learn about the relationships between sounds and letters. Their scribed oral language will also provide another opportunity. They may pick out words in stories that begin with the same letters, or are made up of two little words or collect words that end in ed, ing, etc. Words for special attention should always be separated out of phrases and sentences before letters are separated out of words. Again, many games dependent upon the application of phonic knowledge can be devised. 'I spy' is a favourite which may vary from children having to identify something that begins the same as *b*aby, to something that rhymes with *cat*. (It is important that the sound is presented in the context of a whole word, as additional confusion is often caused when children are expected to pronounce consonant sounds in isolation.) Many board and card games which emphasise specific word patterns or sound/letter correspondences can also be played. Phonics can be fun. Worksheets which present phonics skills in a meaningful context can also be used on occasion, and children can be encouraged to create and share their own jingles, rhymes, puns, etc. Books with rhyming couplets are particular favourites, and children can be encouraged to write their own couplets and create humorous sentences which include the repetition of the same sound. The report from HMI (1990) stresses that phonic skills are best learned when they are embedded in activities that are relevant and enjoyable, and particularly when children are helped to put them to use in writing and in making sense of the texts that they want to read.

In recent years, many teachers have reported that some parts of the Letterland materials (Wendon, 1985) have been very useful in promoting interest in and developing awareness of letters, the sounds they represent, and the structure of words. In these materials, a story has been created for every regular letter and sound pattern in English. (Dippy Duck is dipping and diving at the duckpond and loves a delicious dinner of dandelions and duckweed.) Additional stories have been invented to explain why some letters behave differently in different situations. (Hairy Hat man hates noise so when Sammy Snake comes next to him, he says sh.) Many visual cues are also provided, and the acting out of Letterland stories is encouraged. Some schools have integrated the Letterland characters into many of their school activities and one classroom teacher created 'Christmas in Letterland' for the class presentation to parents. The stories about the letters and how they are made can also be extended and may form an integral part of the discussion in shared writing activities. It is certainly not necessary to purchase or to use all of the wide variety of support materials that are available with this scheme. The published materials could be used in a very trite and overcomplicated manner but many experienced and competent teachers have found them to be a most helpful prop for developing phonic skills with all children and have extended their use across the whole curriculum. Particularly, the scheme has been found helpful for slower readers who enjoy the sound stories and seem to learn about graphic and phonic correspondences almost intuitively. The opportunity to learn this essential phonic knowledge in an amusing, meaningful and interesting context is a very positive contribution to the early reading curriculum. Less fluent readers need many such opportunities, but they also need many other experiences in using all the available cues to create meaning from text. All phonic activities, including the Letterland materials, need to be part of a much wider and more flexible approach to support for reading development.

THE READING RECOVERY PROGRAMME

Aspects of Marie Clay's work (1985) on the early detection of reading difficulties have already been discussed but it needs special attention in a chapter focusing on children whose progress towards independent reading is considerably slower than their peers'. Her Reading Recovery Programme emphasises the importance of early identification of these children (by age 6) to prevent feelings of failure and loss of confidence, and to avoid the learning and practice of inappropriate reading behaviours which may become real barriers to later satisfactory progress. Clay also stresses the importance of the teacher's knowledge of the reading process for making sensitive observations of what children can do with text and identifying the reading strategies that they are using. This knowledge is also essential for the planning and implementing of an intensive, flexible programme which will meet the children's individual learning needs. She emphasises the many differences in children's backgrounds and experiences and suggests that it is impossible to rely completely on any one published reading scheme. Appropriate pacing of the difficulty level of the material and the teacher's regular support are of prime importance. Her total programme is based on book reading rather than words and she recommends that there be lots of reading and rereading of easy and attractive books. In addition, story writing, including the teacher's scribing of children's oral stories for them to read back, is a key element of the intensive help provided. She stresses that it is essential that children develop reading fluency on the simple books that they know well. These books might be special interest books, easy books already read to the child, a story that has been written using the pupil's known vocabulary or a text which the child has dictated. The first two weeks of her tutoring sessions would concentrate on 'roaming 'round the known', thus ensuring the initial and continuing success that is so vital to young inexperienced readers. Clay is also concerned that many opportunities are provided for children to develop basic concepts about print and how it works, and that there be specific and detailed instruction in sounds and their relation to letters. Detailed advice regarding word study in the context of sharing stories is provided in her published programme. Being positive and giving plenty of praise are other essential components for the teacher and the parent.

Clay (1985) recommends that daily tutoring sessions should initially be organised on a one-to-one basis. (Groups of two or three children might later be possible.) The sessions might last for 30–40 minutes or be several shorter sessions throughout the day. A typical tutoring session would include:

1 Rereading of two or more familiar books to practise reading skills and to develop reading fluency.
2 Practice in letter identification using plastic letters on a magnetic board.
3 Shared writing of a story to be read and reread.
4 Rearranging a cut-up story to provide many opportunities to study individual words and their structures.
5 Practice in the sound analysis of words using Elkonin's (1973) and Holdaway's (1979) approaches, which are discussed in more detail later in this section.
6 Introduction and attempted rereading of at least one new book.
7 Individual variations depending on the child's needs. These might be 'an intensive vocabulary spree' or training in predicting what structures come next or extra practice in letter identification.

In spite of Clay's continued insistence that readers should operate on a continuous text, her tutoring programme does include some time for individual sound analysis and word study. She suggests that children may have some difficulty in breaking oral messages into words and that they could have even greater difficulty in breaking up words into a sequence of sounds and hearing the sounds in sequence. She found children in her New Zealand study who could go from letters to sounds (presumably because of the school's explicit teaching) but could not hear sound sequences in the words they spoke. She emphasises that children must be able to *hear* a difference between two sounds before they can learn to *see* the difference and make use of this knowledge in

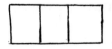

Figure 11.3

Figure 11.4

decoding and encoding words. Clay's procedures for overcoming these difficulties are based on a method developed by the Russian psychologist, Elkonin (1973). He suggests that the concept of the individual phoneme does not exist for many early readers because their experiences have all been with larger meaningful chunks of language. These children, therefore, cannot begin to understand the grapheme–phoneme code of an alphabetic writing system until they have concrete experiences with this meaningless phoneme unit. Elkonin suggests that the tendency in schools to introduce simultaneously the sound and written symbol often creates additional confusion for young children. They fail to understand that the letter is *the written symbol of the spoken sound,* and believe that the sound is only the *name* of the written character (as in their pre-school experience with language as labels). To overcome this confusion, Elkonin recommends phonetic/directional learning which concentrates on the initial learning of the sound structure of words only. Holdaway's (1979, pp.132–43) slightly modified form of this approach includes:

1 *Spoken language sequencing* (Figure 11.3). The child is encouraged to say the word clearly and slowly, and then repeat the sounds as he points to each square or puts a counter on it. There are sufficient squares for each phoneme in the word. The number of letters in the conventional spelling of the word is irrelevant at this stage.
2 *Written language sequencing.*

240

Figure 11.5

    a At this stage (Figure 11.4) the child uses some alphabet cards and some counters for the boxes. Concentration on initial, final and medial consonants is recommended initially. There is no need to work through confusing words like fire or chimney. It is awareness of the sequencing of sounds that is being developed, not the ability to find the appropriate letter for every English sound.

    b The child then practises the skill using vowels and more complex consonant blends (Figure 11.5).

3 *Sequencing in context* (Figure 11.6). Similar learnings are included in sentence, rhyme and story contexts and these activities provide many opportunities for children to use other available cues to confirm and reinforce their predictions.

This detailed approach is usually only necessary with a few examples. Other words are learned by comparing their similar structures (e.g. down, crown, clown).

It is important to emphasise again that all of this sound analysis work should take place in the context of real reading. It is only a small part of Clay's total special recovery programme which is based on helping children to integrate their use of all the available cues for creating meaning from text.

The financial resourcing of most schools may not allow for the intensive one-to-one work that Clay recommends but her basic principles and many aspects of her suggested strategies (which

```
Jack and Jill went up the ▨▨▨    (Initial Consonant)

To fetch a pail of ▨▨▨▨         (Final consonant)

Jack fell ▨▨▨                   (Final Consonant)

And broke his ▨▨▨▨              (Consonant Blend)

And Jill came tumbling ▨▨ ▨.    (Vowels)
```

Figure 11.6

have been evaluated very positively in both this country and in New Zealand) can be integrated into the ongoing group activities of all Early Years classrooms. They are not dependent on any one method for promoting reading development and illustrate the same integrated 'both/and' approach that this chapter has tried to emphasise.

CONCLUSION

The writers of *Building a House of Fiction* (NATE, 1989) have confirmed that less able children responded well to their emphasis on 'reading for real' from the very beginning stages. They suggest that a wider range of books, and the encouragement of some self-selection, reduces the competitive element that often comes into early reading experiences. The emphasis on creating meaning and personal response to text means that even the children making slower reading progress become more confident readers and develop more positive concepts about themselves as readers. These teachers do suggest, however, that more time is needed for them to become independent readers, but this should not matter if we have patience and accept that there is no evidence to suggest the existence of a 'critical age' for becoming an independent reader. The crucial points are that (1) the child's self-confidence and concept of him or herself as a reader is not destroyed, and (2) his or her ability to create meaning from text remains the first criterion for judging his or her reading progress.

This chapter has attempted to summarise some of the key strategies and resources that might be useful in supporting the reading growth of the slow starters. These children do need a carefully planned and structured reading programme but it is a structure based on their teacher's knowledge of the reading progress and the cues that successful readers use. It is not a structure related to one particular published remedial reading scheme which has often been specifically written to emphasise only one type of reading cue.

HMI's report (1990) has emphasised that evidence from all their recent inspections confirms that the quality of the teaching is the most important factor in reading success. Teachers of less experienced readers should concentrate on creating many motivating, challenging and purposeful reading activities which will provide these young readers with many opportunities to use every possible cue in their 'quest for meaning' from text, and lead them towards independence in the recognition of words. Meaning, purpose and enjoyment remain the core of the process in this 'integrated methodology'. Yet, many opportunities are provided for the learning of core vocabulary and the acquisition of the necessary phonic knowledge. Whatever teaching programme is used, any class of children will always have a wide distribution in their standard of reading. Their individual differences have to be accepted. The important thing is that they all continue to make progress. These children, like all readers, will be learning to read for the rest of their lives, and the essential beginning for all children must be pleasure, purpose and meaningful response.

QUESTIONS FOR PERSONAL REFLECTION OR GROUP DISCUSSION

The Reading Process

1 How does the teacher's understanding of the reading process influence the reading curriculum that he or she provides for less competent readers?

Identification

2 What criteria should be considered when identifying children who are making a slow start towards achieving independence in reading?

Strategies

3 Do the teaching/learning strategies provide opportunities to integrate meaning, language, visual and phonic cues when reading?

4 What teaching/learning strategies are particularly helpful to the less fluent reader?

Integration

5 How can reading activities be integrated with and supported by oral language and writing activities?

Reading Recovery Programme

6 Is Clay's programme with its emphasis on individual tuition of any use to classroom teachers?

Resources

7 Do the available reading resources provide a wide range of different types of texts at varying levels of difficulty? Are additional resources needed?

Parental Support

8 What is the role of parents in supporting less experienced readers? How can the school provide the necessary advice?

Monitoring Progress

9 How can progress towards independent reading be monitored? What recording procedures are the most appropriate?

RECOMMENDED READINGS

Marriott, S. (1991) *Picture Books in the Primary Classroom*. London: Paul Chapman Publishing. This very recent book stresses the value of picture books in helping children 'to see reading as a meaningful, enjoyable and satisfying activity'. In addition to many suggestions for using picture books at home and school, it provides an extensive review section of picture books for all readers from the very beginning stages to the independent level.

Guatrey, F. (1990) 'Cross-age tutoring in Frankley'. *Reading*, vol. 24, no.

1, pp.21-7. Shared reading approaches involving older and younger readers have been found to be beneficial to both groups of readers. Such approaches appear to be particularly useful for developing reading fluency through the joint reading of many easy books. This article describes a variety of such projects, and provides very useful advice for the preparation, organisation and evaluation of cross-age tutoring in the classroom.

Phinney, M.Y. (1988) *Reading with the Troubled Reader*. New York: Scholastic. The main purpose of this book is 'to describe ways of recognising and helping different types of troubled readers' (p.3). Its author is described as a 'practical activist' who believes strongly in a holistic approach to literacy. Chapter 3 on universal reading principles contains some very useful strategies for supporting young readers, and the case studies in the following chapters, although sometimes overanalytical, help to increase awareness of children's many individual differences and approaches to the reading process.

Pinnell, G.S., Fried, M. D. and Estice, R. M. (1990) 'Reading recovery: Learning how to make a difference'. *The Reading Teacher*, vol. 43, no. 4, pp.282-95. This article describes in detail the implementation of Clay's Reading Recovery Programme in some Ohio schools. The teaching/learning strategies are clearly explained and the inserted case studies of both a child and a teacher provide further insights into the effectiveness of the programme. The overall evaluation is very positive.

Smith, J. and Alcock, A. (1990) *Revisiting Literacy: Helping Readers and Writers*. Milton Keynes: Open University Press. This very readable book contains many practical ideas for supporting less experienced readers and writers. The authors' stated aim is 'to provide a variety of relevant and enjoyable situations through which children who are not succeeding may be invited to revisit literacy' (p.1). Very useful recommendations are made for supporting reading and writing development across the whole curriculum, and the suggested strategies are exemplified in two brief accounts of children's literacy journeys.

Wilkinson, L. (1990) *Literacy for Young Learners*. Australia: Era Publications. Although this short book does not refer specifically to children who are making slower progress in early reading development, it does stress children's individual learning needs and the importance of the adult role in providing for them. It contains 'a host of practical classroom strategies' for supporting young emergent readers, and also links reading activities with writing and oral language development.

BIBLIOGRAPHY

Ahlberg, A. (1983) *Please Mrs. Butler*. Harmondsworth: Kestrel.

Allen, D. (n.d.) *English, Whose English?* National Association of Advisers in English.

Barrs, M. *et al.* (1988) *The Primary Language Record*. ILEA Centre for Primary Education.

Bradley, L. and Bryant, P. (1985) *Rhyme and Reason in Reading and Spelling.* University of Michigan Press.

Bryant, P. and Bradley, L. (1985) *Children's Reading Problems.* Oxford: Basil Blackwell.

Bryant, P. E. (1989) 'Nursery rhymes and phonological skills in reading'. *Journal of Child Language,* vol. 16, pp.407–28.

Burningham, J. (1970) *Mr. Gumpy's Outing.* London: Jonathan Cape.

Clark, M. (1976) *Young Fluent Readers.* London: Heinemann.

Clay, M. (1979) *Reading: The Patterning of Complex Behaviour.* London: Heinemann Educational.

Clay, M. (1985) *The Early Detection of Reading Difficulties* (3rd edn). London: Heinemann.

Cox, B. (1988) *English for Ages 5 to 11.* DES.

Cox, B. (1989) *English for Ages 5 to 16.* DES.

DES (1990) *English in the National Curriculum.* London: HMSO.

Elkonin, D. B. 'U.S.S.R.'. Chapter 24 in J. Downing (ed.) (1973) *Comparative Reading.* London: Collier Macmillan.

Goswami, U. and Bryant, P. (1990) *Phonological Skills and Learning to Read.* London: Lawrence Erlbaum Associates.

HMI (1990) *The Teaching and Learning of Reading in Primary Schools.* DES.

Holdaway, D. (1979) *The Foundations of Literacy.* New York: Aston Scholastic.

Mackay, D., Thompson, B. and Schaub, P. (1970) *Breakthrough to Literacy.* London: Longman for the Schools Council.

McKee, D. (1980) *Not Now, Bernard.* London: Sparrow Books.

McNicholas, J. and McEntree, J. (1986) *Games to Develop Reading Skills* (3rd edn). NARE Publications.

Melser, J. and Cowley, J. (1981) *Story Chest.* London: Edward Arnold.

NATE (1989) *Building a House of Fiction, Children Becoming Readers.* Sheffield: National Association for the Teaching of English.

Pumfrey, P. (1991) *Improving Children's Reading in the Junior School.* London: Cassell.

Root, B. (1982) *40 Reading Games to Make and Play.* London: Macmillan Education.

Stanovitch, K. (1980) 'Towards an interactive/compensatory model of individual differences in the development of reading fluency'. *The Reading Research Quarterly,* vol. XVI, no. 1, pp.32–7.

Walker, C. (1974) *Reading Development and Extension.* London: Ward Lock.

Waterland, L. (1985) *Read With Me: an Apprenticeship Approach to Reading.* Stroud: Thimble Press.

Wendon, L. (1985) *Letterland.* Walton-on-Thames: Nelson.

INDEX

247

SUBJECT INDEX